From Crisis to Crisis
Soviet-Polish Relations in the 1970s

FROM CRISIS
TO CRISIS

SOVIET-POLISH RELATIONS
IN THE 1970s

Vladimir Wozniuk

Iowa State University Press / Ames

TO MY MOTHER AND FATHER

• •

Vladimir Wozniuk is Assistant Professor in the Department of Government and Law at Lafayette College. He holds graduate degrees from George Washington University, Yale, and the University of Virginia. His published work has appeared in journals such as *East European Quarterly, The Journal of Politics,* and *Studies in Soviet Thought,* among others.

© 1987 Iowa State University Press, Ames Iowa 50010
All rights reserved
Printed in the United States of America

No part of this book may be reproduced in any form or by any electronic or mechanical means, including information storage and retrieval systems, without written permission from the publisher, except for brief passages quoted in a review.
First edition, 1987

Library of Congress Cataloging-in-Publication Data

Wozniuk, Vladimir.
    From crisis to crisis.

    Bibliography: p.
    Includes index.
    1. Soviet Union–Foreign relations–Poland. 2. Poland–Foreign relations–Soviet Union. 3. Soviet Union–Foreign relations–1953-1975. 4. Soviet Union–Foreign relations–1975-   . I. Title.
DK67.5.P7W69   1987   327.470438   87-2911
ISBN 0-8138-0386-1

Contents

☐☐☐

Viability or Cohesion?
Poland and Limited Sovereignty, 1980–1981

Acknowledgments

I owe a debt of sincere gratitude to a number of individuals and institutions for valuable assistance at various stages in the preparation of this book.

First, my appreciation goes to Paul Shoup who gave so freely of his time in reading and commenting upon various drafts of this study as a doctoral dissertation. Thanks to him must also go for challenging my assumptions about Soviet foreign policy and East European politics.

Next, a word of thanks for advice and encouragement along the way goes to Kenneth W. Thompson, Alvin Z. Rubinstein, Vladimir Petrov, John Armitage, Inis Claude, Thomas T. Hammond, and Vladimir Reisky de Dubnic.

My gratitude also goes to the Institute for the Study of World Politics and to the University of Virginia, which provided financial and technical support instrumental in the completion of my research. Sincere appreciation as well goes to Suzanne C. Lowitt, a sensitive and insightful editor.

Finally, I thank my wife Karen, without whose love and spiritual support I should not have completed this book.

All errors and omissions are my responsibility alone.

A NOTE ON SPELLING

In deciding not to use diacritical marks in the rendering of Polish words in this text, the purpose has been to make the text more easily accessible and potentially less confusing to a general audience. In the case of both Russian and Polish, I have tried to retain the original spelling or transliteration of place names and proper nouns whenever possible, except in the case where common usage in English prevails as in Moscow instead of Moskva, Cracow instead of Krakow.

Acronyms

AFP – French Press Agency
ANSA – (Rome) Italian Press Agency
CC – Central Committee
CDSP – Current Digest of the Soviet Press
CMEA – Council for Mutual Economic Assistance (also COMECON)
CPCz – Communist Party of Czechoslovakia
CPSU – Communist Party of the Soviet Union
CSCE – Conference on Security and Cooperation in Europe
CSR – Czechoslovak Socialist Republic
CTK – Czechoslovak News Agency
DiP – Experience and Future
DPA – West German Press Agency
EEC – European Economic Community (Common Market)
FBIS – Foreign Broadcast Information Service
FRG – Federal Republic of Germany (West Germany)
GDR – German Democratic Republic (East Germany)
IMF – International Monetary Fund
KOR – Committee for the Defense of the Workers
KPN – Confederation for an Independent Poland
LCY – League of Communists of Yugoslavia
MBFR – Mutual Balanced Forced Reduction talks
MFN – Most Favored Nation
NATO – North Atlantic Treaty Organization
NEM – New Economic Mechanism
PAP – Polish Press Agency
PCE – Spanish Communist Party

PCF – French Communist Party
PCI – Italian Communist Party
PPR – Polish People's Republic
PRC – People's Republic of China
PUWP – Polish United Workers' Party
RCP – Romanian Communist Party
RFER – Radio Free Europe Research
ROPCiO – Movement for the Defense of Human and Civil Rights
SPD – Social Democratic Party (West Germany)
Scinteia – Romanian News Agency
SRV – Socialist Republic of Vietnam
USSR – Union of Soviet Socialist Republics
Tanjug – Yugoslav Press Agency
WTO – Warsaw Treaty Organization (Warsaw Pact)

Past as Prologue:
Russians, Poles, Communism,
and Crises

WHEN those states which have been accustomed to live in freedom under their own laws are acquired, there are three ways of trying to keep them. The first is to destroy them, the second to go and live therein, and the third to allow them to continue to live under their own laws, taking a tribute from them and creating within them a new government of a few which will keep the state friendly to you. For since such a government is the creature of the Prince it will know that it cannot exist without his friendship and authority and is thus certain to do its best to support him, and a city accustomed to freedom can be more easily held through its citizens than in any other way if it is desired to preserve it.

NICCOLO MACHIAVELLI[1]

Introduction

THE PRECEDING OBSERVATION by the pragmatist Machiavelli is part of his classic advice to the Medici on how to rule foreign peoples most effectively. Machiavelli's incisive comments, though penned nearly five centuries prior to this writing, still have much relevance for a comprehensive understanding of various contemporary states' conduct of policy, foreign as well as domestic.

A natural affinity towards Machiavelli's analyses of politics was evidenced by Vladimir Ilyich Lenin, father of the Bolshevik Revolution and founder/theorist of the modern Soviet state. This affinity was not heretical to Marxist thought, for both of Lenin's mentors, Karl Marx and Friedrich Engels, praised Machiavelli's work for its "materialism." Lenin's favorite maxim, *kto-kogo,* reflects that same incisive quality found in *The Prince.* The necessity for strong authoritative dictatorship in politics is seen in both Lenin's and Machiavelli's thought.[2]

Led by the ideology of Marxism-Leninism, adherents of communist dogma have predicted the eventual unification of the nation-states of the world under a single banner—the victory of the proletariat as represented by the hammer and sickle. This would be the final resolution of man's struggle with his fellowman and would result in the establishment of an utopia.

In a smaller context, Machiavelli too strove for a resolution of internecine conflict. He implied a reunification of the Italian city-states to the previous glory that was Rome, thereby resolving the political conflicts of Italy in his day. What Machiavelli counselled in the Italian and European contexts, Lenin proclaimed on a universal scale in his doctrine of "internationalism," which was directed at no less than the creation of an international hegemony in the name of the proletariat by its vanguard, the communist party. With the success of the Bolshevik Revolution in November 1917, these ideas were given the opportunity to be realized in practice.

This study deals with a small but nevertheless important aspect of Soviet international hegemonist policy—relations between the Soviet Union and its ally Poland during the decade of the 1970s. It embraces both an examination of Russo-Polish relations in the traditional historical sense and international "socialist" relations that developed with the expansion of communism to East Europe in the post–World War II period. To understand Soviet-Polish relations in the 1970s, it is necessary to some extent both to view what came before 1970 and what has happened since the watershed events of August 1980. Hence, the study is divided into three parts.

Part I investigates the background of Soviet-Polish relations during the partitions, Poland's brief period of independence, and the early socialist period up until the ouster of Wladyslaw Gomulka from the leadership of the Polish United Workers' Party (PUWP) in December 1970. Part II focuses on the period of Edward Gierek's leadership of the Polish party, concentrating on the interim between the signing of the Final Act of the Conference on Security and Cooperation in Europe (CSCE) on 1 August 1975 in Helsinki, Finland, and the strikes of August 1980 in Poland, which ushered in a new era of Polish communism. Part III examines the effects of the historic events of summer 1980 upon the Soviet-Polish relationship and the future of East European communism.

In Part II, the heart of the study, Soviet-Polish relations are viewed bilaterally and multilaterally in the context of the Warsaw Treaty Organization (WTO) and the Council for Mutual Economic Assistance (CMEA) and in the broader framework of the pan-European communist movement. External influences and pressures appeared to modify Soviet behavior toward Poland during this time. Important developments within European communism in the 1970s fostered a climate conducive to a weakening of the party and subsequently to a dramatic change in Poland's politics. By gauging the undercurrents within the various East and West European communist parties, a clearer image emerges of the complex dynamics of Soviet-Polish relations in the 1970s.

The account that follows is only comprehensible in light of (1) the historic context of Russo-Polish relations, (2) the advent of the Cold War and Poland's relegation to the Soviet sphere of influence, and (3) the distinctly unique nature of communist relations as articulated in the concept of "internationalism" and its interpretation by the Communist Party of the Soviet Union (CPSU).

A few comments are necessary here on point number three. Several themes recur throughout this study. These themes are developed later and addressed directly in my concluding chapter. The first thematic element in this book is the notion of "doctrinal unity" embodied first in the Comintern and later emphasized by Stalin in his imposition of the Soviet "model" of socialism on East Europe. The book documents Soviet continuity in stressing the superiority of their "way" in the contemporary period, especially when faced with alternative models (e.g., Eurocommunism and Yugoslav self-management).

Another important theme is the notion of "separate roads to socialism." The emergence of the separate roads thesis at the Twentieth CPSU Congress in 1956 signalled a new era in relations between socialist states. East European socialist states, it was now claimed, were to be allowed to develop socialism according to the unique historical features each nation possessed. However, parallel to this notion of separate and unique paths to socialism, the doctrine of "socialist internationalism" was put forward by the CPSU. The East Europeans were now taking part, according to this doctrine, in a new historical development: international relations of a "new type" were said to be operative among the fraternal bloc states and China. Socialist internationalism was an expansion of "proletarian internationalism" (the international solidarity of the working class) to the state-to-state level of relations between communists. The theory indicated that separate roads to socialism would eventually lead to an integration of socialist states sometime in the future.[3]

This notion of socialist internationalism was badly damaged by the subsequent rift in Sino-Soviet relations in the early 1960s and by the Soviet intervention in Czechoslovakia in 1968. These events also served to question the validity of the term "socialist commonwealth" for the Soviet-sponsored state system. The enunciation of the Brezhnev Doctrine, which proclaimed the limited sovereignty of socialist states, put these theoretical concepts of separate roads, socialist internationalism, and growth of a socialist commonwealth into a different light. The Brezhnev Doctrine exposed the major Soviet concern for East European communism in an unambiguous way: the Soviet Union claimed the right to protect its position in East Europe by any means necessary, including intervention to restore communist hegemony. However, the Brezhnev Doctrine did not exhaustively define the parameters of possibilities that would necessitate direct intervention. The question of when the Soviet Union would intervene after 1968, although somewhat clarified by the response to the Prague Spring, was still not entirely resolved. More on this point will be offered later.

Soviet-East European relations were also influenced in the 1960s and 1970s by the reorientation of East-West relations. The dramatic improvement of East-West relations was directly linked to Soviet de-tente strategy and embodied most visibly in the signing of the CSCE Final Act in 1975, which was based on Soviet and East European desires both to reduce tensions in Europe and obtain more technology from the West. Benefits accruing to East European states in this proc-ess were substantial in diplomatic as well as in financial terms. In the Polish case especially, the treaties of 1971–1972, which codified the status quo territorially and politically in Europe, and the Helsinki Ac-cords accelerated the pace and broadened the scope of relations with the West.

The Soviet decision to allow East European regimes to decide their own process of *kto-kogo* (that is, to select their own leaders) also influenced the character of subsequent Soviet-East European rela-tions. The process of leadership selection in Poland in 1956 (Gomulka) and in 1967 in Czechoslovakia (Alexander Dubcek) was not vetoed by the Kremlin, but accepted, despite the fact that in all likelihood these were not "first choice" candidates of the CPSU. This new privilege given to the bloc parties was one reflection of the greater relative autonomy granted these regimes, an autonomy perhaps based on the Machiavellian notion of trusting the loyalty of a "new government of a few" to rule in the Prince's stead.

Finally, after 1956 the Soviet leaders realized that some leeway would have to be granted to the bloc states in developing greater viability in the economic sphere to avoid the most overt forms of oppo-sition to communist domination. This was underscored in the late 1960s after the economic malaise of both Poland and Czechoslovakia fueled political turmoil and was a salient reason for the dramatic ex-pansion of East-West relations during the early 1970s. Soviet recogni-tion of this problem of viability influenced significantly the develop-ment of Soviet-East European relations in the 1970s.

All of the above themes have been explored extensively in Western scholarship on Soviet-East European relations. Notwithstanding the complex interlocking character of these themes, the two most impor-tant considerations that have emerged in the last fifteen years are (1) the nature of the Brezhnev Doctrine and (2) the "viability-cohesion" dilemma that Soviet policymakers face in East Europe.[4]

This book explores the reasons why the Brezhnev Doctrine was not implemented in the crisis period from September 1980 through October 1981 in Poland. It will also attempt to shed some light on the parameters of the doctrine's validity in the post–Solidarity environ-ment in East Europe. What does limited sovereignty imply in a situa-tion where the party is besieged by a nonviolent opposition and strives to "hold the line" with limited success? Clearly, the Polish crisis of 1980–1981 presented a more ambiguous problem to the Soviet leadership than did Czechoslovakia in 1968, not to mention Hungary in 1956.

Without disparaging the validity of J. F. Brown's viability-cohesion concept, an attempt will be made to reappraise it in light of the Polish crisis of 1980. How successful have Soviet leaders been in their maintenance and promotion of cohesion in East Europe, while sanctioning cautious development of greater political and economic viability of the dependent regimes in these countries? The attempt will be made to modify this dual concept in light of the complex developments in East European communism in the 1970s.

The implicit assumption embodied in Western writing on all these issues is that the Kremlin leadership will take firm action when faced with threats such as the Polish crisis of 1980–1981 to protect its interests in this vital sphere of influence. This case study documents a relationship that does not neatly fit this assumption.

An attempt to explain the paradox of why Soviet leaders failed to anticipate and head off the burgeoning crisis in a more vigorous manner is made in the concluding sections in terms of the relative priority of political and economic policies in Soviet-Polish relations and the balancing of long- and short-term concerns in Soviet foreign policy. This is not to say that well-founded wisdom concerning the Soviet position of control and oversight of the East European periphery should be revised. Rather, this is an attempt to place the notion of Soviet "oversight" in a more flexible framework, given the experience of the Soviet response to the Polish crisis. In some ways, Soviet oversight of the bloc may not be as scrutinous as is commonly thought.

It should be pointed out that Soviet-Polish relations contain unique features not to be found in Soviet relations with other bloc states. This relationship retains many characteristics of earlier Russo-Polish relations. More than three centuries of political relations between ethnic Poles and ethnic Russians brings to the study of Soviet-Polish relations certain variables not found in the bilateral relations of the Soviet Union with its other East bloc allies. Evidence of just how this affects Soviet-Polish relations in the 1970s and after is presented in the chapters that follow.

In this regard, the discussion focuses both on the difficulty Poles encountered in developing a "national" communism without slipping into "nationalist" positions and on Soviet caution exhibited in exhausting other options before embarking on an interventionist course. A decision to intervene in 1980 or 1981 could have resulted in resistance and bloodshed substantially greater than in the case of either Hungary in 1956, or certainly Czechoslovakia in 1968. Yet it is clear that the Kremlin leadership was determined, if required, to intervene to protect Soviet strategic interests in this vital area if all other options failed.

The relationship represented in this study reflects less the Leninist ideal of "proletarian internationalism" or its corollary "socialist internationalism" than the cynical but pragmatic Machiavellian understanding of power relationships. The vassallike dependency of the East European regimes on the sole guarantors of their rule in the Kremlin closely resembles the image conveyed by Machiavelli in the epigraph that prefaces this study. As Machiavelli himself might have speculated, a vassal state could strive to play a role in a larger game—in this case, Poland as "mediator" between East and West in the game of detente—in which case the weaker country could accrue some bargaining strength against the stronger. These dynamics also appear in the pages that follow, lending weight to the description of "asymmetric interdependence" as the type of relationship existing between the Soviet Union and its East European allies.[5]

Before going any further, a few words are in order concerning sources and some of the problems of empirical evidence encountered by any study seeking to pierce the screen of secrecy surrounding the decision-making process in the Kremlin.

Throughout the account that follows, extensive use of Russian and Polish primary sources (newspapers and selected journals) has been made. Two respected secondary sources, the *Foreign Broadcast Information Service (FBIS)* and *Radio Free Europe Research (RFER)*, were also utilized. These two sources were especially helpful in conveying various TASS (the Soviet news agency) accounts from radio and television as well as other European media reports on the subject not available to the author primarily because of language considerations. The regular translations, reports, and day-to-day analyses I have used have assisted in providing a more complete picture of events and dynamics during the period in question.

Finally, the issue of empirical evidence and its interpretation is also important in two ways. First, statements by other than authoritative Soviet spokesmen have been used to buttress various arguments in this study. A common Soviet media practice is to air opinions and views by citing other than Soviet sources on a given issue or area of concern. This is often done to test the waters and at the same time obviate a more authoritative Soviet stance than might be desired in a given instance. In this regard, Polish, Czechoslovak, and East German sources are most notable for the purposes of this study. In using Czechoslovak statements in particular, there is some danger of implying a complete congruence of views shared between the CPSU and the Communist Party of Czechoslovakia (CPCz) regarding Polish developments in the 1970s and the issue of Eurocommunism. Certainly, CPCz leaders had their own reasons for taking a hard line against the emergence of pluralist ideas in the international communist movement and developing problems in Polish communism. However, it appears that Prague more often than not faithfully reflected Moscow's perspective on these matters.

Second, as all Sovietologists know, understanding details of the decision-making process in the Kremlin is an extremely difficult, and sometimes impossible, task because nothing is open to public scrutiny in the Soviet Politburo. In some cases during and after crises, Western analysts have been able to pierce at least partially the shield of secrecy surrounding Kremlin politics. The case of the Prague Spring is perhaps most relevant here. Both individual and institutional conflicts of interests within the Kremlin and the effect of this struggle on Soviet foreign policy decision making have been inferred from the record of the Czechoslovak crisis.[6] It is also from this crisis that much has been learned of Soviet crisis management. These achievements were possible largely due to the plethora of information available on the Prague Spring from a variety of Soviet and Czechoslovak sources.[7]

Although data from Soviet sources on the Polish crisis become more readily available *after* 31 August, 1980 (the date of the Gdansk Agreement's signing between Solidarity and the Polish government), nothing like the amount and quality of information on the Prague Spring exists on this more recent crisis.[8] Moreover, there is also a relative paucity of information from Soviet sources stretching over a much longer time frame – that of the five years of the crisis' development from 1975–1980. This period, of course, is the central focus of this study.

Despite the fact that there was no *open* debate among Soviet and East European leaders and party organs during this time as there was during the Prague Spring, growing Soviet concerns about both the course of Polish communism and the gradual but continuous deterioration of Polish economic and social conditions in the 1970s can be discerned. These concerns become apparent from the analysis that follows of the complex interplay between Polish domestic factors (about which there is no dearth of information) and the variety of external determinants of the course of Polish communism in the 1970s.

1

Background:
Collaboration and Resistance,
Imperial Period through
Stalin's Reign

FROM the inception of the Polish and Russian imperial eras in the fifteenth and sixteenth centuries, the princes of Muscovy and the lords of the Polish-Lithuanian state vied for the same territory, the vast steppes or plains between them. As the imperial powers of Poland and Muscovite Russia alternately waned and grew in the area now known as East Europe, conflict and confrontation between the two was the hallmark of their relationship. They competed for cultural, religious, political, and military hegemony in the region. The lack of any significant natural boundaries between these Slavic neighbors led to a blurring of distinction between East and West Slavic ethnic territories.[1]

Linguistic affinities were eclipsed by the nature of the cultural asymmetry between the two: Poland was Latinized relatively early by the Roman Catholic Church, while the lands of the *Rus'* were Christianized by Byzantine scribes and monks who created an alphabet for the natives based on the Greek, and not the Latin script. The clerical split between Rome and Byzantium in the eleventh century guaranteed parochial hostility between the two nations. Years of oppression under the Mongol yoke between the thirteenth and fifteenth centuries further orientalized the political culture of Muscovy, while Poland acquired the benefits of such Western influences as the European cultural renaissance.

In 1569 the Acts of Lublin officially proclaimed a res publica of the two nations of Poland and Lithuania. The Polish-Lithuanian state appeared to be a distinct federation. Circumstances emerged that actually led to the brief possibility of a union between the Russian and Polish-Lithuanian states.[2] According to Nikolai Karamzin, one of the earliest Russian historians, the election of the Polish king's son, Wladyslaw, to the Muscovy throne during the Time of Troubles in Russia could have changed history significantly:

> . . . he could have remained Tsar of Russia and changed her
> fate by weakening autocracy. Perhaps the whole of Europe
> would have changed too for many centuries. . . .[3]

However, instead of union, something quite different transpired. Late in the seventeenth century, Polish imperial power was completely eclipsed. Wars with Turks, fellow Slavs, and Germanic peoples weakened the Polish state substantially. This process was exacerbated by a weak constitutional monarchy, which had increased the power of the nobility at the expense of the power of the throne.[4] Historians of Poland continue to refer to this era as the "deluge."

It is in the eighteenth century that a new trend in Polish politics begins to emerge – collaboration with the imperial Russian power during the precipitous decline of Poland's own position.[5] Perhaps the most renowned example of collaboration in the eighteenth century is that of Stanislaw II, August Poniatowski, the last King of Poland who attained the Polish throne in 1764 through his romantic connection with Grand Duchess Catherine at the court of St. Petersburg. In one sense, he saw himself as the first of a new bloodline replacing the defunct Jagiellonian dynasty. However, the unfortunate Poniatowski was unable to restore the country to greatness, as pressures from the surrounding imperial powers forced him to pursue a strategy of compromise. Poniatowski actually presided over the first partition of Poland in 1772, which was effected by the Russians after civil turmoil in Poland. The forces of Poniatowski (backed by those of Empress Catherine) prevailed over a broad coalition of Polish nobles who were disenchanted with Poniatowski's Russian connection.[6]

In the 1780s forces of opposition to Russian domination grew in strength, culminating in the adoption of a Polish constitution on 3 May 1791. This Polish declaration of independence was construed by Catherine the Great as a dangerous attempt to kindle Jacobinism in East Europe. The following year, a successful Russian intervention (with the help of sympathetic Polish nobles) returned the situation to the status quo ante, but a second partition of Poland quickly followed.[7]

The forces of revolution, however, were not to be quelled easily.

The growing threat of Republican France to the European monarchies created an atmosphere of reaction. An insurrection led by Tadeusz Kosciuszko, begun in Cracow in May 1794, was swiftly suppressed by superior Russian forces and led to the final partition of the Polish state. This third partition resulted in not only the truncation, but the complete dissolution of Poland as an independent political and national entity. Poland was swallowed up by Prussia, Austro-Hungary, and the Russian Empire, all of whom were glad to end the troublesome problem of Polish insurrection in a climate of growing instability on the continent. Russian suppression of Polish independence had the unintended effect of fueling the growth of a distinctly Polish national identity even before the Age of Nationalism properly began in Europe.

Hopes for the reestablishment of an independent Polish state were briefly rekindled by developments in the early nineteenth century. Adam Jerzy Czartoryski (a kinsman of Poniatowski) befriended the young Prince (and soon to be Tsar) Alexander, who reportedly had sympathy for the Polish cause and even admiration for Kosciuszko. In 1804 Czartoryski became Tsar Alexander's foreign minister. Despite Polish participation in the Napoleonic campaigns against Russia, the years of Alexander's reign held out the prospect of eventual restoration of a Polish state. In 1812, upon the defeat of Napoleon, Alexander declared:

> In the name of heaven and earth . . . I restore the Kingdom of Poland, to include the Duchy of Warsaw and the Polish provinces, which, following the partitions of 1772, 1793, and 1796 were annexed to Russia . . . *I place upon my head* the Royal Polish Crown, but united in My Person, with Russia . . . I regard as the fundamental law of the Polish people the Third of May Constitution, which is beloved and respected by all of you; and I propose to govern you in accordance with it.[8]

Congress Poland was created by the allies in 1815; its people enjoyed constitutional rights nonexistent in Russia. Had Alexander continued as tsar for another generation, Polish desires for independence may have been fulfilled to an even greater extent. As it happened, the advent of Nicholas I in 1825 changed the face of the "Polish Question."

Nicholas was concerned only with the strategic importance of Poland. This change of tone and policy towards Poland beginning in 1825 dashed the hopes of Polish elites who saw the road to Poland's restored independence linked to the Russian imperial power. The insurrection of 1830, supported and encouraged by the growing Polish emigration in France, was brutally suppressed by Russian forces. Russian elite

opinion weighed heavily against the "ungrateful" Poles after this episode, as can be seen in the belligerent attitude of writers such as
Pushkin and Dostoevsky. Until his death in 1855, Nicholas ruled Poland with an iron hand. During this dark period in Polish history,
emigré activity against Russian rule of Poland increased. The aging
Czartoryski, now living in self-imposed exile in Paris, actively participated in the campaign against Russian rule. This change in Czartoryski's position added credibility to the Polish cause in Western Europe.[9]

The reform-minded Alexander II attempted to mitigate the effect
of thirty years of Draconian Russian policy towards the Polish province. He appointed a Polish nobleman, Alexander Wielopolski, to assist in developing better relations with the Poles. By this time, however, Polish opposition to Russian domination was strong and
collaboration was largely viewed with contempt.[10]

This loosening of the imperial grip encouraged separatist forces in
Poland and assisted in the fomenting of the 1863–1864 debacle. The
tragic aftermath of this revolt included a long and fruitless attempt by
the tsars to Russify Poland completely, which ultimately resulted in a
complete breakdown in relations, " . . . making the alienation between
the nations as complete as possible." The "Polish Question" had now
been eclipsed by the "Russian Idea"—the unification and "protection"
of Slavic peoples in East Europe by their Russian big brothers.[11]

Even among Russian "liberals," sympathy for Poland was couched
in extremely paternalistic terms and emphasized Russian security concerns:

> The interests of both countries require them to strengthen
> the last action of unification. Poles, our brothers, are also
> the guardians of our front borders, because of their geo-
> graphic location. Therefore, they are our most natural allies,
> in spite of our domestic quarrels. We need an arrangement
> similar to that of the English and the Scotch, in order to take
> our place among the European nations and realize our na-
> tional destiny.[12]

Only among the more radical groups of politically conscious intelligen-
tsia within the empire was there an appreciation of the Polish desire
for complete independence. Instances of collaboration have been re-
corded between Russian and Polish Marxists at the end of the nineteenth century. Ties between the Polish proletariat and the Russian
group *Narodnaia Volia* (People's Will) were originally based on an understanding that it would sometimes be necessary to combine efforts
against tsarist oppression. Although it remains an open question as to
how close these ties were, a "secret document" of 1884 (*Umowa Konfi-*

dacjonalna), spoke of collaboration and the future creation of an independent Poland.[13]

Collaboration and Opposition in the Twentieth Century

The character of Russo-Polish relations did not change substantially as the two nations entered the twentieth century. Both strands of collaboration with and opposition to the imperial structure remained as vital forces in Poland and became clearly visible in the political differences between the two Polish nationalists Roman Dmowski and Jozef Pilsudski.

Dmowski, conservative Polish representative to St. Petersburg, was willing to work with the Russians in hopes of eventually achieving a free, independent Poland. As leader of the National Democratic Party (*Endecja* or *Endek*), his perspective was purely Polish and highly nationalistic. Until 1906 Dmowski retained the belief that reform in the empire would include a revision of Poland's status. However, after the debacle of the Russo-Japanese war, the Russian Duma did not have among its priorities the Polish problem.[14]

For three decades, Jozef Pilsudski remained Roman Dmowski's chief political adversary. Although their goal was the same—Polish independence—their means of achieving it were not. Pilsudski's nationalism was affected considerably by his early socialist views. Five years in Siberian exile (1887–1892) stemming from his brother's involvement in an attempt on Alexander III's life also contributed to the formation of his political views. He quickly rose to power in the Polish Socialist Party upon his return from exile, relinquishing leadership of that party only in 1914. After the Russo-Japanese war, Pilsudski participated in acts of political terrorism against the empire. He emerged from the First World War the most respected Polish spokesman and quickly attained the leadership of the reconstituted Polish state.[15]

Dmowski was Poland's representative to the Paris Peace Conference in 1919, which gave birth to the independent and reconstituted Polish state. The territorial boundaries of this new Poland were drawn along ethnic lines, in accordance with the conference's pledged goal of giving the right of self-determination to minorities of the now defunct imperial powers. This was completely in line with Dmowski's own nationalist ideals and the Endek Party's platform, which sought an ethnically "pure" Polish nation-state. The new boundaries were also consistent with two decades of Endek policy towards Russia (now Bolshevik): the Endeks had renounced Polish claims to all Ukrainian and Belorussian ethnic territory that had previously been a part of the historic Polish-Lithuanian Federation.[16]

The Endek Party espoused a "middle class democracy" heavily ladened with nationalism. However, this was not the source of the major differences between Dmowski and Pilsudski. The major conflict between the two stemmed from fundamentally different perceptions of Poland's position between the great powers of Germany and Russia. Dmowski saw the Germans as the major nemesis of Poland's aspirations and therefore worked for a "reconciliation" of Russo-Polish relations on a pan-Slavic basis. Pilsudski, on the other hand, viewed the Russians as the chief threat and looked for expansion and security against the East. The contrast between Dmowski's and Pilsudski's vision of Poland's security is essentially the geopolitical dilemma of modern Poland.[17]

It has been suggested that Pilsudski had anticipated the consequences of the Great War of 1914 and accordingly busied himself with preparing Poland for statehood on the heels of the breakup of the imperial giants.[18] He broke his socialist party ties and began to follow his vision of a Poland restored to its former greatness. As it happened, this vision did not completely conflict with the peace settlement reached among the great powers at Versailles. Although this agreement was couched in highly idealistic terms (self-determination for the newly created East European states), the reality of the Bolshevik success in the former land of the tsars threatened to undermine this new order in Europe. Consequently, Poland was perceived by the allies as an important part of the *cordon sanitaire* that isolated the dangerous Russian revolutionary virus from the rest of the war-weary continent. Poland was, according to some, a bulwark against Bolshevism – the "red tide" that sought to engulf Europe.

Indeed, the success of the Bolshevik Revolution and the defeat of its enemies during the civil war that followed encouraged the Soviet leaders to attempt an expansion of the revolution to the heart of Europe (Germany), where it was thought that the proletariat would rise to the occasion and overthrow the weak Versailles system. The occasion for such an attempt presented itself during the Polish-Soviet War of 1920.

Pilsudski, with the restoration of Polish power to its former greatness in mind, made a compact with Ukrainian nationalist forces to defeat the Bolsheviks and support Ukrainian separatism.[19] Success of this policy would result in a buffer for the Poles and allow for a Polish expansion to the East in Lithuania. Marshal Pilsudski led Polish forces to the gates of Kiev, where success seemed to be his.

However, the ensuing Red Army counterattack forced a quick retreat across the steppes, eventually to the outskirts of Warsaw itself. Meanwhile, the Comintern was convening in Moscow and taking great interest in the seemingly fortuitous turn of events. According to Grigory Zinoviev:

> In the congress hall hung a great map on which was marked every day the movement of our armies. And the delegates every morning stood with breathless interest before this map . . . all perfectly realized that, if the military aim set by our army was achieved, it would mean an immense acceleration of the international proletarian revolution.[20]

Notwithstanding this enthusiasm, the European revolutionary visions of the Bolsheviks were crushed after a decisive defeat was handed the Red Army at Warsaw by the Poles. Lord d'Abernon, British ambassador to Berlin, called the Warsaw victory "the eighteenth decisive battle in world history."[21]

Indeed, the result of this defeat was the stifling, for the time being, of the expansion of Soviet Russia. The armistice concluded by Poland and Soviet Russia on 12 October 1920 led to a peace treaty signed at Riga on 21 March 1921, which resulted in the ceding to Poland by the Soviet government of parts of Belorussia and Lithuania.

Despite these setbacks, the international aspirations of Soviet communism were not discarded. Passage of twenty-one conditions for membership in the Comintern by the Second Comintern Congress solidified Soviet control of the international communist movement. Unconditional support of the Soviet state, rejection of social-democratic positions, and the binding nature of central decisions upon all parties were the most critical of these conditions.[22] In this manner, the Bolsheviks guaranteed their hegemony in the international communist movement; they could now dictate to communists everywhere what path was to be followed. This would prove to be disastrous for Polish communists in the next decade.

The Communist Workers' Party of Poland (CWPP), formed at the end of the First World War, desired an "organic incorporation" of Poland in the Soviet Republic. The interwar activity of the CWPP was, as was the case with all such parties, directed from Moscow. However, Pilsudski's coup d'etat of 1926, which claimed to establish a "dictatorial democracy" in Poland, was supported by the CWPP without the blessings of the Comintern. The CWPP apparently hoped that a general revolution would follow Pilsudski's coup.[23] This turned out to be a catastrophic error used against the Polish communists by Stalin in the 1930s. Polish communist leaders lived and worked in Moscow and thus were especially vulnerable during the mass purges of the 1930s in the Soviet Union. The Polish party was dissolved sometime in 1939, though exactly when is unclear.[24] Accusations of unreliable and subversive elements within the CWPP preceded its destruction, as the error of backing Pilsudski's coup came back to haunt the Polish communists. The dissolution of the CWPP had consequences for the future of Poland that were not fully apparent at the time. During the war, these consequences would become clearer as Stalin implemented his policies towards Poland.

Official Polish policy towards the USSR during the interwar period for the most part mirrored Pilsudski's vision of the Russian threat. From 1926 to 1932 Poland faithfully played the role of the Western powers' outpost against the Soviet threat, which was perceived to be greater than that of a still weak Germany. Despite the "anti-Soviet policy" of the Polish government, a treaty of nonaggression was concluded on 25 January 1932 between Poland and the Soviet Union. However, this pact did not indicate on the part of the Soviets either a recognition of the Versailles system or Polish boundaries set by the Versailles Treaty. It was an agreement merely stating that both parties would not "resort to war." Poland's reasons for concluding such a treaty were simple and clear, as can be seen from Polish Foreign Minister Jozef Beck's evaluation:

> In connection with the happenings in Germany, [Poland] must foresee grave troubles with her. An indispensable preparation for this is a relaxation of tensions with Russia. The West is of the opinion that we are caught between the pincers of two enemies. . . . We must prove that we can tear the pincers apart.[25]

Poland also signed a nonaggression pact with Germany on 26 January 1934. Pilsudski's government was striving to steer a course between its two neighbors without offending either one. Given the fact of Poland's de facto weakness, this course was bound to run into trouble.

After Pilsudski's death on 12 May 1935, Poland's fortunes declined steadily. Poland did not object to the Munich agreement, nor to the absorption of Czechoslovakia into the Third Reich. Its own interests were served by these events: Czechoslovak territory was also incorporated into Poland. Even after 1935 there remained a distinct sense in Poland that Germany was less a threat than the Soviet Union. In the late 1930s Poland suffered from the same inability to accept the dangers of Hitler's rearmament of Germany as did the Western powers themselves. Yet there did appear some late signs that Polish leaders were becoming wary of Nazi designs on the East. On 7 November 1938 Poland and the Soviet Union issued a joint declaration which reaffirmed the nonaggression pact of 1932. This was soon followed by an extensive trade agreement signed between the two states on 19 February 1939.[26]

It soon became apparent, however, that the Soviet Union was not concerned with Polish security. The Nazi-Soviet Pact of 23 August 1939 sealed the fate of Poland by giving the Nazis a free hand in the East. It was a death warrant for the reconstituted Polish state, allowing the Soviet annexation of Eastern Polish territories, including the cities of Lublin and Lwow. Beck's confidence that the pincers of Soviet and German power could be avoided by Poland proved unwarranted. Poland was not strong enough to play the balancer in the East European balance of power game.[27]

War-time Changes

It is not beyond reason to assume that Stalin was already at the time of the conclusion of the Nazi-Soviet Pact preparing for the eventual Soviet takeover of Poland. From 1939 until the German attack on the Soviet Union in June 1941, Poland no longer existed according to Soviet and German views. It had become a province of Germany in the West and incorporated into the Ukrainian and Belorussian republics of the USSR in the East. The Soviet occupation of Eastern Poland caused much misery and destruction—leaving hatred for communism in these areas that would not abate after the war.[28]

In 1941, after the abrogation of the "unholy alliance" by the Germans, Stalin quickly moved to mend fences with his new Western allies. One product of this move was an agreement concluded on 30 July 1941 between the government of Poles-in-exile in London and the Soviet government. This agreement included the recognition of Poland by the USSR, a rescinding of the territorial changes made in the Nazi-Soviet Pact, and establishment of diplomatic relations. Stalin could not have been very sincere in this maneuver, as the question of *future* Soviet-Polish relations was kept open.[29] Soviet dealing with the London Poles was, of course, necessitated by the need to keep relations with the allies as good as possible. However, Stalin's creation of the Polish Workers' Party (*Polska Partia Robotnicza*) in January 1942 spoke more clearly of Soviet intentions regarding future relations with the Poles.

The mass grave of several thousand Polish officers discovered by the Germans in Soviet-occupied territories in April 1943 further clarified the nature of Soviet intentions in Poland.[30] The long-term significance of what became known as the Katyn Forest massacre cannot be overestimated. Any future postwar political settlement would be affected, as Stalin well knew, by the presence of Polish nationalist elites. The eradication in one bold stroke of an estimated 15,000 of this elite — certainly part of the core of any possible opposition in a postwar Poland — could be counted on to alter substantially Poland's attitudes towards the Soviet Union. This was especially true in light of Soviet willingness (with German complicity) to dismantle Poland. Katyn would never be forgotten by the Poles. Perhaps more importantly, this event hindered the national communist movement in Poland in achieving legitimacy after the war.

Creation by the Soviet Union of a "Union of Polish Patriots" in Moscow enhanced Soviet claims of supporting the Polish resistance. Despite the disbanding of the Comintern in May 1943, plans for communist control of Poland continued methodically. A Moscow-trained Stalinist, Boleslaw Bierut, the first chairman of the Polish Workers' Party, was appointed head of the "National Council of Poland." This, along with another Moscow front organization, a "Committee of National Liberation of Poland," suggested that Moscow was creating the necessary mechanisms for the communist transformation of Poland's domestic politics.

The final elimination of opposition to what was becoming more apparent as Soviet manipulation of Polish politics came in August 1944, during the liberation of Poland from the East. The Polish underground (Home Army) attempted to liberate Warsaw, in full knowledge that Soviet forces were within striking distance to assist. Evidence seems clear that there was Soviet encouragement of an uprising in Warsaw and the suggestion that an assault on the capital city would be coordinated with the resistance. But Soviet forces held back, resulting in the destruction of the Home Army. This assured little resistance to the imminent Soviet occupation of all Poland. One Polish communist official was cited in 1946 on the debacle of the Warsaw uprising and its significance for the future of Poland:

> Had General Bor-Komorowski (Head of the Home Army) . . . succeeded in liberating Warsaw, they would have been heroes of Poland and would have formed the nucleus of

the government within Poland. It would have been most difficult under such circumstances for the Soviet government to maintain in power the Lublin Committee of National Liberation.[31]

Soviet-sponsored Communism in Poland

Despite the agreements reached by the Allies at both Teheran and Yalta on the nature of governments in Eastern Europe, the Red Army's presence dictated what was to be. Communist contrivance in the results of elections held in 1947 in Poland is well known.[32] The London Poles were being squeezed out of the domestic political arena by Moscow-controlled communists.

Wladyslaw Gomulka, one of the few Home Army communist survivors, succeeded Bierut as secretary of the Polish Workers' Party. Gomulka was a homebred communist who had no Moscow training — he had spent the 1930s in Poland while the party was being dissolved in Moscow. Gomulka faced a difficult task in broadening the political base of communism in postwar Poland:

> (the Polish Party) faced a harder task during 1944–45 than did other CP's in East Central Europe. Out of the ordeal of war, the Polish nation, although bled white, emerged more homogeneous than ever, both socially and politically; class distinctions were largely obliterated and party differences blurred, thus blunting the slogan of class struggle; religious sentiments both broadened and deepened. This also tended to increase resistance toward the new regime.[33]

In December 1948 the Polish Party of Socialists (Pilsudski's old party) merged with the Polish Workers' Party to form the Polish United Workers' Party (PUWP).[34] Democratic alternatives became a remnant of Poland's "bourgeois" past. Gomulka, who espoused a Polish road to socialism, was denounced in September 1948 as a "national deviationist" and was removed from the party in November 1949. Loyal Moscow-educated communists Edward Ochab and Boleslaw Bierut took the reins of party control.

Gomulka's differences with the Kremlin centered on his "national" approach to Poland's building of socialism and his lukewarm attitude to the establishment of the Cominform in 1947. His position was too easily identifiable with that of Josip Broz Tito in Yugoslavia, who, by 1948, was considered a traitor to international communism by Stalin. All nationally oriented elements were purged so that the example of

Tito might not be emulated by others in Poland as well as the rest of East Europe. The ideological platform of the PUWP, issued at its founding congress in 1948, emphasized the proper orientation for Polish communists:

> ... every tendency aimed at loosening collaboration with the Soviet Union endangers the very foundation of People's Democracy in Poland and, at the same time, the independence of the country. ... (the party) indissolubly links the cause of consolidating Poland's independence and her march towards socialism with the struggle for peace conducted under the leadership of the Soviet Union.[35]

The last years of Stalin's rule were characterized by the brutal exploitation of Poland and the other satellite nations. Extraction of economic resources and matériel from these countries approached phenomenal proportions in the years 1948–1953. By some estimates, the total was equivalent to the amount of dollars the Marshall Plan injected into Western Europe.[36]

Yet Poland was once again a national state. Although purging of unreliable elements continued, few were shot as had been the case in the 1930s. Gomulka remained alive, a prisoner of the Stalinist government. Stalin's primary concern was to keep Poland under strict supervision to guarantee Soviet control of the pathway by which invaders had devastated Russia twice in the twentieth century. Poland was now the linchpin in the newly formed Soviet security system. The territory of the Soviet Union had been enlarged by the annexation of former Polish lands (taken as a result of the Nazi-Soviet Pact). In return for this, Germany ceded eastern lands to the Polish People's Democratic Republic. Poland was now completely dependent upon the Soviet Union for its security and territorial integrity. There was no recourse for redressing grievances on any count.

During the course of nearly two centuries, Poland had existed as an independent entity for but twenty years, from 1919–1939. Except for this brief period of independence, Poland had been first subservient to, and then completely subjugated by, the Russian Empire. National identity and aspirations had survived despite attempts to extinguish them and integrate the Poles more completely into the imperial system.

The modern dilemma of Poland, survival between two powerful neighbors, came to the fore in the twentieth century and was embodied in the rivalry between the two most charismatic Polish political figures of the modern era, Roman Dmowski and Jozef Pilsudski. Each represented one aspect of continuity of Poland's geopolitical dilemma: Pilsudski represented opposition to first Russian and then Soviet imperialism and Polish reliance upon Russia as a protector, while Dmowski saw alliance with the Russians (and later the Soviets) as the more natural and less dangerous course to follow, given the power and ambitions of Germany.

With the defeat of Nazi Germany and the occupation of Poland by Russians once again, both dynamics of Poland's historical political dilemma continued to be manifest. Opposition to and collaboration with the Soviet power could be seen clearly in the Stalin period. The experiences of World War II and Stalinization had a lasting effect on Soviet-Polish relations in several ways.

First, a substantial widening of the gulf between Poland and the Soviet Union occurred as a result of the Katyn Forest episode and the Warsaw uprising. These tragic events emasculated the political elite of Poland and assisted the Soviet Union in exerting its complete control over postwar Poland.

Second, these Soviet actions sealed the fate of the PUWP itself in the communization of Poland by dictating the nature of the PUWP—a Moscow-controlled organization bereft of its prewar cadres (the purge of the Polish party in Moscow in the late 1930s achieved this result). This became the determining factor behind the inability of Poland to move in the direction of developing a "national" communism akin to what Tito achieved in Yugoslavia.

Third, one temporary (but important) result of the lack of Polish communist elites completely loyal to Moscow was the emplacement of Soviet overseers at key levers of control and responsibility within Poland. Perhaps this is best illustrated by the well-known example of Soviet Marshal Konstantin K. Rokossowsky, a war hero of Polish origin who served in several different capacities in postwar Polish government.

Poland now found itself completely dependent upon the Soviet Union to defend its national integrity and protect it from any threat that might arise from Germany again. It is not beyond the realm of possibility that Stalin planned just such a result. In any event, this guarantee of Polish security from the East was hardly enough to balance the record of Soviet actions towards Poland during the war or the postwar occupation of the country by the Red Army. These issues could not find any channel through which to be articulated in the face of tight Soviet control over political life in the Polish People's Republic (PPR). But they would not be forgotten.

2

De-Stalinization
and the Gomulka Years

THE parameters of Soviet-Polish relations had been, to a great extent, set by the Stalinist method of socialization of Eastern Europe. The collective Soviet leadership after Stalin had to resolve the twofold problem inherited from Stalin's legacy in East European countries: (1) popular disaffection with socialist regimes seen as nothing more than puppets of the Kremlin, and (2) persistent economic problems exacerbated by harsh Soviet demands. The nature of the challenge facing the new Soviet leadership in this regard was underscored by the outbreak of riots in 1953 in Soviet-occupied zones of Germany. This turmoil was a direct result of the serious economic situation created by Draconian Soviet policies.[1]

The destruction of Stalin's "cult of personality" by Nikita S. Khrushchev was a necessary career vehicle for the new leader, given the factions in opposition to him. But the upshot of the destruction of the Stalinist myth included the "collapse of the infallibility of the dogma," which led to increased disillusionment with both the Soviet party and Marxism in Eastern Europe. Even before Khrushchev's "secret speech" at the Twentieth CPSU Congress in February 1956, discontent of East European communists with heavy-handed Soviet policies was widespread.[2] The debunking of Stalin led to increased questioning of the Soviet role in East Europe. Although "separate roads to socialism" were validated by the Soviet leadership at this congress, the parameters of acceptable behavior in this pursuit were not clearly defined. No explicit prescriptions or Marxist-Leninist formulae were made available to East European party elites to help them deal with the new set of assumptions about Soviet-sponsored communism. An explosive situation developed in Poland that could be tied directly to the process of de-Stalinization occurring across East Europe.

Rehabilitation of Stalin's purge victims during the thaw period of de-Stalinization brought Gomulka back into the Polish political arena. Gomulka proved able to move quickly into the ranks of the party leadership and then rise to the very head of the party in October 1956 in part because he had attained the reputation of a national hero for championing the cause of Polish national rights and standing up to Stalin. However, a popular "national communist" leader was not what Khrushchev had in mind when proposing the separate-roads thesis. After Bierut's death in March 1956, Khrushchev had personally selected Edward Ochab, a Stalinist, to head the Polish party, which:

> . . . had the effect of assuring Moscow that, as in Czechoslovakia or East Germany, a loyal regime was established in Poland and that the newly legitimized theory of many ways to socialism would be interpreted by Ochab in keeping with the broad interests of the Soviet bloc.[3]

Yet popular opposition to the Moscow-backed regime of Ochab was so deeply seated even among old-line communists that the change to Gomulka was effected by the PUWP itself.

The touchstone of credibility in the new interpretation of Soviet-East European relations was loyal support of Soviet positions internationally and solidarity within the Warsaw Treaty Organization (WTO), which had been created in May 1955 as a security system in response to the remilitarization of West Germany and its inclusion in the North Atlantic Treaty Organization (NATO). In autumn 1956 Hungary under the leadership of Imre Nagy crossed the point of no return in this regard by announcing Hungary's secession from the WTO. The subsequent intervention of Soviet forces to "save socialism" in Hungary underscored the limits of national sovereignty of East European states. In the words of Wolfgang Kraus:

> . . . the inherent and crucial limitation upon the possibility of success was the strategic interest of the USSR, which made armed intervention a virtual requirement where these interests seemed threatened. Where, as in the case of Poland, a reintegrated party leadership with strong popular backing was clearly committed to the maintenance of the Moscow bond, there was no need for armed intervention.[4]

This, then, is why the "Polish October" escaped Soviet intervention. Moreover, the *unity* of the Polish regime with the Polish people through the summer and autumn of 1956 posed a crucial dilemma for the Soviet leadership. The degree of this unity would not reoccur. Certainly of greatest importance was Gomulka's provision of ample evidence to the Soviet leadership of Poland's intention to remain firmly within the Soviet security system.

Gomulka and the Kremlin

It has been suggested that the most important Polish gains under Gomulka's leadership were largely psychological in nature, including the perception of relative autonomy within the Soviet sphere of influence and the end of neocolonial exploitation.[5] However, the Soviet model of collectivization was in fact abandoned in the face of peasant resistance and religious instruction was again permitted, two factors of vital importance for subsequent Polish developments. Initially, Gomulka posed some problems for the Kremlin in 1957–1958 by opposing Soviet preference for multilateral (instead of bilateral) ties among communist parties. Gomulka also showed considerable opposition to the Soviet role as self-appointed arbiter of ideological questions. He wrote in 1957 that "the practice of directing all parties from one center is frequently harmful." While the Hungarian events of October 1956 were labelled "counterrevolutionary" by the Soviet media, *Trybuna Ludu,* the Polish party organ, blamed Stalinist excesses in Hungary for the situation. Furthermore, the Polish representative to the United Nations did not vote with the USSR on the issue of admitting impartial observers into Hungary, but rather, sided with the Yugoslavs, beginning a history of close contacts between these parties.[6]

Gomulka's initial support of polycentrism and a Polish road to socialism was not acceptable to the Soviet leaders. Under increasing Soviet pressure, Gomulka hardened his positions and brought them more into line with the Kremlin's views after 1957.[7] But this successful Soviet pressure did not prevent a far-reaching transformation from occurring in relations among East European regimes. The Polish events of 1956 and Gomulka's limited success in forging a quasi-independent approach to the Kremlin during 1956–1957 were instrumental in this change.[8]

Adam Bromke has suggested that Gomulka's behavior in 1956–1957 influenced Hungarian and Romanian leaders in their subsequent development of relatively autonomous positions in the East bloc. Both Gheorghe Gheorghiu-Dej, the Romanian leader, and Janos Kadar, the new Hungarian leader, had only positive regard for "Gomulkaism." Increasing criticism of remaining Stalinist elements in Antonin Novotny's regime in Czechoslovakia is also attributed by some to Poland's success in carrying out a leadership change without Soviet reprisal.[9]

While the influence of Poland's experience helped other East European peoples to find their own paths in the 1960s, Gomulka's return to a firm pro-Soviet line interrupted reform in Poland. In matters of foreign policy, Gomulka fell into step behind the Kremlin. He consistently supported the CPSU in its heated polemics with the Chinese (while, for example, Romania did not). His personal prestige was heightened among the Soviet leadership by his increasingly close association with Soviet foreign policy initiatives.[10]

Perhaps Gomulka's major point of agreement with Moscow was on the issue of a strong stand *vis-à-vis* the Federal Republic of Germany (FRG). The lack of a peace treaty between the FRG and East European states (including the Soviet Union) played an integral role in this stance. The postwar Oder-Neisse line was unacceptable to the FRG as Poland's western frontier, and West German Chancellor Konrad Adenauer's unequivocal refusal to recognize the statehood of the German Democratic Republic (GDR) further complicated the resolution of the German problem in Europe. Of course, a combination of (1) the renunciation of the Hallstein Doctrine (formal refusal to have diplomatic relations with any state recognizing the GDR), (2) the acceptance of postwar borders by the West, and (3) conclusion of peace treaties would serve to legitimize the Soviet postwar position in East Europe as well as bring formal Western recognition of the existence of two separate Germanys. Khrushchev's statements on the German question beginning in 1957 indicated how badly the Kremlin wanted to achieve these goals. Early Soviet pressures on Berlin were aimed at achieving this recognition of the GDR and a de jure Western affirmation of the Soviet position in East Europe.[11]

The spectre of a revanchist Germany seeking to redress border grievances with Poland was used by the Kremlin leaders to prove to Poland that the Soviet-sponsored East European security system was its only guarantee against a hostile and possibly aggressive West Germany now integrated into the NATO alliance. Although fear of a resurrected Germany might have held sway among Poles in the early postwar period, this image of the German threat became less effective as Europe recovered from the ravages of World War II.

By the mid-1960s, with the advent of the Kurt Kiesinger-Willy Brandt coalition, the possibility of a revaluation of West German positions presented itself in the guise of the FRG's *Ostpolitik*. But Leonid Brezhnev and Alexei Kosygin had been successful in 1964 in ousting Khrushchev from the Kremlin leadership. The new collective leadership in the Soviet Union reacted negatively to unregulated attempts at West German "bridges" being built into East Europe without the formal resolution of the German problem. The unresolved German problem, in turn, formed an important part of the background against which Czechoslovak events of 1967–1968 were played out.

Poland and the Czechoslovak Crisis of 1968

The Czechoslovak events of 1967–1968, which culminated in the Soviet-sponsored WTO intervention in Czechoslovakia in August 1968, have been expertly detailed and analyzed elsewhere.[12] It is enough for the purpose of this study to recapitulate the salient elements of the Czechoslovak reform movement and Soviet and Polish reactions to it. This will assist in providing a clearer understanding of later Soviet and Czechoslovak reactions to Polish developments at the end of the 1970s and in 1980–1981.

Policies of the CPCz from December 1967 through the spring of 1968 were aimed at reforming the sad economic state of affairs which long years of economic malfeasance under the regime of Antonin Novotny had fostered. The party itself desired a change and selected Alexander Dubcek to lead Czechoslovakia in a new direction. Debate over economic reform had already begun to broaden before Dubcek assumed party leadership. Under Dubcek, this process accelerated. On 24 April 1968 the government of the Czechoslovak Socialist Republic (CSR) officially recognized that "democratic trends" in the FRG were now visible and seemed to favor normalization of relations with Bonn without the settlement of the German issue to the satisfaction of Soviet and Polish leaders.[13] The spectre of bilateral relations developing between East and West European countries without Soviet sanction threatened to weaken the unity of the WTO against NATO, and particularly against the threat of a ravanchist Germany.

An anti-Zionist campaign on the heels of Polish student protests (influenced by the situation in the CSR) in early March 1968 had brought severe criticism from the Czechoslovak media. Apparently, Prague had been reevaluating its policy towards Israel as well.[14] Official Polish protests concerning "slander" of Poland in the Czechoslovak press became the first sign that Czechoslovak events were perceived by the PUWP as threatening. Polemics escalated in the Polish media in spring 1968 against "antisocialist tendencies" in Czechoslovakia and the dangerous situation that was emerging there.[15] Polish party press organs were utilized by Moscow to criticize the course of events in the early going. The threat of a Czechoslovak rapprochement with West Germany without a mutually accepted understanding between East and West was also of serious concern to the GDR. These three actors, Poland, East Germany, and the Soviet Union, played the most important roles in the offensive launched against the Prague Spring. The oft-repeated accusation of "subversion from within" implied that a betrayal of socialism was taking place not only within the country, but within the party as well.[16]

Polish Premier Jozef Cyrankiewicz assessed Czechoslovak developments as: (1) threatening the leading role of the party, (2) propagating principles of bourgeois democracy, (3) undermining the unity of socialist countries. All this was allegedly in preparation for an "antisocialist counterrevolution."[17] Throughout the summer, the shadow of another Hungarian-type intervention to "save socialism" hung over the CSR. Indeed, it was bluntly asserted that anything to save socialism would be done if socialism was threatened anywhere in East Europe.[18] Continued revisionism in the CSR could provide a new model of socialism for other East bloc states. Moreover, during the summer of 1968, there appeared evidence suggesting that unrest in Western Ukraine was related to Czechoslovak events. Nationalist problems had resurfaced in Ukraine in the 1960s and it has been said that Dubcek, Slovak by nationality, had admiration for Ukrainian nationalists' programmatic aspirations. Radio broadcasts from Slovakia into Ukraine ostensibly threatened to spread "bourgeois anti-Leninism" into the Soviet Republic. Rumors of strikes in Southern Ukraine during the summer also surfaced. It has been said that Petro Shelest, Ukrainian party boss and Soviet Politburo member, was the most outspoken advocate of crushing the revisionist elements within the CPCz and restoring socialist order to Czechoslovakia.[19] "Socialism with a human face" could not be left to develop and threaten CPSU-defined "real socialism" anywhere in the bloc.

The significance of the phenomenon of the Prague Spring for both Soviet-East European relations and international communism at large became fully apparent only in the wake of the military intervention of 21 August 1968, which stifled the reform movement in the Czechoslovak state. Romania, the only WTO member that did not assist in the intervention, put its militia on twenty-four hour alert and denounced the WTO action. Perhaps the Romanians were wary of reprisals against them, for they had been following a substantially independent foreign policy for some years.[20] Yugoslav and Spanish communists expressed "deep sympathy" for the tragic upshot of the Czechoslovak experiment.[21] The ensuing communist polarization over the WTO intervention was only the beginning of a more lengthy process of reappraisal by various parties in the communist movement of the nature of Soviet leadership.

Moscow, still considering itself primus inter pares in the international communist movement, declared one month later that the Kremlin had the right to defend the interests of socialism anywhere it was threatened.[22] Even before the enunciation of the Brezhnev Doctrine, which claimed limited sovereignty of socialist states, *Polish* justification for the necessity of intervention emphasized the crucial nature of the problem. The loyalty of the Polish People's Republic to the foreign policy of the Soviet Union was apparent in the words of Mieczyslaw F. Rakowski, editor of the Polish journal *Polityka:*

> A trend towards a free-play of forces is unacceptable in the situation where the basic problem of our epoch—kto kogo— has not yet been finally resolved . . . it becomes clear that the development of socialism without the leading role of the party is impossible.

Indeed, this was unacceptable because a change in the "balance of forces" between socialism and capitalism on the European continent was threatened by the Prague Spring.[23] *Zolnierz Wolnosci,* the Polish party's military newspaper, criticized both Yugoslavia and Romania for their stance against the WTO action.[24] Staunch support by the Polish leadership of the Soviet-sponsored intervention throughout the summer and autumn signified Polish acceptance of the CPSU's definition of the proper path towards achieving socialism and Polish affirmation of the CPSU's leading role in the movement.

Economic questions were not at the core of the debate surrounding Czechoslovak reformism. After all, significant steps toward economic reform had already been undertaken in Hungary earlier in 1968 with the introduction of the New Economic Mechanism. An internal PUWP debate regarding stagnation in the Polish economy and methods of dealing with it had also been in process for some years.[25] The paramount issue was political in nature. How far could reform go before political repercussions began to manifest themselves? The Soviet response to Czechoslovak events of 1968 seemed to establish clearly the parameters of reform. Political developments threatening the suprem-

acy of the communist party put into question the feasibility of economic reform. Moreover, without a general European recognition of
the immutability of socialism in East Europe, bilateral contacts, particularly with the FRG, would not be allowed to develop.

Aftermath of the Prague Spring and Gomulka's Demise

Alternatives to single party dominance of the CPCz, independence
from the USSR, and development of a different road to socialism were
the main themes of the Prague Spring. The Soviet Union defended the
intervention by condemning external forces (primarily in the FRG) and
internal "opportunism" seeking to change the system in the CSR:

> The right opportunists give their own interpretation of the
> changes taking place in the world. . . . They identify the
> possibility of a peaceful road to socialism with parliamentar-
> ianism, and seek to justify the unscientific contrapositioning
> of the "democratic" road to the road of revolution. . . . The
> offensive of right opportunism was of the most violent na-
> ture in Czechoslovakia where it threatened the social sys-
> tem. Czechoslovak events were further reminder of the im-
> portance of consistently fighting right opportunism. . . .[26]

Such reminders were not primarily directed at the CPCz, for the political situation had been stabilized in the CSR. By 1969 Dubcek had been
replaced by Gustav Husak as CPCz leader and the levers of control
within the party passed into the hands of loyal Moscow-oriented communists.[27] Rather, such analyses by Soviet ideologues were directed at
the international communist movement at large and signalled the
Kremlin's categorical reaffirmation of its role as sole arbiter of doctrine
and individual parties' validity in their search for paths to socialism.

Because of the furor arising in the international communist movement over the Czechoslovak intervention, plans for an international
conference of communist parties sometime late in 1968 were set aside.
The Communist Party of Italy (PCI) denounced the invasion and validated the rightness of the Dubcek path, rejecting at the same time
Moscow's doctrine of limited sovereignty.[28] Although the CPSU still
had the support of important communist leaders such as Gomulka and
GDR chief Walter Ulbricht, criticism of the Soviet party soon increased and sharpened elsewhere in the communist movement. The
problem of deteriorating relations with the Chinese very likely was
behind the Soviet desire for an international conference as soon as

possible to reestablish general communist support for Soviet positions internationally.[29] Postponement of this conference to 1969 was necessary so that the preoccupation with the intervention could subside both in the West and throughout the communist movement.

When the conference was finally convened in June 1969, it proved to be an embarrassment to Soviet foreign policy, for Czechoslovakia was discussed at length. The final document produced by this conference, which included a guarantee of "no internal interference in party relations" but no mention of the CPSU's "leading role" in the movement, indicated an erosion of the CPSU's prestige.[30]

Earlier, in March 1969, when the Warsaw Pact nations jointly issued an invitation to the West Europeans to participate in a mutual security conference (what later became the Conference on Security and Cooperation in Europe), it was suggested that part of the impetus behind this action had been rooted in the Soviet desire to erase memories of the WTO intervention and proceed with state and party affairs as before the crisis.[31]

Gomulka developed a noticeably muted tone regarding the FRG early in 1969, seemingly in line with the fledgling Soviet detente initiative. This change was apparently in response to overtures from West Germany concerning normalization of relations, possibly through the conclusion of a peace treaty.[32] Gomulka publicly announced an official change in policy towards the FRG at a rally in Warsaw on 17 May 1969.[33]

Negotiations on the German peace treaty and border questions continued throughout 1970. The crowning achievement of Gomulka's foreign policy, in unison with the Soviet detente effort, was the signing of the Bonn-Warsaw Treaty on 7 December 1970, finally resolving the issue of borders. This agreement was followed by similar agreements between the FRG and GDR, and the FRG and the USSR. This entire process was only possible with the direct sanction of the Kremlin within the broader framework of Soviet detente strategy.

Despite the historic nature of this achievement, within two short weeks Gomulka was ousted as secretary of the PUWP in the wake of food riots that erupted in Szczecin and Gdansk after the announcement of significant price increases in food stuffs.[34] In the final analysis, internal forces directed toward change toppled Gomulka, similar to those forces that had brought him back into the party leadership in 1956. Economic problems had contributed to growing factionalism in the PUWP in the 1960s. Several months prior to Gomulka's demise, a clear indication of the nature of the problem was voiced in the Polish daily *Zycie Warszawy*.

> . . . we should make it clear to the heroes of the past cen-
> tury, who are now trying to rest on their laurels, that if they
> refuse (although they can and know how) to achieve new
> skills, if they fail to be open to innovations, the slowly rising
> but already visible New Wave will sweep them from their
> positions in society.[35]

Feeble reforms initiated by the Gomulka regime in 1969 were not sufficient to resolve the deep-seated problems of managerial ineffi-ciency and technological backwardness of the Polish economy. Edward Gierek, Silesian party secretary and leader of the "younger generation of technocrats," came to an understanding with his chief rival and leader of an influential and markedly nationalist "partisan" faction, Mieczyslaw Moczar; they were able to convince the Central Commit-tee of the PUWP that it was time for a change.[36] In line with the growing Soviet impetus towards detente, the time was ripe for seeking solutions to economic problems in the expansion of relations with the West.

In autumn 1956 Polish relations with the Soviet Union were put on a new footing: the parameters of exploitation were narrowed by the Gomulka regime and a modicum of independence was granted to Po-land in the framework of the new "socialist commonwealth" sponsored by the Soviet Union. The essence of the 1956 "revolution" in Polish politics was twofold. It included both the ending of crude Soviet ex-ploitation of Poland and the rebirth of a national identity on the level of national politics. This new direction in Polish politics did not include a visible anti-Russian or anti-Soviet character. To exhibit such a charac-ter could have risked a Soviet response similar to the one in Hungary during that same autumn.

After several initial forays that appeared somewhat independent of Soviet policy, Gomulka quickly returned to a staunch pro-Soviet posi-tion (1957). Gomulka's loyalty to the Soviet Union continued right up until his ouster from the PUWP leadership in 1970. In retrospect, Gomulka was able to reassert, to a large extent, PUWP control over Poland. Yet victories such as the removal of Marshal Rokossowsky from Polish politics could only be accepted by the Kremlin with the firm knowledge that Moscow loyalists would continue to guide PUWP policy, especially in the foreign sphere.

By 1970 the de facto resolution of the German problem (de jure by 1971–1972) created new opportunities for Poland, as well as for the rest of the East bloc. Poland was already by the late 1960s becoming an important actor on the international stage, taking advantage of its

role as the Soviet Union's largest ally. The collaboration of the Gomulka regime with the CPSU on international issues of crucial importance to the Soviet Union identified Poland as a true friend of the
USSR and an example for others to follow.

However, 1970 would also set a precedent for Soviet behavior in
the Polish crisis as it developed in the late 1970s. The Soviet leaders
would stick with "their man" in Warsaw despite serious economic
failures. Gomulka's departure from the Polish political scene was attributed to an illness, while direct criticism connecting him with the
economic problems that had forced him from the party leadership were
avoided. The autarkic policies of the Gomulka era would be challenged
by the new PUWP leader Edward Gierek to take advantage of the new
opportunities open to Poland in the international arena and to move
towards solving Poland's economic problems. This new direction plotted by the "technocrats" now in charge of the PUWP would subsequently generate an entirely new slate of economic and political problems.

Popular disaffection with the Polish road to socialism under Gomulka was mirrored in the riots and demonstrations of December
1970. This disaffection was, in part, the product of a broader disenchantment with Poland's international position, both within the Soviet
bloc and in the wider European context. The new PUWP leadership,
under Gierek, would strive to manipulate this dissatisfaction to its
advantage as Poland began to modernize its economy in the 1970s.

II

Interplay of Determinants:
Soviet-Polish Relations, 1970s

3

Gierek, the Kremlin, and Detente

ECONOMIC viability may be the only domestic basis of legitimacy that East European leaders have.[1] Since 1956 the Kremlin leadership has evidenced some flexibility in allowing East European parties greater leeway in determining their processes of leadership succession without excessive Soviet interference. Moscow has appreciated the necessity of allowing East European regimes more independence in pursuing greater viability, while at the same time it has attempted increasing the cohesion of the bloc.[2]

Edward Gierek was able to produce a consensus in the PUWP which, on the one hand, agreed to a drastic change in domestic economic policy, and on the other, soberly realized that this change in policy could not be allowed to feed the political unrest already evidenced in the riots at Gdansk, Gdynia, and Szczecin in 1970. The example of Czechoslovakia in 1968, where economic problems had led to a political threat to the communist system itself and subsequently to Soviet intervention, could not be ignored. Any reforms were to be orderly and limited to the economic sphere without allowing any spillover of this process into the political arena.

In order to secure Soviet support of his new position as leader of the PUWP, Gierek journeyed to Moscow shortly after his assumption of power. Loans were granted by the Soviet Union to assist in defusing the precarious economic situation. The Soviet Union granted to Poland one billion rubles of credit (including hard currency) to help the new leadership stabilize the domestic situation. The price hikes that had precipitated the food riots were rescinded within several weeks; other economic concessions were made by the Gierek regime to Polish society, including a price freeze of two years.[3]

A new direction was promised for Poland as Gierek supplanted old-line Gomulkaists with the younger generation of technocrats like himself. Modernization of the Polish economy was at the core of Gierek's promises to the Polish people. Under the aegis of detente and with the German question finally resolved to the satisfaction of the Soviet Union and Poland, this seemed to be a concrete possibility. Yet this new direction plotted for Poland did not alter the nature of Poland's relationship to the Soviet Union. Gierek, just as Gomulka before him, realized the crucial significance of the Soviet-Polish relationship to the very existence of the Polish state.[4]

Gierek was unique among East European leaders in that he had spent time in the 1930s in the Belgian trade union movement (he was a miner by trade) and spoke fluent French. His views of the Soviet Union could be considered to be somewhat different from Gomulka's. Although Gierek, like Gomulka, had not been schooled in Moscow, he was not, like his predecessor, a "home-grown" communist. He was unaffected by the tragic fate of Polish communists in the 1930s. These factors, it could be suggested, helped to shape a view of both the Soviet Union and the future of Poland that was not purely Polish but rather seasoned substantially with West European leftist perspectives.

In pursuing the number-one priority of improving the domestic economy, the new regime did not limit itself to critiquing only the ousted leadership. Management at all levels was indicted for the steadily deteriorating economic situation that began in the mid-1960s:

> Dissatisfaction with economic and social policy with the way the affairs of the party and state were being managed, has been growing and spreading for a considerable time. . . . Everyone of us bears a part of the responsibility . . . unfortunately, somewhere in the mid-1960's, after the 4th PUWP Congress, the crisis in the leadership of the party and state became more and more apparent.[5]

Embarking on the path of better ties with the West under the rubric of detente was part of the solution to Poland's problems. Shortly after the leadership change, the nature of "special ties" between West Europe and Poland were alluded to by *Zycie Warszawy* in an article entitled, "Historical Variants and Contemporary Polish Politics."[6] It was implied that Poland was an equal partner to the Soviet Union in efforts towards detente with the West:

> While dynamically comprehending Polish politics, we have a
> great opportunity in support of the Soviet Union and the
> entire socialist community. Simultaneously, the USSR has in
> Poland, in consideration of her spiritual ties with the Euro-
> pean culture, a valuable alliance in the struggle . . . for col-
> lective security on our continent. From this perspective, de-
> spite all our internal and economic problems, we are obliged
> as a nation to fully appreciate our opportunities and latest
> achievements in international politics.[7]

It appeared that changes in both the domestic economy and Poland's
foreign policy would go hand in hand. However, this did not imply
eagerness for institutional reform in People's Poland. As A. Ross Johnson has noted, the initial trade-union reforms that followed on the heels
of the December 1970 demonstrations were limited in scope and not
analogous to institutional reforms undertaken in the 1960s in either
Hungary or Yugoslavia. Limited concessions were made as a result of
pressure "from below" in Poland, but this did not mirror to any significant degree the reforms implemented "from above" in both Hungary
and Yugoslavia. Indeed, Gierek was able to convince Brezhnev and
other East European leaders that he was not a "reformer" and thereby
secured Kremlin sanction of his position. He was "a sincere friend of
the Soviet Union, a convinced communist and internationalist" who, we
can presume, would not allow domestic pressures to jeopardize his
position vis-à-vis his Soviet allies.[8]

The deep-rooted problems of Poland reflected a substantially different socialist commonwealth from a decade earlier. The CPSU took
note of the considerable changes in the socialist world during the latter
part of the 1960s on the occasion of its twenty-fourth congress in 1971.
The Central Committee report to this congress recognized that certain
"difficulties and complications" had arisen in the world socialist system. Events in Czechoslovakia in 1968 and in Poland in 1970 were the
primary problematic developments since the last party congress in
1966. Although the process of detente was proceeding apace and the
German problem was being resolved, achievement of unity *within* the
socialist camp was considered a "complicated task" due partially to
nationalistic tendencies, "left-" and "right-wing" opportunism, and efforts of Chinese "splittism."[9]

According to the international report of the Central Committee of
the CPSU, the capitalist system had succeeded by 1971 in "adapting to
new conditions," which, as Franklyn Griffiths has suggested, implied:

> . . . the opposing social system was doing sufficiently well
> in the economic and technical competition to justify a
> greater Soviet commitment to East-West economic coopera-

tion and technology transfer to compete more efficiently in areas in which the USSR was threatened with being left behind.[10]

In tandem with Soviet initiatives in this regard, Gierek and the Polish party were prepared to take advantage of this new climate as well.

1970–1975 was a period of general expansion of East-West trade in a climate of "relaxation of tensions" in the framework of an all-European Conference on Security and Cooperation (CSCE). The nature of the expansion in trade could briefly be described as exchange of raw materials (and some manufactured goods) for technology and hard currency loans to provide for the intensive development and modernization of East European industry.[11]

Within the framework of growing East-West detente and with the object of exploiting Poland's "special ties" to West Europe, the Polish Republic's economic relations with the West, specifically the European Economic Community (EEC), increased dramatically. Some economic figures will assist in communicating the magnitude of this change in policy from Gomulka's relatively autarkic (in relation to the West) policies and the attendant implications for Polish politics.

While total indebtedness in hard currency of the six East European socialist countries (excluding the USSR) increased from $4.6 billion in 1970 to $19.1 billion in 1975, Poland's debt rose from $0.8 billion to $6.9 billion during the same period.[12] These figures reflect a percentage increase of 415 percent total East bloc indebtedness and an 862 percent increase in Poland's debt. In other words, the hard currency debt rose twice as fast for the Polish People's Republic as it did for the Council for Mutual Economic Assistance (CMEA) nations (minus USSR) in the aggregate (Table 3.1 and Table 3.2).

Moreover, the contribution of hard currency debt to growth of

TABLE 3.1.   Eastern European Net Hard Currency Debt 1970–1975
($ Billions)

	1970	1974	1975
Poland	0.8	3.9	6.9
Czechoslovakia	0.3	1.1	1.5
Hungary	0.6	1.5	2.1
GDR	1.0	2.8	3.8
Bulgaria	0.7	1.2	1.8
Romania	1.2	2.6	3.0

Source: Extrapolated from Paul Marer, "The Economies of Eastern Europe and Soviet Foreign Policy," in *The Domestic Context of Soviet Foreign Policy,* ed. Seweryn Bialer (Boulder: Westview, 1981), 279.

TABLE 3.2. Exports from Eastern Europe to Western Europe, 1975
(percent)

	Fuels	Primary Products	Manufactures
Poland[a]	37.0	25.0	38.0
Romania	20.8	28.3	50.8
Czechoslovakia	14.3	20.3	65.4
GDR	6.8	23.2	70.0
Hungary	2.1	43.1	54.8
Bulgaria	1.9	48.2	49.9

Source: Thomas Wolf, "East-West European Trade Relations," in JEC, *East European Economies Post-Helsinki* (Washington, D.C.: USGPO, 1977), cited in Marer, 285.

[a] Terms of trade with West Europe increased favorably only in Poland during this time. In all other cases, terms of trade deteriorated except in Romania, where they remained roughly the same (see Marer, 285).

GNP, as calculated by Paul Marer of Indiana University, was largest in Poland in comparison with the rest of the bloc during the first half of the 1970s. This figure is 20 percent.[13] Substantial increases in the standard of living seemed to suggest that Gierek's economic program was working during this time. Soviet commentary indicated that this was not contrary to proper communist orientations:

> It stands to reason that the immediate tasks of the further development in the socialist countries are essentially different from those in capitalist countries. The representatives of the communist and workers' parties that are in power confirmed their striving to use the favorable international conditions for the further strengthening of economic power and for the raising of the living standard of the working people and for perfecting the new social system.

This evaluation, however, was under certain caveats. Expansion of relations under favorable conditions was to be based on "unity of action of the socialist community in the international arena."[14] A repeat of the Czechoslovak experience of 1968 was to be avoided, in part, by greater integration of the bloc. Individual socialist countries' independent development of relations was not encouraged.

The continued success of Gierek's plans for modernization in Poland was predicated upon continued expansion of East-West ties. Beginning in 1972, a noticeable trend emerged: while Poland's trade with the West was rising quickly, the PPR's share of CMEA trade was declining. There was no sign that either this reorientation of Polish trade or the rising Polish debt to the West was considered harmful by the Polish leadership or by the Soviet leadership itself as late as 1975. Soviet and East European press organs waged a tireless campaign for the realization of the Final Act of CSCE during the period 1972–1975.[15] Poland was especially visible in this campaign. Reservations about the Helsinki process, which included increased trade contacts, were voiced only intermittently about certain unnamed aspects of Basket III, the so-called human rights component of the talks. It was recognized that CSCE developments were not necessarily "irreversible."[16] But these were minor reservations. Soviet analysis of the first half of the decade depicted an emergent "equilibrium" between the blocs as the "correlation of forces" stabilized in the climate of detente.[17] We can assume that this would continue to be the case so long as unity and socialist internationalism continued to characterize East bloc actions.

By 1975 a definite self-perception of Poland may be discerned, which could be described as one of "mediator" between the superpowers in the game of detente.[18] President Nixon had visited Warsaw after the Moscow summit of 1972, where the principles of detente were approved and the SALT I agreement was signed. Poland's prestige was enhanced both by this visit and the return visit paid by Gierek to Washington in 1974. Internationally, as well as domestically, the PPR was basking in the warm glow of detente's success. The crisis of 1970 very likely seemed to be a distant historical event to the Gierek regime, one not linked to the current leadership with its domestic successes and growing international prestige. CSCE's progress suggested that, despite some minor reservations, expansion of both the good life in Poland and Poland's international prestige was to continue, a situation unprecedented in modern Polish politics.

The first five years of Gierek's rule in Poland were not characterized by the implementation of economic policies unpopular with the masses. Price increases on basic commodities were avoided in appreciation, no doubt, of the disastrous results price hikes had for the Gomulka regime. Despite enormous state subsidies of basic commodities, the problem of pricing in the economy remained serious.

There were no visible signs indicating that the Kremlin leaders perceived the Gierek regime as going too far in expanding trade with the West or going beyond the basic principles the Soviet leadership itself had laid down in 1971.[19] In October 1974, during Gierek's visit to Washington, a long-term trade agreement was signed between the Polish leader and President Ford. Further expansion of Polish trade with the West was especially important during this time because of effects being felt in East Europe from the general world energy crisis. This Polish-American agreement meant an expansion of Polish coal production.[20] France also continued to be a major target of Polish economic interest. For example, during a state visit to Poland in June 1975, President Giscard d'Estaing of France granted f7 billion of credit to the PPR, in addition to the f4.5 billion already granted in the early 1970s.[21]

Gierek's policies not only enhanced his own stature as a world leader, but also benefited the Soviet Union in two ways. First, increased trade with the West lessened Polish reliance on Soviet economic assistance. Second, the success of Polish policy deepened the process of detente with the West. Gierek's loyalty to the Soviet Union during this time was unquestioned. He has been described as going "out of his way" to cater to Brezhnev's foreign policy in the first years of his leadership of the PUWP. Both leaders desired increased technology transfer to enable their countries to compete more effectively with the West. Gierek's loyalty prompted a characterization of the PPR as not only a trusted ally, but a prime example of "international relations of a new type" in its staunch support of Soviet foreign policy.[22]

Despite all this evident Polish success as loyal executor of Soviet detente policy, the Final Act of Helsinki brought with it unexpected problems to the East bloc as a whole and to Poland in particular. It soon became apparent that neither the problems of the Polish economy nor the crisis that the party experienced under Gomulka's leadership had been adequately resolved.

First Signs of Soviet Concern

The implications of the Helsinki process for Soviet policy in East Europe began to clarify themselves in late 1975. Whatever reservations Soviet leaders might have had about the possible domestic repercussions in East European countries of expanded East-West contact *prior* to the conclusion of the Helsinki Final Act, *after* July 1975 it began to seem that these reservations were indeed warranted. The first indication that Helsinki's effects on East Europe were not wholly positive came in the form of a constitutional debate in Poland beginning in autumn 1975 ostensibly in preparation for the Seventh PUWP Congress, scheduled to convene in early 1976.

Diverse forces both within and outside the ranks of the PUWP, taking strength from the new political climate created by Helsinki, mounted a challenge to the wording of certain proposed changes to the constitution recommended by loyal pro-Moscow elements within the PUWP. Edward Babiuch, president of the PPR, supported these proposed amendments to the twenty-four year old constitution, in order that the role of the PUWP in Polish society be more clearly defined:

> The historic fact that the PPR is a socialist country in which
> power belongs to the working people of the towns and vil-
> lages and *the leading force is the PUWP* must be confirmed
> in the constitution.[23]

The amendments offered in September were to mirror the "new type of
international relations" between the PPR and the USSR. They included statements reflecting:

1. Unshakeable fraternal bonds with the USSR
2. Affirmation of the PUWP's leading role
3. The nature of citizens' rights to be dependent upon fulfillment
   of duties to the state
4. An increased restriction of dissent in two clauses[24]

The intense debate over these amendments lasted through to the
party congress in February 1976 and ended, surprisingly, in their resounding defeat. In place of these changes, watered-down versions
appeared stating that Poland was:

> . . . guided by the interests of the Polish nation, its sov-
> ereignty, independence and security and the desire for peace
> and international cooperation . . . (and) the noble tradition of
> solidarity with the forces of freedom and progress
> strengthens friendship and cooperation with the Soviet Un-
> ion and other socialist states.[25]

The PUWP was referred to only as "a leading force" in the process of
constructing socialism. As one German observer noted, these were
rather "dry words" compared to the original changes offered just after
the Final Act of Helsinki was signed. The broad array of social forces
that participated in the debate and the defeat of Moscow loyalists on
this issue included the church, disenchanted intellectuals and workers,
and elements within the party itself.[26]

It has been suggested that the PUWP was being pressured in the
immediate aftermath of Helsinki to reword the Polish constitution to
"accelerate ideological integration" within the bloc and to reflect Poland's "falling into line" behind the rest of the WTO states, whose
constitutions without exception clearly enunciated a more orthodox,
pro-Soviet line.[27] The extent of Soviet disappointment over this defeat
of Moscow loyalists within the PUWP can only be surmised. Clearly,
the backing down of the regime was a blow to "business as usual" in
the conduct of Soviet policy and influence within the PUWP. National
Polish interests, as depicted in the wording of key clauses, were identi-

fied in clear contrast to Soviet-defined *internationalist* interests of socialism and the class struggle.

The Road to the Berlin Conference

In 1976 larger issues in the international communist movement were also at the forefront of Soviet policy towards Europe. The CPSU was planning an international European communist conference to present a picture of communist unity behind the Soviet Union's foreign policy and to dispel the rumblings of disaffection with Soviet policy that had been in evidence since the WTO intervention in Czechoslovakia in 1968. It will be recalled that the intervention precipitated unprecedented criticism on the part of the West and some East European parties regarding Soviet motivations.

The growing influence of the large West European parties in the movement, especially the Italian and the French, could have been a primary reason why this conference was considered so important to the CPSU. "Eurocommunists," as they had been christened by a Yugoslav spokesman, were to be drawn back into the fold at the conference, as the spectre of Czechoslovakia in 1968 faded from public consciousness.

At the CPSU's Twenty-Fifth Party Congress in February 1976, Secretary Gierek was given the honor of speaking first among the foreign delegates in attendance. His speech centered on detente, implied ideological unity with the CPSU, and reported that preparations were proceeding successfully for the forthcoming East Berlin Conference of Communist Parties, which was to take place in June. Since the initial October 1974 announcement of this conference, the PUWP and the Communist Party of Italy (PCI) had been jointly cooperating as heads of the preparatory commission for the meeting. The PCI had emerged as perhaps the most outspoken critic among the West European parties about the Czechoslovak invasion and Soviet control of the international communist movement.

The presence of the PCI on the planning committee of this important conference was, in and of itself, enough of a reason to suspect Soviet apprehension about the possible content of the conference. But the lapse of time between the Czechoslovak intervention and this conference was perhaps thought sufficient assurance of a more favorable climate for a general reassertion of the CPSU's leading role in the movement. Soviet leaders no doubt wanted to avoid another debacle like the last conference of European parties held in Moscow in 1969. As noted earlier, Soviet prestige had been damaged by pointed criticisms at the Moscow conference.[28]

The CPSU had attempted to ensure against possible repetition of the embarrassment of the 1969 Moscow conference by continuously stressing orthodoxy and castigating those who would damage international communist unity. Lines were clearly drawn at the party's Twenty-Fifth Congress in 1976 around these issues:

> Unfortunately, some people have begun to interpret [proletarian internationalism] in such a way that in fact, little remains of internationalism. There are people who openly suggest that internationalism be renounced. In their opinion [it] has become outmoded.

The Central Committee report from this congress also claimed that "primary attention" had been given to alliance relations since the last congress in 1971.[29] This clearly indicated increased Soviet concern about the bloc during the height of detente. The CPSU could not view with equanimity the possibility that increasing Eurocommunist criticism of Soviet international policies could begin to fuel criticism among ruling parties as well.

The French Communist Party (PCF) had boycotted the Twenty-Fifth CPSU Congress in 1976. Reasons for this snub included the PCF's unhappiness with Soviet leader Brezhnev's apparent courting of French President Valery Giscard d'Estaing, seemingly in disregard of the French Left's struggle and PCF leader George Marchais's own electoral aspirations. The PCF had allied itself with the French Socialist Party (PSF) earlier in hopes of buttressing its own electoral strength and challenging Centrist control of the government. At its own Twenty-Second Congress in February 1976, the PCF had criticized the Soviet Union and stricken from its records all reference to the Leninist tenet of "dictatorship of the proletariat." Increasing Soviet polemics against such developments in the West European parties implied that the CPSU was concerned with the possibility of the spreading of such dangerous ideological revisionism to the Eastern parties. This is why the issue of international communist solidarity was so vital to the Soviet party and why it would continue to struggle with resurfacing revisionist tendencies, so evident already by 1975–1976.

The Poles enthusiastically fell into line behind Brezhnev's detente policy towards France and Germany in particular. This drew PCF criticism of the PUWP as well. The PCF sharply criticized the Polish government concerning the visit of Premier Piotr Jaroszewicz to Paris in May of 1976.[30] It seemed that Eurocommunists, particularly the

French, were being left to fend for themselves in a climate of expanding detente between East and West—a situation in which East bloc leaders, particularly Brezhnev and Gierek, were, in effect, sanctioning the rule of Centrist politics in the West to the detriment of the Left.

CPSU leaders no doubt hoped that the presence of the PUWP in the planning process of the East Berlin Conference would help to buffer the growing disagreements between the nonruling Western parties and the CPSU. After all, the PUWP had evidenced its loyal support of Soviet policy during the first five years of Gierek's tenure as PUWP leader.

When the conference finally convened on 29 June 1976 Gierek, as co-planner of the meeting, spoke first and indicated that unity was to be the hallmark of the conference. He expressed his

> . . . confidence that the document of the conference of fraternal parties will facilitate the development of internationalist bilateral and multilateral ties among them and the strengthening of their unity.[31]

However, an expansion of bilateral ties with parties already discussing "pluralism" as a political orientation and revising Marxist-Leninist dogma was hardly what Kremlin leaders had in mind. In an atmosphere of de facto fractured unity (since the Prague Spring), such moderate statements by Gierek failed to reflect Soviet concerns.

Just prior to the conference, Italian sources had predicted how the meeting would differ from what the Soviet leaders either desired or expected:

> The Italian Party intends to reiterate the innovative principles contained in the document stated by the preparatory commission. The principles are: each party's autonomy, consensus as a work method, reaffirmation of the Helsinki Pan-European Conference and starting with the principles of Marxism-Leninism, *in absolute equality of rights—each party freely chooses its strategy for the construction of socialism* (emphasis added).[32]

That these "innovative principles" were jointly composed by the PUWP and the PCI in the preparatory sessions of the conference suggests, at the very least, a disappointing performance by the PUWP in its support of CPSU positions. When compared to the public statements of both the Bulgarian and Czechoslovak representatives to the conference, Todor Zhivkov and Gustav Husak, Gierek's position at the conference could be interpreted as somewhat moderate and independent.[33]

The PCI was picking up where it had left off at the Moscow conference in 1969 when it denounced the Soviet invasion of Czechoslovakia. It is likely that the PCI was bolstered in its "independent" stance by the fact that just two weeks prior to the conference in Berlin, the Italian party had come out of its own national elections with an increase of more than 7 percent over the previous elections. The 34.4 percent it received seemed to sanction the increasingly "pluralist" positions taken by the PCI since the Czechoslovak intervention.

Evidence that this Eurocommunist variant held some attraction for at least some East European ruling parties was given by Nicolae Ceausescu, the Romanian leader, when he withdrew his prepared text and returned to the podium with a revised speech. He supported the PCI on the issues of independence of each party and the pursuit of national self-interest:

> In no way can the concern of a party to defend the interests of the working class and of its own people be considered national narrow-mindedness, as an attitude which is likely to weaken international solidarity. The very notion of international solidarity can be conceived only in organic connection with . . . struggle for safeguarding of the interests of each people, of the independence and sovereignty of each nation.[34]

This statement, along with others at the conference, appeared to be an implicit rejection of the prime communist tenets of "socialist" and "proletarian internationalism." The CPSU had been tenaciously defending these precepts, particularly since the attempted "counterrevolution" of the Prague Spring. Never before had these precepts been so directly and forcefully criticized or a Soviet interpretation of doctrine so clearly rejected as at this public forum in East Berlin.

Enrico Berlinguer, PCI chief, publicly reminded the conference of the Czechoslovak intervention and implied that this was the reason for the ballooning rejection of solidarity and internationalism as defined by the CPSU. After the conference, *Le Monde,* which followed the conference closely, reported that several East European ruling party leaders came to see the Italian delegation and privately congratulated its members "on having expressed a viewpoint which they themselves could not express publicly."[35]

It is not surprising that embarrassing references and speeches were substantially truncated or deleted by the Soviet press in order to salvage some vestige of unity from this conference.[36] Obviously a *Pravda* reprint of PCI criticism of East European social development or references to the Czechoslovak crisis from a dissenting perspective could not be allowed.

It is interesting to note, however, that PCI criticism of distorted development in East European societies was not attacked in the Polish press. On the contrary, although *Trybuna Ludu* did censor some of Berlinguer's comments, it reprinted sections *Pravda* had left out, including commentary on:

1. Affirmation of the value of individual and collective freedoms and guarantees
2. Plurality of political parties
3. Possibility of alternating government majorities in the electoral process
4. Autonomy of trade-unions
5. Religious freedom
6. The nonideological nature of the state and its democratic organization[37]

The willingness of a Polish party organ to reprint these comments, all heresy in the Soviet view, is significant. Although the PCI leader was referring mainly to West European institutions, reproduction of these articles by *Trybuna Ludu* exhibited both a disregard for the dangers of "ideological contamination," about which Soviet ideologues continually warned, and a possible willingness on the part of the Polish party to broaden the debate regarding the process of constructing socialism. Apparently, alternatives to the Soviet model of socialist development continued to hold interest for at least some elements in the PUWP.

Signs of Volatility

During the first six months of 1976, expansion of East-West trade continued to be encouraged in the official media of the East bloc, including within the Soviet Union itself. Prague Radio, consistent with the Soviet line on the issue, communicated to West Germany:

> As far as the CMEA countries are concerned, West Europe remains the target of foreign trade activities for the foreseeable future among the capitalist industrialized countries.

Repetition of terms such as "cooperation," "specialization," and "joint investment policy," underscored long-term East European interests to promote intrabloc trade.[38] The dual impetus for more trade with the West, on the one hand, and for greater cohesion and integration of the bloc on the other, was also prominent in the Soviet press during this time.[39] An article in the journal of the influential and authoritative Institute of World Economics and International Relations (IMEMO) cited 30 percent as a "mutually beneficial" figure for CMEA trade with the West and implied that more was needed.[40]

However, the unrest in Poland precipitated by announced price increases of foodstuffs on 24 June 1976 seemed to put into question the continued efficacy of expanding trade relations with the West. Memories of 1970 were rekindled as workers at factories in Radom and Ursus rioted in reaction to the price hikes, despite the justification of this government action in rational economic terms.

At the East Berlin Conference, Gierek avoided direct reference to these riots. However, some of his comments seemed to imply flexibility regarding the sacrosanct principle of party dictatorship:

> Through the development of its socialist democracy, the state of proletarian dictatorship is being transformed into a state of all the people—a state whose main support is the working class and its alliance with the peasants and the intelligentsia. This is reflected in the newly made amendments to our constitution. *On all matters important for the country, before making a decision, we consult society about them.*[41]

That the PUWP had retreated on both issues of constitutional amendments and the short-lived price changes (revoked the next day) gave a curious flavor to Gierek's comments on the positive development of socialism in Poland. There was, in fact, no evidence that Gierek was forging a "consultative dictatorship," the very meaning of which is difficult to comprehend.

A conspicuous silence of Soviet and East European organs obtained, both regarding the tumultuous events in Poland and the de facto disunity in the international communist movement evidenced at the East Berlin conference. Beyond a very few indirect references to the evils of "consumption as the main point of existence" and the danger of placing national interests above those of the communist movement, no qualitative assessment was offered as to problems in either international trade or deficits contributing to the pricing difficulties of Poland.[42]

The lack of authoritative Soviet pronouncements indicated that the CPSU was anxious to let the events of both Radom and Ursus and East Berlin fade into history. After all, the Polish price hikes had been rescinded as Gierek attempted to save face with his promise to consult society about future actions. Calm had been restored to Poland just as it had several times previously after domestic unrest. Moreover, there was no direct evidence that the Helsinki process was adversely affecting social stability in East Europe. "Eurocommunists" had not challenged the CPSU *directly* on issues crucial to the movement or the Soviet position in East Europe.

Disagreements were disagreements. The benefits of CSCE still far outweighed meager evidence in Poland that perhaps there were problems on the horizon.

Evidence would quickly mount that these hypothetical Soviet perspectives were not, in retrospect, justified.

Soviet-Polish Relations
and the Issue of Eurocommunism

The "June events" . . . produced a chain reaction which led
to the emergence of a fundamentally new political situation
in the country. Opposition, which in the past had been
largely passive and scattered, has now become active — it has
taken an organized, vocal, and increasingly influential political form.[1]

D ESPITE clear indications in the mid-1970s of deteriorating economic conditions in Poland, the Kremlin did not veto expanded relations with the West. On the contrary, the Soviet
media stressed continued expansion of East-West trade, ostensibly as
one part of the solution to economic problems. For example, in reporting Gierek's 20 July 1976 speech to Polish party regional secretaries,
Pravda only alluded to unspecified "problems" in the Polish economy
while directly reiterating Gierek's call to improve economic efficiency
and further "expand economic relations with the capitalist countries."[2]
Apparently, the June riots at Radom and Ursus and the serious instability these events underscored were not considered sufficiently threatening to the bloc for a reappraisal (and possible reorientation) of trade
relations with the West to begin. However, Soviet spokesmen would
make clear through the summer of 1976 and beyond that the vital issue
was political and not economic in nature.

The PUWP's response to the June events was not particularly
orthodox. Initial sentences conferred upon the rioters arrested during

the June 24–25 price-change fiasco were rescinded after West European communists, particularly in the PCI, intervened with the Polish party. The PCI interceded on behalf of the jailed rioters in response to a letter of petition by Jacek Kuron, dissident intellectual. Just how much PCI influence was present in the remarkable decision by the Supreme Court of Poland to reduce the initially harsh sentences is unclear, but it seems reasonable to conclude that some influence was indeed present.[3]

In July, shortly after the June events and the disappointing Berlin Conference of Communist Parties, *Pravda* reviewed a theoretical work on the relevance of peaceful paths to socialism. The book, *Three Revolutions in Russia and Our Time,* claimed that "general laws" of establishing and maintaining socialism had not changed since Lenin's time.[4] This book, written by Konstantin Zarodov, editor of the journal *Problems of Peace and Socialism* and a key member of the CPSU Central Committee's International Department, presented itself as a staunch defense of Lenin's revolutionary method. It particularly singled out and warned those who thought that "twenty years" of socialist development was enough to guarantee against "restoration" of the old capitalist order—reminding all that vigilance was necessary to protect socialism's gains and a willingness to resort to violence in so doing.

By implication, Western European parties, most notably the PCI, were being taken to task for their ideas of pluralism and the possibility of peaceful communist transition to power. But the warning to ruling parties—not to languish in a sense of false security as had the CPCz in 1968 according to Zarodov—was also clear. As noted earlier in the discussion of the Berlin Conference, the self-espoused pluralist path of Western European communists in their quest for electoral gains was making a considerable impression on "some" East European ruling elites. The meaning of linking the "bankruptcy" of the pluralist path with the dangers of counterrevolution in the East bloc seemed clear—if a pluralist path could work in West Europe for communists, this might in turn have an impact on socialist development in the East. This was, of course, far from desirable in Soviet eyes.[5]

Veiled attacks against pluralist ideas continued in two major articles in the August issue of the authoritative CPSU organ, *Kommunist.* According to these articles, the "ideology of anticommunism" was responsible for the development of pluralistic ideas in socialism. "Models of socialism" apart from the Soviet experience were also attacked—leaving the objects of attack to inference.[6] Shortly thereafter, and more than coincidentally, the Soviet weekly *New Times (Novoe Vremya)* drew an analogy between Czechoslovak events of 1968 and the possibility of such a threat reemerging at some unspecified time and place in the future. Citing "ideological subversion" by Western forces in the Prague Spring, the article scored those who:

> ... try to supplant the Marxist-Leninist ideology with reformist and bourgeois theories. From this it is only a step to creeping counter-revolution and the subversion of socialist society.[7]

This apparent anxiety was being displayed on the heels of public weakness exhibited by the PUWP in backing down from economic austerity measures, as well as in the reduction of sentences to rioters—a result in which the PCI, the most "reformist" of all communist parties, had played a significant role. Moreover, a Committee for the Defense of the Workers (KOR) was established 7 September by Polish dissident intellectuals and workers.

The willingness of the Polish press to refrain from taking part in escalating polemics with the Eurocommunists, as well as its openness in reporting on issues important to the PCI, helped provide a climate where a phenomenon such as KOR could develop in a socialist state. Clearly, the PUWP was allowing dissent to gain a foothold in the PPR to an extent which could not but worry the Kremlin. KOR was not immediately repressed or destroyed; the fledgling coalition was to be tolerated for the time being. Apparently the Gierek regime was concerned with the domestic effects such a crackdown could have so soon after the riots of June. Moreover, beyond criticism by analogy, the Soviet media stayed silent concerning this serious turn in Polish domestic affairs. Perhaps it was believed that comrade Gierek could adequately manage the situation on his own.

Throughout August consultations between WTO members took place in preparation for military maneuvers to be held in the autumn under the rubric "Shield '76."[8] These preparations were watched carefully in the West, as it was suggested that the situation in Poland could be perceived by the Kremlin to be jeopardizing the PUWP's position. Polish Politburo candidate member, Tadeusz Wrzaszczyk, carefully reassured the Warsaw Pact in a *Pravda* article in August of the firm basis of Soviet-Polish relations, Poland's firm commitment to proletarian internationalism, socialist integration, and the socialist division of labor.[9] Despite such testimony, it was becoming increasingly clear towards the end of 1976 that the CPSU was apprehensive about developments in the PPR.

On 7 October 1976 Gierek embarked on his first official visit to Romania since his coming to power. Considering that Gierek was well-travelled both in the East and the West, it could be seen as somewhat curious that Gierek and Ceausescu had not exchanged official state visits in five years. It has been suggested that this new Polish interest in Romania, with the object of fostering closer "fraternal" relations between the two, was a product of Soviet encouragement.[10] However, in light of the East Berlin conference of the previous June, it can also be suggested that mutual interest was developing between the two in establishing greater independence on their roads to socialism in the face of increasing reassertion of Soviet hegemonic policies in intrabloc affairs. Certainly Ceausescu's example in the realm of foreign policy was not one which the CPSU would have encouraged Gierek to emulate.

More direct concern by the CPSU for Polish party affairs could be seen in the increase of bilateral party contacts between the two beginning in October. A special delegation of the CPSU CC's Organizational Department paid a visit to Warsaw in October in order to better "acquaint themselves with the experience acquired by the PUWP in the field of strengthening the party and its leading role." This appeared to be the first indication that the CPSU was seriously concerned with the PUWP's organization and its relationship to society in the PPR. *Trybuna Ludu* reported that this high-level delegation's visit had taken place, but only after the representatives had returned to Moscow. The stated purpose of the meeting was to discuss problems of "socio-economic development, ideology, and organizational work of the party."[11]

A visit by Gierek on 8 November to Moscow resulted in the sale of more grain and consumer goods to the Poles during a time of economic difficulty. But, as one analyst has suggested, the main purpose in having Gierek come to the Kremlin was to ". . . imprint on the minds of the two nations the preeminence of the Polish-Soviet alliance."[12] This conclusion does not seem extraordinary when considered with the June events in Poland, the formation of KOR, the willingness of the PUWP leader to flirt with ideas emanating from the Berlin conference (specifically from the PCI), and expanded "bilateral" contacts with the maverick Ceausescu.

Moreover, during this PUWP visit to the Kremlin, it was reported that Brezhnev departed from his prepared text while addressing the visiting Polish delegation and emphasized the significance of " . . . this brotherly family of nations *led* by Marxist-Leninist parties," remarking that "This is a very important matter, comrades, a very important matter." The joint communiqué issued at this meeting stated that "staunch defense and consolidation of the achievements of socialism . . . are the internationalist duty of the socialist states."[13]

Sometime between 17 and 22 December CPSU CC Secretary Mikhail Zimyanin, former editor in chief of *Pravda,* headed a delegation to Warsaw, where the experiences "in ideological, educational, and propaganda work of the PUWP and the CPSU" were discussed. It is not surprising that more emphasis by the CPSU on PUWP ideological-propaganda work was appearing. Zimyanin, considered a hard-line "orthodox" CPSU representative, seemed a good choice for such a delegation, given the nature of the problem.[14] With the experience of the Prague Spring to draw upon, the Kremlin was attempting to nip in the bud any potential weakness that the PUWP was evidencing in these vital areas before a crisis in the party developed.

After the Election of Carter

The increase of human rights activity in the Soviet bloc followed the election of Jimmy Carter to the U.S. presidency in November 1976. Dedication to human rights was openly stated as a centerpiece of the Carter administration's foreign policy. The nations of the WTO were immediate targets of this accentuated emphasis in American policy, an emphasis based on the agreements included in Basket III of the Helsinki Final Act.

The East European response to the prominent support of the Final Act of Helsinki by the Carter administration quickly followed. Upon the appearance of the "Charter '77" human rights document in Czechoslovakia, issued clandestinely on 8 January 1977, official attacks on human rights activity increased markedly. Vasil Bilak, second in command of the CPCz, portrayed renegades and foreign provocateurs as still attempting to foment counterrevolution in the CSR. In a *Pravda* editorial entitled "Distorting Mirror," Western interference in East Europe was denounced (particularly in Poland and the GDR) as distorting Basket III, ostensibly "under the guise of defending liberties."[15]

A rigorous and apparently coordinated campaign followed in the Soviet and Czechoslovak media, claiming that anticommunism was gaining a foothold in the CSR, GDR, and Poland.[16] *Trybuna Ludu* echoed these perspectives and added, "to be against socialism is to be against Poland." It was claimed that some Poles were disseminating propaganda from the West, while a "handful" were labelled "bourgeois liberals" exhibiting nationalism, revisionism, and calling for anarchy in Poland.[17] Relations between Poland and the United States, which had been very good since the Nixon visit to Warsaw in 1971, were now undergoing noticeable strain. Poland was loath to jeopardize its Most

Favored Nation (MFN) status in trade with the United States as well as the prestige it had accrued in its role of "mediator" between the super-powers. However, the continued stress on human rights by the Carter administration through the winter of 1977 provoked a frank question from *Zycie Warszawy* on the nature of detente:

> Is not the White House aware that its interference into the internal affairs of other countries, parties to the dialogue on relaxation of tensions, largely complicates the talks on this topic, difficult as it is?[18]

The continued self-perception of Poland's importance concerning its voice in the process of detente can be seen in a number of articles at this time.[19]

Eurocommunist support of the human rights movement in the bloc was also part of the reason for the indignant response of East bloc regimes to this activity. The PCI sanctioned the validity of Charter '77 just as it had done with KOR in September 1976. Furthermore, the PCI continued to promote disgraced CPCz leaders' ideas on the Prague Spring. Zdenek Mlynar, a former leader of the Prague Spring, appealed directly to the West and to Eurocommunists to defend human rights in the East bloc in January 1977. The noted Czech historian, Jiri Pelikan, indicted the CSR and USSR for coordinating repression in Czechoslovakia.[20]

In fact, Eurocommunist support for East European dissidents had noticeably increased in late 1976. French CP member Jean Kanapa echoed dissidents' criticism of East European regimes in rejecting the East European model of socialism, while *L'Unita*, the PCI daily, referred to "general laws" governing socialist development as an "historical absurdity." The PCI bluntly announced that relations between pro-Soviet ruling parties would not in the future be mirrored in relations among other parties.[21] The French, Greek, Spanish, British, Swedish, Belgian, and Japanese parties all lined up on the side of the PCI on the issue of East European human rights. Edward Kardelj, Yugoslav party secretary, went further in his support of the nonruling European parties, hailing Eurocommunism as an historic "turning point." In February of 1977, the Yugoslav party (LCY) forwarded to the CPCz a list of LCY signatories who supported the Charter '77 members.[22]

The East bloc media campaign against human rights activism was largely carried out by Soviet and Czechoslovak press organs, while a lack of participation (particularly regarding criticism of Eurocommunism) by other East European party organs was especially conspicuous. Tanjug, the Yugoslav news agency, had even cited the Hungarian party's willingness to consider that *in principle*, "socialism can be materialized under the conditions of a multi-party system."[23] It would be an understatement to say that this was not in line with the Soviet stance on this issue.

While *Zycie Warszawy* might have been castigating "antisocialist" developments in the East bloc, its rhetoric did not reflect party action to stem such developments within Poland. During Gierek's visit to the Ursus tractor plant on 3 February 1977 (where considerable violence had manifested itself during the June riots), the Polish leader offered partial clemency and pardons for those who had been prosecuted and sentenced, also admitting that there were serious "difficulties" in the economy.[24] The same day a letter was sent to the workers of Radom with the same message. This apparent spirit of compromise was part of Gierek's attempt to restore PUWP legitimacy, which had been badly tarnished by the increasingly poor performance of the Polish economy since 1975.

Just how much this remarkable attitude on the part of the Polish leadership was a product of the Brezhnev-Gierek meeting of the previous November in Moscow is unclear. However, it would not be out of the realm of possibility to assume that Brezhnev himself sanctioned a conciliatory approach to the Polish workers by Gierek, in hopes of averting a challenge to the party on grounds of PUWP economic failures. To a certain extent, Gomulka had been able to decouple the foreign policy component of loyalty to the USSR from the domestic program of the PUWP. By doing so, he was able to attain a degree of legitimacy without provoking the veto of the CPSU. Possibly a similar dynamic was now operating in Gierek's case. That is, as long as Gierek was able to maintain the leading role of the PUWP and thwart any genuinely "counterrevolutionary" developments, his style of dealing with Poland's domestic problems would not be opposed by the Soviet leadership. It is quite possible that the apparent tolerance for dissent was meant to head off pressures for change in Poland, rather than actually promote reform.[25] In any event, no clear policy of the Gierek regime was evident in dealing with mounting domestic problems.

However, evidence was mounting that political pressures were developing as a result of the economic situation. Jacek Kuron, cofounder of KOR, stated in an interview with *Le Monde* that he was "more or less" in favor of a status of Finlandization for the PPR. According to Kuron, a "Third Poland of Socialist Movements" would be launched at some time in the future. Concerning Gierek's apparent magnanimity in reducing the sentences of rioters at Radom and Ursus, he drily added, ". . . we tolerate the state, not vice-versa."[26]

Adam Michnik, another leader of the opposition (cofounder of

KOR), assessed Polish past gains and future possibilities to a Western correspondent in the following manner:

> We owe a great amount to the Italian communists. Not only has their intervention helped to free many Polish workers from prison, but it is also thanks to the PCI that people consider it possible to create socialism with a human face in East Europe or elsewhere. Nevertheless, the Italian comunists' criticism of East European regimes is merely symptomatic and does not go into an analysis of social and political relations. It is our duty, the duty of men outside the party, to create a socialist public opinion and a socialist resistance movement outside the party. To hope that a Prague Spring can reoccur in Poland is Utopian . . . it is much more important that [they] learn to demand rights guaranteed by the constitution and the penal code: to strike, freedom of association, assembly, of the press, and of expression.[27]

Michnik seems to contradict himself on the nature of Polish aspirations, for indeed, they seem to resemble those developments that were part and parcel of the Prague Spring. The apparent contradiction notwithstanding, candid expression of opposition to the continued party attitude of "business as usual" stands out.

Poland and the Flowering of Eurocommunism

Signs that the situation in Poland was not likely to return to one of passive acceptance of the status quo ante Helsinki continued to appear throughout the spring of 1977. The palpable negative effect that Eurocommunism was having on the East bloc is apparent by the Soviet response to the issue of human rights. Polemic surrounding this issue appears in increasingly vituperative tones in the spring. The Soviet and Czechoslovak media continuously portrayed the dangers of infection by these ideas spreading from West to East.[28]

Further institutionalization of dissent appeared in Poland in March 1977 as the ROPCiO (Movement for the Defense of Human and Civil Rights) was born. The gathering strength of activism across East Europe was to be addressed by the Soviet party at an international conference of East bloc party secretaries on 2–3 March. It was not a coincidence that this affair took place at the same time that the Eurocommunist parties were meeting in Madrid. It was speculated that at this summit, highly touted in the Western press, a strategy vis-à-vis the CPSU was to be planned.[29]

While the Madrid summit produced a broad consensus among the

PCI, PCF, and the PCE (Spanish Communist Party) regarding problems in the communist movement, the Sophia conference, which had
been convened to resolve "ideological problems," had little apparent
success. It was suggested that Soviet initiatives to obtain a consensus
of opinion against Western communist criticism of Soviet policies in
East Europe were outflanked. Vasil Bilak, CPCz secretary and Moscow loyalist, took the "point" for the Soviets on the issues of human
rights and Western communist support of dissent in East Europe. Bilak
had previously categorically stated that there was "no room for dissidents in the CSR." That spring Bilak emerged as the most outspoken
critic of both dissent in East Europe and Eurocommunists, openly denouncing the latter as "traitors" to the cause of world communism.[30]

The PUWP, unlike the CPCz, was not publicly associating Eurocommunists with human rights activity in Poland, even after repeated
and openly defiant statements by Kuron and Michnik in the Western
media, which, in effect, linked the phenomenon of Eurocommunism to
East European opposition:

> There is no doubt that in East bloc countries people turn to
> Eurocommunism . . . out of self-interest, as a precaution, or
> as a political or ideological alibi. The fact remains, however,
> that Eurocommunism is a very important phenomenon, es-
> pecially because it shows the possibility of another kind of
> communism.

Michnik even suggested that PCI leader Enrico Berlinguer publish his
speeches every three months, "so that they can be confiscated by the
police in my country." Berlinguer's open support of Polish dissent could
only improve his standing in the eyes of the trade-union movement in
Italy, upon which he heavily relied, and raise his hopes for future PCI
electoral gains. This appeared to be a mutually beneficial situation for
both the Polish opposition and the PCI.[31]

After their visits to West Europe, both Kuron and Michnik were
arrested by Polish authorities under Article 132 of the Polish Code—
acting on behalf of foreign organizations. However, internment turned
out to be a temporary state of affairs. Apparently, a KOR appeal to
Eurocommunist leaders played a role in the release of both Kuron and
Michnik. They also became beneficiaries of a general amnesty, what
would later be referred to victoriously as the "July Amnesty." The
authorities appeared reticent to provoke the opposition. This hardly
resembled the treatment of Czechoslovak dissidents during this time.
Jiri Pelikan was forced to emigrate from the CSR, as Bilak's words
seemed to ring true about the CPCz's stance on dissent.[32]

More indications of problems in the PUWP appeared during March–April 1977. Stefan Olszowski, PUWP Politburo member, spent five days in Moscow 13–18 March during which time he met with K. V. Rusakov, close advisor to Brezhnev and Chief of the CPSU CC's Department for Liaison with Communist and Workers' Parties of Socialist Countries, to discuss the "party management of the national economy."[33] This extended working visit by Olszowski suggested that the Kremlin leadership was now regarding the PUWP's poor management of economic affairs as a noteworthy problem.

Edward Babiuch, a Gierek ally in deposing Gomulka, visited Moscow from 19 to 21 April to "acquaint himself with the experience of the CPSU in the field of party work." He discussed problems of "cooperation" with Brezhnev himself, as well as with Rusakov, B. N. Ponomarev, head of the CPSU CC's International Department, and I. V. Kapitanov, head of the Organizational Party Work Department.[34]

This apparent deepening Soviet concern for deficiencies in the PUWP's organizational work and its responsiveness to Soviet "advice" suggested disarray within the Polish party. Indeed, that spring party differences began to surface in public forum. M. F. Rakowski, editor of *Polityka,* the widely read weekly strongly supportive of Gierek, expanded on certain of Gierek's ideas concerning "socialist democracy."[35] Rakowski wrote in April 1977:

> The creators of Poland's socialist system was the generation of inter-war communists who, at the turn of 1945 had only one experience to fall back upon: the Soviet one. At present, in the more than thirty years that have elapsed since the end of the Second World War, there exists a world socialist system; there exist powerful communist parties with diverse views as to what socialism should be. The wealth of forms and ways of resolving various economic and social problems used by the individual socialist countries and communist parties cannot help but *encourage a successive generation of Polish communists to conduct a creative search.*[36]

It has also been suggested that *Polityka* favored a "rule of law" in Poland, in contrast to the more orthodox lines of both official papers, *Zycie Warszawy* and *Trybuna Ludu.*[37] These organs took a hard line against dissidents during May and June, which indicated that there was a difference of opinion on what to do with the opposition. However, the July Amnesty seemed to mute severe criticism of KOR and the opposition.

A Soviet-sponsored conference set for 27–29 April in Prague sought to clarify ideological (and by implication, organizational) issues.

Seventy-five parties were slated to attend. But this conference seemed to backfire as the leaders of major West European parties did not show up, sending lower level central committee members in their stead.[38] If Soviet ideologues were attempting to somehow reestablish even the facade of unity at this meeting, they were sadly disappointed.

The Appearance of Eurocommunism and the State

In May of 1977, a new book by Santiago Carrillo, Secretary General of the PCE, was published. The book, entitled *Eurocommunism and the State,* was an extensive critique of the development of socialism in the Soviet Union and East Europe, bringing into question whether the Soviet Union itself had ever experienced "real socialism."[39] Silence prevailed for a while in the East European media regarding this highly critical work. Then a flurry of attacks was generated by first Czechoslovak, and then Soviet, representatives in important journals. The polemical offensive was led by Vasil Bilak in *Voprosy istorii KPSS (Problems in the History of the CPSU),* as he struck at revisionist ideas:

> We know what happened when Leninist norms of party life were violated . . . deplorably in the second half of the 1960's certain people in the party began to succumb to the influence of "fashionable" but in essence old petit bourgeois revisionist theories and methods of opportunist practice . . . falsifying the content and distorting the principles of socialist internationalism, counterposing them to patriotism and maintaining that proletarian internationalism means the limitation of state sovereignty.

This attack by analogy heavily implied that the ideas of the Prague Spring were again being resurrected. National communism, revisionism, reformism, and socialism with a human face, were all now being merged, according to Bilak, with "democratic socialism" to subvert socialist states.[40] In *New Times* Carrillo was taken to task directly for these "anti-Soviet" ideas. For the Soviet media to dispense with veiled polemic and come out into the open in this manner, the CPSU must have had bigger fish to fry than just Carrillo.[41] It is more likely that the attack was really directed against the power behind the Eurocommunists – the PCI.

These sharpened Czechoslovak and Soviet polemics were not, however, mirrored in other East European media, which largely refrained from joining the fray. In this regard, Polish party organs were especially conspicuous by their silence. *New Times* soon tempered its initial assault on Carrillo, indicating that the Kremlin did not wish to risk an open rupture by continuing the attack on Carrillo personally. The sudden retreat was due in part to the wide publicity the book received in the West and to Eurocommunist defense of the Spanish leader's right to speak his mind.[42]

It was only after the polemics subsided that *Trybuna Ludu* dropped its silence and commented on the episode. While recognizing that certain remarks were "superficial" and "irresponsible," the commentary went on to praise the PCE for all the good it had done in the communist movement and then generally noted the need for better relations between parties.[43] Clearly, the PUWP was neither anxious to take sides in the dispute, nor to criticize Western European communists for their divergent views. Appearance of this article only on 3 August, long after the initial furor had subsided, indicates significant reluctance of the PUWP to engage in *any* polemics regarding the Eurocommunists.

Gierek himself revealed an ambiguous position on the entire issue of Eurocommunism in an interview with *Le Monde* in September 1977. Admitting that Poland did indeed have serious economic problems generated by a "rapid growth rate," he also said he did not want any "political prisoners" in Poland, an astonishing comment for a ruling party's leader to make.[44] Gierek seemed to be adopting a "mediating" position between the polarized sides of the debate surrounding Eurocommunism. One section of the interview reveals this clearly:

> Q: Do you believe Eurocommunism is a lasting phenomenon?
> A: Let us await history's verdict.
> Q: In any case, do you condemn this phenomenon?
> A: It is not a question of condemning—it is a question of discussion. But it must be understood that I could not like a situation in which certain non-communist politicians make capital out of this problem to divide the communists.[45]

It could be suggested that Gierek's early experiences in Western Europe influenced this rather liberal (from a communist perspective) approach to these issues.

There were also rumors, however, that Gierek himself was independently following a somewhat "liberal" course in Poland. In March a French journal cited "current Warsaw rumors" that it was Gierek who authorized the release of Andrzej Wajda's monumental film, *Marble Man,* over the dissent of the majority in the Polish Politburo.[46] The film is generally regarded as embodying Polish national antipathies towards the period of Stalinization of Poland from the perspective of workers.

In September public discussion was rekindled over the Katyn Forest episode of World War II. It had only been since 1975 that *any* discussion had been allowed on the subject at all.[47] Official blame was placed on the Germans, of course, and only details referring to July 1941 and after were available. It will be recalled that the Soviet Union occupied the area until August 1941, the massacre occurring most likely during the previous spring. Obviously, no discussion could be officially sanctioned if it implied any Soviet responsibility in this affair at all. The resurgence of discussion about Katyn accompanied the appearance of Polish documents that detailed the official censorship of the massacre by Polish authorities. That this discussion was not nipped in the bud either by stepped-up censorship or by attack in the media is revealing. The resurrected issue of Katyn reflected a further change of the political climate within Poland – the significance of which could not have been entirely lost on those observers in the CPSU Central Committee who were responsible for monitoring relations with East bloc parties.

Also at this time the Catholic Church directly criticized the socialist system in Poland. In September a pastoral letter condemning "godless ideology" and the "cult of the man robot" was circulated without any substantive response from party organs.[48] The lack of firm response from the party to such clerical criticism could not have been favorably viewed by the CPSU, especially in light of the substantial efforts it had been making in reorienting the PUWP's organizational and propaganda work during the preceding nine months.

Up until this time, evidence *seemed* to suggest serious problems within the PUWP. The first *clear* evidence that factionalism was taking its toll on the party appears in November 1977. On 8 November a blistering *Zycie Warszawy* editorial attacked *Polityka* editor Rakowski's "revisionism," a charge based on *Polityka*'s advocacy of greater decentralization of the economy, in recognition of the serious economic problems that could be dealt with only by substantially reorganizing the levers of control.[49]

That Rakowski had long been a proponent of Gierek's views suggests that high-level sanction of these opinions was present. Rakowski quickly rebutted this charge and the debate disappeared from the public eye.[50] That this debate did not continue in public suggests that the hard-line faction in the PUWP was being outmaneuvered by the more pragmatic Gierek-led "modernizers," who were ostensibly searching for new solutions to the growing Polish economic crisis. This search for new solutions to economic problems was a primary factor in the developing political disarray within the party.

Rather than distancing himself from the now clearly defined evils of Eurocommunism, Gierek met with PCI representatives in December 1977 while on an official visit to the Vatican. Gierek said of this meeting:

> ... we also met with the leadership of the Italian Communist Party and with its leader Comrade Berlinguer. Our cooperation with this great party, together with which we prepared the Berlin Conference, is traditional and we want to deepen it further.[51]

This assessment of PUWP-PCI relations was reproduced in the 7 December issue of *Trybuna Ludu*.[52]

There was no indication that Gierek was at odds with the PCI for supporting human rights and the worker-intellectual coalition in the PPR. To "deepen further" this relationship implied a disregard for the clearly drawn Soviet line on the subject of Eurocommunism. Apparently the Kremlin was either unwilling or unable to force Gierek to fall into step behind the CPSU on these issues. Moreover, it is possible that Gierek was attempting to conclude a modus vivendi with the Vatican during his visit—by which more tolerance of the church would be evidenced if it would refrain from directly attacking the regime itself. Beleaguered as he was by mounting domestic problems, the Polish leader was probably seeking to keep the church from joining the opposition or taking a more active role. This remains a matter of conjecture, but the success of this strategy, if that is what it was, is somewhat less ambiguous. On 16 December Vatican radio broadcast to Poland (in Polish) the message that communist youth organizations are "contrary to Christian philosophy."[53] No rebuttal of this serious social criticism could be found in the Polish press. The church in Poland would have more to say in the coming months.

After the 1976 price hikes and the resulting domestic unrest, the Polish leadership appeared to retreat from a number of positions that orthodoxy in Marxism-Leninism demands must be upheld. The compromises that apparently had been reached to secure domestic tranquility included tacit agreements with the opposition and the church. Although repression by state apparatuses did not altogether disappear, it was apparent that the regime did not wish to mount an all-out offensive against opposition elements. To do so could endanger Poland's image as "mediator" between East and West in the detente process, as well as its status in West European and American public opinion – both important concerns for a regime that needed to retain favorable trade relations if it hoped to avoid further unwelcome political ramifications of a rapidly deteriorating economy. The regime had chosen to come to an *unwritten* accommodation with the opposition, the precise terms of which were not entirely apparent to either side. The PUWP leadership also chose to ignore Soviet warnings about Eurocommunism and remained aloof in the debate on this issue. These policies, if they can be appropriately so called, were being forwarded despite indications on the part of hard-line elements in the PUWP, as well as in the CPSU, that this was by no means a healthy course to follow.

The PUWP was in the process of desperately trying to salvage legitimacy in the eyes of the Polish people and to prove to Europeans that Polish socialism was more like a benevolent "social democracy" than a mere reproduction of Soviet communism. It remained to be seen how much longer the Gierek regime could continue to avoid constructing a coherent policy to deal with mounting domestic problems. It also remained to be seen how much further the Soviet leadership would allow the Gierek regime to advance on this risky, dual path of compromise with the opposition and currying of favor in the West.

5

Road to Crisis:
Increasing Disarray
in the PUWP

Y the beginning of 1978, it became increasingly clear that the PUWP was in disarray over a number of issues. The debate between so-called moderate-liberals and hard-liners was reflected in the polemics aired in both *Zycie Warszawy* and *Polityka* on issues of reforming the administration of the economy. Ryszard Frelek, PUWP secretary, openly acknowledged the seriousness of the problems facing the PPR during a trip to Italy in January 1978, when he focused on the substance of the debate:

> Development . . . has created a contrast between structure
> of the society and political superstructure which has re-
> mained bound to the 50s. . . . We must have an institutional
> solution.

On the question of burgeoning dissent in Poland over constitutional guarantees and "democratic socialism" (which the PCI continued to support in Poland) Frelek "shared" the assessment that formal freedoms are the basic precondition for the building of a real socialist society. He added:

> . . . once the phase when the Dictatorship of the Proletariat
> was over, Poland undertook the task of building a national
> state . . . even formal freedoms must therefore have precise
> guarantees in the forms most suited to the traditions of our
> society.[1]

These comments in themselves are enough to warrant careful attention to the developing nature of Polish communism during this period. Evidently eager to please Western observers, the Gierek regime was presenting a picture of restrained dictatorship of the party, deemphasizing the crucial communist concept of dictatorship of the proletariat. Implicit criticism of the Gomulka period and the Soviet model (superstructure . . . bound to the 50s) indicated an attempt on the part of the Gierek leadership to distance itself from the PUWP's Stalinist past.

The PUWP was actually receiving assistance from unexpected quarters in this regard. During President Carter's whirlwind tour of Poland (29–31 December 1977), the American leader extolled the virtues of what he called three of the most important human rights documents in world history: the French Rights of Man, the American Declaration of Independence, and the Polish Constitution of 3 May 1791.[2] By February Carter was even cited by the Polish journal *Ideologiya i Polityka* in defense of the Polish human rights record. The Polish press praised Carter and emphasized the positive results of detente, continuing to project the image of the PPR as being in a mediating position between the two superpowers.[3] That the 1791 Polish Constitution reference was clearly an anti-Russian comment must have raised some eyebrows in the more orthodox factions of the PUWP. It will be recalled that this document was directed against Russian domination of Poland before the formal incorporation of Poland as a province in the Russian Empire.[4]

The Czechoslovak press, however, playing the role of loyal Soviet vassal, belittled Carter's assessment of human rights and his "three documents" address. The CPCz apparently was carrying the banner of ideological orthodoxy in the CPSU's stead. While the Czechoslovak press reported in negative terms the Carter State of the Union address upon the president's return to the United States, the Polish press promoted a relatively positive image of this event, especially concerning Carter's position on East-West relations. The Polish press continued to present a positive portrait of the United States in world affairs through the winter of 1977–1978, including what can be construed as a comparatively neutral stance concerning the Camp David process in the Middle East—a position that was far from reflecting the Soviet view.[5]

Just after the Carter visit to Poland, the Czechoslovaks reminded communists that events in the CSR in 1968 had made the Soviet action inevitable due to three factors:

1. Norms of party life were violated

2. Marxism-Leninism and proletarian internationalism were betrayed
3. Democratic Centralism as a principle was violated[6]

No mention was made of developments in Poland, but the emphasis on problems leading to a betrayal of socialism in the CSR implied a warning by the orthodox to those who might be considering a reformist course elsewhere. This image of an error-prone Czechoslovak party was being emphasized during a time of decidedly questionable activities by the PUWP in Poland, the only East bloc country where the party was apparently undergoing significant stress.

It was also in January 1978 that Eurocommunists held a three-day seminar on "Problems of the History of the USSR" in Italy, where "restrained liberty" and "backwardness" in Soviet socialist development were criticized. A direct attack was made on Czechoslovakia also by the leading Eurocommunist parties in the period following this conference. The regime in the CSR was condemned as "harsh and repressive." These polemics were in essence commemorating the birth of the Prague Spring ten years earlier. Czechoslovak denunciation of the seminar included castigation of former Prague Spring leaders now in the West, one of whom was Jiri Hajek, foreign minister under Dubcek.[7]

By 1978 there remained little doubt that opposition had become unofficially institutionalized in the PPR in a manner unlike any previous opposition in East Europe. At least twenty *samizdat* papers were being published regularly with monthly subscribers totalling more than twenty thousand.[8] Noted dissidents discussed in both *samizdat* and Western publications the notion that Poland should become a "model" for East European development — in the political sense.[9] Criticism of obstacles to progressive development included the identification of Soviet hegemony in East Europe and Russian imperialistic policy toward Polish and Soviet minorities:

> There is no such thing as a Polish-Russian boundary, and anyone who constructs one does so at the price of enslaving the Ukrainians, Belorussians and Lithuanians. For Poland, this program means a lack of sovereignty and a constant deadly menace; for the Russian people, this is a dictatorship which depraves society. . . . Enslaved nations and nations which enslave are equally poisoned by hatred and contempt.

Discussion in the underground was now broaching the entire gamut of grievances regarding the Soviet-Polish relationship: Katyn, borders, the nature of socialism, a Polish "model" for East Europe—all anathema from the perspective of Soviet communism.[10]

It was reported that "nonconformists" were elected to the Writers' Union Presidium in the spring, including some with close ties to Polish *samizdat* papers.[11] With increasing heterogeneity of representation in official organizations, the threat of further dilution of orthodox communist control increased. Whether this development was a contributing factor to the evident deterioration of firm party leadership, or a result of this deterioration was still unclear. The only thing certain was that the PUWP took no substantive action to address the danger of a growing opposition threatening to affect party control of vital institutions.

Already by the spring of 1978, an "Organized Committee of Free Trade Unions" in the underground was reported to be demanding "genuine democracy" in Poland. A retired Sejm representative, Stefan Kisielewski, predicted that repression would surface sooner or later and that major reforms had little likelihood of ever being passed by the regime.[12] Opposition to reformism in the PUWP, not to mention in the CPSU, made any alteration of economic mechanisms a risky business.

A key meeting took place between Gierek and Brezhnev in Moscow from 17 to 19 April 1978. It appeared that some pressure was being applied to Gierek to demonstrate greater solidarity with his Soviet allies. This was reflected in statements issued from the meeting. Gierek and Brezhnev were cited as strongly supporting "real socialism."[13] During the Moscow visit, Brezhnev made much of the Soviet-Polish relationship and its connection to Poland's national revival after World War II.[14] It was also perhaps more than coincidental that this meeting between the two leaders took place on the eve of the Ninth Spanish Communist Party Congress in Madrid, where the PCE rejected Leninism on 19 April.[15] Some Moscow loyalists attacked the PCE for this heresy, while the Soviet media remained silent. The Poles still remained above the polemics surrounding the issue of Eurocommunism.

There was little evidence, however, that the PUWP was closing ranks and charting a more orthodox course at home. On 16 May the Soviet Ambassador to Warsaw, Stanislaw Pilotowicz, was replaced by Boris Aristov. Pilotowicz reportedly was disliked by the Poles and considered to be a "meddler" in Polish cultural affairs. Although it was unclear at the time whether this removal of Pilotowicz was because of successful pressure by the PUWP to relieve itself of a troublesome Moscow representative, or a move designed to improve Moscow's voice in Warsaw, this reshuffling in the diplomatic corps at this time suggested a changing climate in Soviet-Polish relations.[16]

Domestic pressures on the Gierek regime continued to mount. By June Poland was reported to be seeking an easing of credit terms on its U.S. loans and attempting to resolve the serious problem of export-import imbalances. "Organizational" problems in the administration of the domestic economy were also being identified in the Polish media as needing attention. Increasing internal pressures were not making it easy for the Polish party to conform more closely to the Soviet line on any issue.[17]

During a trip to Yugoslavia in May, Gierek remained uncritical of both Eurocommunism and the East Berlin conference. Although he claimed that he was not an "adherent" of the term Eurocommunism, he also stated that he saw "no substantial deviations from that conference" in the European communist movement.[18]

Also in May the appearance of a book entitled *Proletarian, Socialist Internationalism* reminded communists everywhere that the Soviet perspective on international communism was the definitive one. Eurocommunism was attacked along with various "models" and "falsificators" of proletarian internationalism—those who deny party unity. Rejections of Leninism were also condemned, while it was also admitted that nationalism had regrettably cropped up again.[19] These assessments were later reaffirmed in Soviet warnings of ideological "sabotage" in the movement threatening communist unity. A sense of urgency in the struggle against all revisionists (from both the left and the right) also soon became evident in warnings that nationalism was not a healthy course to follow.[20]

Of course, of any party in the bloc the PUWP was evidencing the most problems and ambiguities in these categories. The PUWP was still uncommitted to the Soviet struggle against Eurocommunism and displayed tolerance for the growing opposition in the PPR instead of stifling it. The PUWP's limited accommodation with the opposition continued through the summer and autumn of 1978. In September, purportedly as a favor to the visiting French President Giscard d'Estaing, Gierek released convicted dissidents.[21] Also in September, the Catholic Church increased its criticism of communism in Poland. A pastoral letter distributed by Polish bishops on behalf of Cardinal Wyszynski deemed it imperative to "limit or even abolish state censorship." Both the Vatican and the Polish church denounced censorship as a weapon of totalitarian regimes.[22] Just several weeks before in August a secret meeting had been held on the Polish-Czechoslovak border between KOR and Charter '77 representatives that resulted in an open letter (issued on 20 September) expressing solidarity of both groups with all East European dissidents, including those in the Soviet Union itself. This event was highly publicized in the West European media. The PCI daily *L'Unita* looked upon this as a positive development also.[23]

Despite no fewer than six high-level CPCz-PUWP party contacts whose central focus was reportedly ideological in nature, which took place between February 1977 and September 1978, PUWP action vis-à-vis the coalescing opposition appeared ineffective.[24] Notwithstanding public pronouncements on the "decisive significance" of these joint efforts regarding "key problems" of ideological work, there was little evidence to support this claim.

The Continuing Struggle for Orthodoxy

On 22–23 November 1978 the WTO ministers gathered in Moscow. This conference produced a surprising result: Romania reportedly announced a policy of "selective cooperation" with the WTO on military questions. Over the previous summer the Romanian Communist Party (RCP) had supported the development of a "new type of unity" among communists. This position was stated in Bucharest during a meeting with representatives from the PCI and the PCF.[25] The Romanian leader Ceausescu had also bluntly stated in August that West European communists were on their own paths to socialism and that as long as the content was there, they did not even need the label of Marxism-Leninism. Over the summer Ceausescu had even entertained Chairman Hua of the People's Republic of China (PRC), a visit that was assessed as a "resounding success." By December the RCP was proclaiming that "unity in diversity" in world communism was a positive phenomenon.[26]

The problem of orthodoxy in international communism was now becoming a central focus of CPSU concern. The Soviet party began to press for a clear line to be drawn on ideological matters crucial to its control of the movement. An ideological conference was convened in Sophia, Bulgaria, on 12 December to address these problems. It was no surprise that the discussion was heavily weighted toward the Soviet perspective, since the planners of the conference were Vasil Bilak of the CPCz, Boris Ponomarev of the CPSU, and their Bulgarian host, Todor Zhivkov, all proponents of strict orthodoxy.[27]

Apart from the usual formulaic pronouncements, a considerable hardening of positions was noticeable on the issue of internationalism as interpreted by the CPSU. The conference not only denounced Chinese and Eurocommunist revisionism, but it also "pointed out the harmfulness of 'neutral' attitudes to anti-socialist propaganda."[28] That this was directed at both the Poles and the Romanians was almost certain, for only in their behavior could "neutrality" on key ideological concerns to the CPSU be ascertained. The virtues of the Great October Revolution and the Soviet experience in building socialism were the centerpieces of the conference.

After this meeting, a CPCz spokesman further explained just what a neutral stance implied in the midst of the struggle with revisionism:

> Failure to take part in the ideological struggle and the maintenance of "good relations" with the enemies of communism . . . weakens the ideological resistance of the workers' movement. Experience shows that the parties which describe themselves as "Eurocommunist," and which have taken a stand of negative criticism of existing socialism . . . disorientate the masses . . . and sow doubts about the experience of socialism as a whole.[29]

Orthodox opposition to the avowed pluralism of Western communist parties was broadening into criticism of those who would deviate from the Soviet method (and experience) of building socialism. This criticism, compounded with Western communist support of reforms in East Europe (and particularly in Poland), resulted in further disarray in the Warsaw Pact's political positions.

The issue was far from settled. A three-day conference of both West and East European leftists on the nature of dissent in the Soviet Union and East Europe was convened on 19 January 1979 in Italy. A PCI academician at the conference identified the problem of the socialist bloc as reflecting a "third type of society," one which was "stagnant, stable, but including no liberties for the masses." On 31 January *Pravda* responded in a harsh manner: the dissidents at this meeting were labelled "rabble" (*okhvost'e*).[30] Continuing the Soviet attack, the CPCz denounced a Spanish communist theorist as a leader of the "violent anti-communist campaign" of the previous year. Ridiculing his theory, the article compared his espoused goals for East Europe with the goals of the Prague Spring, both being:

> . . . nothing but spreading the contagion of liberated Eurocommunism from West to East Europe and the takeover of power by Eurocommunists in socialist states.

The article also linked these ideas to those of Western anticommunists who claim:

> the very same mixture is undermining and changing so-called socialism of East Europe . . . the Soviet power is collapsing . . . the WTO is breaking apart.

However, a more direct reason for the virulence of these polemics was revealed by *Rude Pravo* shortly thereafter: the Czech paper bluntly reminded communists everywhere that the legacy of the dissolution of the Comintern *did not* include the notion that parties would begin to operate independently. This was an unambiguous proclamation that loyalty to the USSR must be equated with obedience to the CPSU on matters of doctrine.[31]

At this time, evidence suggests that the Kremlin leaders were attempting to bring Gierek more into line with Soviet international positions. The CPSU issued a formal invitation to Gierek to visit the Kremlin on 12 March 1979. The results of this meeting were several. A joint statement was issued denouncing the PRC and its dispute with the Socialist Republic of Viet Nam (SRV).[32] The SRV had invaded Cambodia in January and hostilities had broken out between China and Viet Nam over this incursion. More economic cooperation was also offered to Poland and greater Soviet assistance promised in preparation for the next Five-Year Plan.[33] That the economic side of the meeting was perhaps more important to Gierek is suggested by his own comments concerning the trip to Moscow. He stressed vital domestic matters, emphasizing the three important problems of the Polish economy—raw materials, exports, and management.[34] It is entirely possible that this united front against the PRC (and possibly promises of future "solidarity" with the CPSU) was traded by the Poles for guarantees of future Soviet support for Poland's ailing economy. A noticeable increase in Polish criticism of the Camp David process became evident as well during this time—more in line with Czechoslovak and Soviet perspectives.[35]

Despite the apparent willingness of Gierek to fall into step behind the Kremlin on some foreign policy issues, it was soon obvious that this apparent shift was somewhat limited in scope. At the PCI's Fifteenth Congress in April, three weeks after Brezhnev's talks with Gierek, Stanislaw Kania, the PUWP emissary to the Italian Congress, spoke warmly of the friendship between himself and Berlinguer, the leader of the PCI. Emphasis on the positive aspects of this relationship with the PCI was clearly the PUWP party line, as the entire Kania speech was reprinted in *Trybuna Ludu. Rude Pravo,* on the other hand, voiced its dissatisfaction with the congress, claiming that the "new internationalism" and "Eurocommunism" issues were dealt with by some "who fell out of the framework of a class approach."[36] The CPCz's own participation in the conference was distinguished by formulaic commentary on Leninism and internationalism. Compared to the negative Czech portrayal, PAP, the Polish News Agency, assessed the PCI Congress only in positive terms, characterizing the "historic compromise" (the PCI coalition with other Italian leftist groups five years earlier) as a success, implying that a pluralist approach by some communist parties was not detrimental.[37]

Despite continued Soviet attempts to discredit the Western parties (particularly the PCI), the PUWP was not moving closer to the CPSU on the question of Eurocommunism. It still apparently reserved for itself the right to determine what was, and what was not, acceptable behavior regarding the quest for "separate roads to socialism." That it was in the PUWP's best interest to retain good relations with the PCI and possibly expand them was far from clear. It was now becoming obvious that a power struggle within the PUWP at this time was influencing Polish foreign policy positions. It could be construed that support of the PCI, or at least the refusal to engage in polemics against the Eurocommunists and remain neutral, was a sign of the continued strength of the more moderate forces within the PUWP. It is also possible that this strength was growing as problems in Poland mounted. After all, there was no direct evidence as yet that the Polish party was being taken to task *directly* for these questionable positions. Despite increasing pressures to fall into step behind the CPSU, the Gierek leadership had been able to hold its ground *and* to receive promises of greater economic assistance in the bargain.

The Visit of Pope John Paul II

The election of former Archbishop of Cracow, Karol Cardinal Wojtyla, to the papacy of the Roman Catholic Church was an historic event on two counts: it was the first time that a Pole had risen to this position, and it was the first time that a priest from a communist country had achieved such a high honor. Initial Soviet reference to the event in October 1978 was limited and reflected ambivalence. Soviet leaders were no doubt wary and waiting to see what the new pontiff would do. The Polish press, on the other hand, portrayed the event in positive terms.[38]

Announcement of the planned visit of the Polish pope to his native

land evoked national pride and produced excitement even in the official media. Rakowski, editor of *Polityka,* evaluated the significance of
the impending visit in terms of national prestige:

> the announced visit of John Paul II to Poland also has its
> state dimension because the Pope is also head of the Vatican
> state.[39]

After the visit was announced in March, preparations were of substantial magnitude. It is unclear whether the Kremlin disapproved of this
historic event, or grudgingly accepted it as a fait accompli. Although
the Soviet media failed to comment on the visit, the CPCz revealed
what was behind the official silence. The 30 May edition of the communist journal *Tribuna* carried an article entitled "A Chapter from the
Battle for Rule over the World." In it, an academician described the
church-state struggle for power in the Middle Ages. The ostensibly
"historic" value of the article was eclipsed by its references to the
present. The impending visit of John Paul II in June to Poland was
linked to the anniversary of Saint Stanislaw (1130–1179) of Poland.
This martyr was described as a prominent fighter in asserting the
church's claims as defined by Pope Gregory VII at that time. Furthermore, Stanislaw

> . . . received the halo of a saint in the struggle for the
> church's aspirations in the world. . . . What remains to be
> done is to wonder what leads the present Pontiff, John Paul
> II from Rome to Poland, on the occasion of the celebrating
> of a bishop-martyr who wanted to implement the principles
> and demands for unlimited world rule by the Pope and the
> Church.

In the event that the tone of the article had not made itself clear, a
warning was issued directly to the pope to pursue his pastoral duties
and ethics and to stay out of politics, which "*is the only sound alternative*" (italics in the original).[40]

   At the least, this attack reflects the general orthodox Leninist fear
that the renaissance of religious feeling in Poland would spell more
trouble for the regime. Unwilling to criticize the PUWP directly for
allowing the visit, the attack concentrated on religious meddling in
political affairs. This diatribe was prepared in the full knowledge that
not only had Gierek been courting the church in his attempt to deal
more effectively with domestic problems, but that he had also been
allowing an unprecedented level of criticism of the regime by the
church. Apparently, apprehensions were developing in the bloc about
how Comrade Gierek was approaching problems on the home front.

On 2 June 1979 John Paul II arrived in his native Poland. Before a multitude of his countrymen, he spoke at Gniezno Cathedral about a special place that Slavs held in the universal church and displayed pride in his nationality, while emphasizing the unity of Christians throughout Europe.[41]

The Polish appraisal of the entire visit was unqualifiedly positive. *Slowo Powszechne,* the official Catholic daily, claimed that the visit was not only of political importance, but affirmed the basic identity of Poles, gave prestige to Poland, and was a "cathartic" experience.[42] Soviet reportage of the visit was very limited and at one point was presented in a rather bizarre historical potpourri—trailing off into sarcasm about religion and fanaticism in Iran.[43] Meanwhile, the Czechoslovak media evaluated the visit negatively, implying that the pope was not a friend of Poland and reminded its readers that grave errors had been committed by the church in World War II.[44] It was clear that orthodox Marxist-Leninists (as defined by the CPSU) were less than pleased with a visit by a Polish pope to his native land during a time of increasing political instability.

The Increasing Threat to the PUWP and the CPSU

After the summer of 1979, realization increased in the opposition and within the party that a deteriorating economic situation was leading to social and political crisis in Poland. The debate on economic reform between *Polityka* and *Zycie Warszawy,* which emerged only temporarily at the end of 1977, remained unresolved and out of the public eye. Apparently, there was not enough backing in the PUWP to risk reform, even if this meant only limited decentralization of the economy. It is unclear just what Gierek's stand on the issue of reform was, although it is highly possible that he was manipulating it for his own political gain. Nonetheless, questions of administrative reform and decentralization of the economy remained important topics in Poland through 1978.

At the beginning of 1979, the debate broadened to include political power itself and how it was wielded by the party and regime. Jerzy Wiatr, Polish sociologist and political analyst, wrote in *Polityka*:

> Power is based on respect of people—it is not a one-time thing. . . . Strong power leads, weak power is satisfied with the solution of current problems.[45]

Here was a clear implication that the regime was resting on the laurels it had won during the boom period of 1971–1975. Gomulka had been criticized by Gierek in this same manner upon the latter's assumption of power at the end of 1970.[46] In October 1978 the founding of the group called "Experience and Future" (*Doswiadczenie i Przyszlosc*) reflected the growing realization among some elements within the party that it was time for reevaluation. This group was comprised of a broad cross section of both party and nonparty elements. M. Rakowski, editor of *Polityka;* A. Wajda, film producer; and S. Bratkowski, writer and sociologist, were among its membership.[47] The task of the group was announced to be "discussion" of the problems facing the PPR. These problems included the growth of church influence, the proliferation of dissent, and most of all, the deterioration of economic conditions.

It should be noted here that declining economic performance was not exclusively a Polish problem, but was becoming apparent elsewhere in East Europe as well. The energy crisis, which had begun in the West with the increased price of oil and had contributed to recessionary pressures, was now also evident in the East bloc. This problem was confirmed at a CMEA session in Moscow in late June 1979. Some austerity measures involving energy conservation were implemented in Poland and other East bloc states, prompted by an increase in the price of Soviet petroleum to CMEA members in 1979 and the poor prospects for a quick resolution of the world pricing problem of petroleum in general. The impact of the energy crisis upon Poland compounded the effects of the general economic decline. Political effects of the oil crisis were soon in evidence as well. In August 1979 a shake-up of the power ministry hierarchy in the PPR resulted in the well-publicized dismissal of several ministers.[48]

Suspicions regarding the growing seriousness of the Polish economic situation deepened during the summer of the papal visit, as rumors surfaced that Poland was seeking to join the International Monetary Fund (IMF) to alleviate its export-import imbalances with more Western aid. The Poles had been members of the IMF for several years until 1950, when they resigned under Soviet pressure during increased East-West tensions of the Cold War. According to some, the suggestion of renewed membership was rejected by Soviet leaders, who "refused to hear of it."[49] This veto was apparently prompted by evidence of Poland's poor economic performance since 1975 *with* extensive Western credits. The Soviet leadership likely concluded that any deeper PPR collaboration with Western institutions – and dangerous penetration of Poland by these institutions – would only adversely affect the country and contribute to an already destabilized situation.

This did not mean, however, that support of East-West trade declined in the East bloc. On the contrary, economic necessity made this an attractive policy to pursue. It was more a matter of the character of the relationship needing to be defined. In July the Czechoslovak press had reiterated the CMEA proposal to the EEC to conclude a "concrete" trade agreement.[50] This implied that the expansion of trade was preferred on an interbloc basis between transnational institutions rather than bilaterally, between individual countries of both blocs. This, of course, would fit more neatly into the Soviet scheme of greater integration of the bloc. However, this did not mean that all the East bloc states would readily accept such an arrangement, for there had been considerable foot-dragging regarding the Soviet idea of integration in general.

After the papal visit to Poland, evidence accumulated that the Gierek regime was either unable or unwilling to curtail effectively the growing opposition. For example, on 22 July, Poland's national holiday, a march of 4,000 people to the tomb of the unknown soldier in Warsaw culminated in a speech that was loudly applauded when the nation was urged to "struggle for Poland's total independence and sovereignty." On the anniversary of the German invasion of Poland, 17 September 1939, Polish television broadcast an official apologia for the Soviet Union, which, according to the broadcast, "had to intervene." Nothing, of course, was mentioned of the Nazi-Soviet Pact of 23 August 1939 or the infamous note of 17 September 1939 informing Poland that Soviet troops were moving into eastern Poland.[51]

Both KOR and the more recent Confederation for an Independent Poland (KPN) commemorated the same event by proclaiming:

> . . . any normalization of relations between the Soviet Union
> and Poland would come only on the basis of recognition of
> crimes committed by the Red Army on Polish territory.[52]

KOR also published in its organization's journal a workers' charter for the right to strike. Still there was no effective response by the PUWP. Lack of firm party response to broadening opposition criticism suggested, in part, the preoccupation of the party with the domestic economic situation. There was little doubt that the PUWP was dealing improperly with burgeoning opposition, if one considers the "proper" response of the CPCz to the same problem in Czechoslovakia. During the papal visit to Poland, for example, priests were arrested in the CSR and Charter '77 signers had been, for the most part, either jailed or exiled. Polish dissidents had even shown solidarity with the purged Charter '77 members in the CSR by staging a hunger strike in Warsaw.[53]

The Soviet media continued to present a picture of Polish loyalty to the Soviet Union. In October *Pravda* reprinted a *Trybuna Ludu* article hailing fifteen years of Brezhnev's foreign policy.[54] A campaign against the possible deployment of Euromissiles by NATO seemed to be well coordinated by the Polish and Soviet media late in the fall of 1979, as criticism of the Strategic Arms Limitation Talks (SALT II) and Mutual Balanced Forced Reduction talks (MBFR) also increased. By this time it had become apparent to the Kremlin that the likelihood of the U.S. Senate's passage of SALT II was slim. Detente, it seemed, was on the rocks.

The broadening solidarity of the PUWP with the CPSU on foreign policy issues could not mask the serious domestic situation in Poland—the party was in increasing disarray. In October the group known as Experience and Future (DiP) concluded its analysis of the Polish crisis. The written document, a copy of which was obtained by the French press, was entitled "Report on the State of the Republic and on Ways of Restoring Order." This remarkably candid document, composed by a group of more than 100 influential Polish intellectuals, outlined the major problems that the party and the Polish nation faced. Broad criticism of the party's corruption of power was the main feature of the report. The admission that the problem was primarily a *political* one defied the official party evaluation of social conditions.[55] Specific recommendations that the parliament (*sejm*) should rule and that "real elections" should be held, along with recommendations to limit censorship and create genuine trade-unions, constituted a true "bombshell." Warning that another explosion akin to the ones of 1970 and 1976 was likely, the report reflected a realism that the PUWP could not publicly afford to display. The seven basic principles the DiP report encompassed have been summarized by one writer as follows:

1. Authority should not be autocratic
2. A broadening of public participation in politics is necessary
3. The party should be responsible for the national heritage
4. The party should be responsible for social values
5. The assessment of people according to their work is necessary (against corruption)
6. The party should be responsible for legality
7. There should be openness in public life[56]

The quest for reform was reaching the heart of the party itself, yet no reform was in evidence. The dangerously pluralistic overtones of DiP's analysis could not have been accepted by the PUWP without a substantial overhaul of the political system itself. To say the least, this would no doubt "violate the norms of party life," not to mention force the party to relinquish its monopoly of political power in Poland. One is reminded of the Two Thousand Words Manifesto during the Prague Spring by this important Polish document. However, the significant difference between the two is that the Soviet Union did *not* directly respond to this widely circulated report of DiP.

Instead, two international communist conferences in October, ostensibly organized to discuss ideological matters, became forums for a sharpened Soviet attack on revisionism, opportunism, and Eurocommunism. In Cavtat, Yugoslavia, an international symposium on Marxism convened on 1 October hosting 113 Marxists from fifty-seven countries. The Soviet and Yugoslav representatives reportedly quarreled over a "center" existing in the communist movement and the nature of economic self-management in Yugoslavia.[57] The LCY had been polemicizing continuously with the CPSU over these issues as well as supporting both the emerging worker-intellectual coalition in Poland and Eurocommunism.

Less than two weeks after the Cavtat Conference, another ideological conference was held in Moscow (16–17 October), in which Boris Ponomarev strongly attacked Eurocommunists. Revision of his comments in *Pravda,* toning down the attack, led some to suggest that a split in the CPSU itself on the issue of Eurocommunism was possible.[58] However, it is perhaps more likely that the Kremlin toned down the criticism to avoid escalating polemics at a time when more important issues were arising on the agenda of the CPSU. In several weeks the Soviet Union would intervene in Afghanistan to "preserve socialism." Moscow would need all the support of communists it could manage to obtain.

Meanwhile, the increasingly anti-Soviet character of the opposition in Poland prompted Rakowski to remind the people of the dangerous implications of such behavior. In an article entitled "Chief Orientations," in the 10 November issue of *Polityka,* he counselled a "realistic" orientation, condemning at the same time revitalized Polish nationalism in the "face of realities."[59] The implication was clear: Poland's position in the Soviet sphere of influence, given the Soviet preponderance of power, was unchangeable. Despite this warning, on 11 November, the sixty-first anniversary of Polish independence (Reconstituted Poland) was celebrated by crowds estimated at five thousand in both Gdansk and Warsaw.[60]

In the very next issue of *Polityka* (17 November), it was clear that

Rakowski thought the PPR could successfully straddle the fence—stay loyal to the Soviet Union in matters of foreign policy, while reforming domestic politics and the economy at the same time. He urged "militancy" against "negative features" in the country, referring to the "positive changes" that had become evident in the PPR during the 1970s. Referring also to a draft plan being prepared by the *Sejm* on the economy, he urged as well that both workers and "those who occupy positions of command" join together to work for solutions. He heartily endorsed activity "from below," not waiting for "directions from above" in this process of public discussion. This discussion of economic problems was to be in preparation for the Eighth PUWP Congress, slated to begin 11 February 1980.[61]

In these two articles, 10 and 17 November, Rakowski spelled out the contemporary dilemma of Poland—attempting to mitigate the effects of an alien political superstructure while at the same time reassuring its Soviet allies that its position in the bloc was not threatened by domestic developments. Despite veiled warnings from both the CPCz and the CPSU that this was a dubious path to follow, especially for a nation of Poland's strategic importance and in light of historic anti-Russian nationalism, many Poles were apparently convinced that this was a real possibility, perhaps on the model of Hungary. To be successful in dealing with the domestic component of this dilemma, the PUWP would have to assure the Kremlin that the stability of the regime was not threatened. Yet signs of erosion of the party's "leading role" continued to surface.

At this juncture the church attacked the regime, directly condemning "state capitalism" in Poland. In a formal communiqué issued at the conclusion of the one hundred seventy-first Plenum of the Polish Episcopate in December 1979, the authorities were blamed for the "economic, moral, and social situation" in the country.[62] The church appeared to be in complete accord with the opposition in its disapproval of a "business as usual" attitude on the part of the government.

If the Gierek leadership had any hopes that this opposition would dissipate without Draconian measures taken against it, by the end of 1979 this was indeed fantasy. During marches staged to commemorate the December 1970 riots, when workers were killed by the police, placards were carried, declaring "We have not forgotten December 1970."[63] There was no evidence that the regime had formulated any policies to address the growing problems on all fronts. All eyes were now on the upcoming PUWP Congress, where, it was thought, solutions to the growing crisis would be discussed.

The Eighth PUWP Congress: Too Little, Too Late

The Eighth PUWP Congress convened from 11 to 15 February 1980. The central topic of concern was, of course, the economy. Gierek proclaimed in his address to the congress that socialism "contains within itself the antibodies capable of overcoming the infection of the crisis emanating from the West." The blatant refusal to take any degree of responsibility for the crisis characterized the public posture of the regime. Despite the announcement of major leadership changes at the congress, nothing substantive was offered to address the growing crisis. Edward Babiuch was elevated to the post of prime minister, while the names of Stanislaw Kania and General Wojciech Jaruzelski appeared at the top of the list of party secretaries.[64] These changes, however, appeared more cosmetic than anything else. No substantive plans were put forward to address the deteriorating economic situation.

Indications that the congress did not go as smoothly as was presented in the Polish press came in the form of a more lucid analysis by the PCI daily, *L'Unita*. In an "unofficial" interview with an "authoritative party figure," the political democratization debate going on in the party was described:

> No socialist country has yet managed to resolve problems of interdependence between politics and economics. All we can say is that the realization has been reached that the present relationship does not work. For the time being we have stopped at the brink of the question: what is the sense of democratizing the economy without democratizing politics.

L'Unita also added some comments by a Polish journalist on the real problem avoided by the congress:

> We have done much more than the Czechs set out for themselves in 1968. In Yugoslavia also, they tried in 1966, seeking to redefine the party's leading role. But they too stopped along this path and the reason for this is clear: it is that there is a danger of reaching a questioning of the single party and the need to start thinking about a real form of pluralism.

This unidentified journalist was also quoted as dismissing "outside pressures" in the Polish party debate, while he admitted that the presence of a center, left, and right faction in the PUWP had inhibited the resolution of political problems.[65]

The credibility of these observations is substantial. The PCI had continually been remarkably candid and concise in its portrayal of the situation in the PPR, as reflected in its organ, *L'Unita*. Two points stand out in this view of PUWP problems: a political debate within the PUWP and the lack of *effective* Soviet pressure on the course of Polish developments. However, the party was handcuffed by internal factionalism and fear of the workers—*forcing* the party to deal with opposition elements on a compromise basis. Attempts at repressing the opposition continued, but by this time seemed sporadic and ineffective. Limited Soviet interference in Polish developments through the winter of 1979–1980 does not mean that the situation failed to be of grave concern to the CPSU. Lack of overt denunciation of Polish events was not a true gauge of Soviet concern. Czechoslovak and Soviet criticism of Eurocommunism centered on the effects that "reformism" in the international communist movement could have on East European socialism.[66] The only East bloc country where such effects could be seen clearly was Poland.

The unwillingness of the PUWP congress to address the crisis directly appeared to lead to even greater boldness on the part of the opposition. By 14 February it was reported that a KOR affiliated paper, *Robotnik* (the Worker), was being distributed at the rate of 30,000 copies per edition. Its editor proclaimed that terror as a political tool was now ruled out by the government and that the authorities were obliged to accept a form of "socialist pluralism." The task of *Robotnik* was to contribute to this broadening "pluralism" by reporting on "historical topics such as the 1947 elections and Polish relations with the Soviet Union before World War II." In April leaflets were distributed in major Polish cities urging the Polish people to "commemorate the Fortieth anniversary of the Katyn massacre" in a memorial to the Polish officers "murdered by the Russians." Still, there was no Soviet response.[67]

The spring of 1980 saw Gierek move still closer to his Soviet allies. In April he agreed to assist in preparing a Soviet peace initiative along with the PCF in Paris. Ostensibly, the proposed conference would be aimed at disarmament; according to some, it was actually staged to take attention away from the Soviet incursion into Afghanistan. Invitations to the Paris Conference were declined by the PCI, PCE, LCY, and RCP. The Romanians gave their reasons for not attending in blunt terms: the conference would not exhibit unity, it was unrealistic, it did not seek to give answers to "acute" questions, and such a meeting should be preceded by bilateral contacts. None of these parties was willing to go along with the CPSU and PUWP on what appeared to be nothing more than a propaganda venture.[68]

Gierek was likely attempting to trade for continued Soviet support of his embattled domestic position by acting as cosponsor of this affair. Similarly, Gierek had come out in support of the Soviet intervention in Afghanistan.[69] However, the Polish leader could not expect to deal successfully with his domestic problems by simply reorienting himself on a wider range of Soviet foreign policy issues. By the spring of 1980 the crisis in Poland was coming to a head. Mismanagement was now identified by the Polish media as a central problem, while harsh weather and unfortunate droughts were officially blamed for increased shortages of food. Further analysis of hard currency and raw material problems facing Poland indicated that some government action was in the wind. Party action against administrators and managers who were deemed by *Trybuna Ludu* as "unsatisfactory" included massive dismissals. In May and June the pricing of meat was again before the public. Something had to be done.[70]

In contrast to government inertia, DiP once again recommended the "way out" in a five-point scheme:

1. Create indispensable trust between the authorities and public opinion
2. Change methods of government and introduce economic reforms
3. Create the right climate and mechanisms to insure public support
4. Guarantee the permanent nature of changes
5. Institute a system to forestall or settle social conflict

It was also recommended that the government show society that "all fundamental decisions concerning the nation are taken within Poland itself." In direct contrast to the official explanation of the crisis as economic, DiP claimed again that it was "mainly political and social."[71]

During the escalating crisis in Poland, a poignant reminder to those who would veer from the path of Leninism appeared in the Soviet army journal, *Kommunist vooruzhenikh sil.* In its May issue, a Czechoslovak general, reminded of the "lessons" of Czechoslovakia in 1968–1969, extolled Gustav Husak who had ended "opportunism, adventurism and irresponsibility" in the CPCz and "restored the leading role of the party," which, in turn, led to a "principled" Leninist policy and a "unity of the people and the party." It was, quite coincidentally, in May 1968 during the Prague Spring that another article in the same journal, entitled "Party Principledness," also discussed the necessity of party unity. It also stated that a "liberal, unprincipled attitude towards the violators of party and governmental discipline is always fraught with grave consequences."[72] The gravity of the situation in Poland in 1980 was just beginning to be recognized.

Despite official Soviet restraint in criticizing developments within the PPR, it had become increasingly clear by 1979 and early 1980 that the performance of the PUWP vis-à-vis the opposition was, from the Soviet perspective, less than effective. Yet the Soviet party did not publicly take the PUWP to task for this or for its "neutral" stance on issues relating to orthodoxy (particularly heretical Eurocommunism). Some reasons for this Soviet restraint may be surmised.

The examples of previous Polish unrest (1956, 1968, 1970, 1976) perhaps led the CPSU to believe that endemic Polish problems would straighten themselves out without more vigorous action. In addition, Brezhnev had met with the Polish leadership many times since 1975 (not to mention numerous other high-level party contacts), and he no doubt had made clear his concern that stability was of prime importance. The Gierek regime desired stability as much as did the CPSU. The Soviet leaders themselves were experiencing difficulties both domestically and internationally: it has been suggested that the impending succession problem in the CPSU fostered an attitude regarding East Europe that could be described as "just keep things quiet, comrades."[73] This same factor could have militated against more pronounced Soviet action in dealing with the weakened PUWP, especially if there was a lack of consensus on what steps were to be taken. The PUWP was still in control, despite strong opposition and internal party disagreements. Loyalty to the CPSU seemed to be solid, especially on the issue of the PPR's position in the Warsaw Pact. No major dangerous reforms had been officially sanctioned, as they had been "from above" in Czechoslovakia in 1968.

Second, Polish nationalism in the population, with its keen anti-Russian component, had to be dealt with more carefully than nationalism in other East bloc countries. Though this did not apply to the leadership ("collaborators" with the Russians), it indicated that extreme care was necessary precisely because grass-roots anti-Russian fervor was a great danger to the Soviet Union.

Third, imprudent actions in East Europe could be costly to the Soviet Union both politically and economically in the international arena. Polish dependence upon Western credits and assistance was substantial: a sudden political turn to more Draconian measures in Poland could jeopardize this situation and force Moscow to take over the burden of Poland's economic crisis. This was, no doubt, an undesirable result. Also, Soviet leaders had been awaiting the passage of

SALT II by the U.S. Senate. Until 1979 American public opinion was still "sitting on the fence" regarding the SALT and detente processes. Manipulation of internal Polish affairs in a more overt manner could have further jeopardized the still hoped-for positive outcome, albeit in a deteriorating climate of already damaged detente. There had been no such agreement awaiting approval, nor had there been a mutually accepted climate of detente during the Prague Spring.[74]

Fourth, CSCE could be seen as restraining Soviet actions vis-à-vis Poland as well, especially considering the improving Soviet image in Western European countries, which were monitoring developments in Poland closely. Barring a serious deterioration of PUWP control (in effect, the party losing or giving up control), the Kremlin would be extremely reticent to risk its diplomatic gains in West Europe and its improved image.[75] Heavy-handed action towards Poland could derail Soviet foreign policy strategy towards West Europe, particularly in the context of the CPSU's "peace offensive" and Euromissile deployments.

Finally, by 1980 the Soviet Union was ensconced in Afghanistan. The Christmas invasion of 1979 to "defend socialist gains" in Afghanistan was greeted both in the West and in some East European countries quite negatively (by this time, hopes for SALT II's passage had been abandoned). Romania immediately announced that it deplored a "policy of domination" and sought to assist in working out an international agreement for the withdrawal of Soviet forces.[76] Yugoslavia labelled the action as "astonishing" in its interference and represented the nonaligned nations in calling for a Soviet withdrawal.[77] Soviet leaders were likely not very anxious to exacerbate further international tensions as well as risk more communist disunity over the more "European" issue of Poland.

Clearly, the "limits of sovereignty" enunciated in the Brezhnev Doctrine had not yet been reached in Poland. But the summer of 1980 in Poland would present both Polish and Soviet leaders with a fundamentally new situation. It remained to be seen just how the PUWP and the CPSU would react to a more "clear and present" danger to Polish communism and Warsaw Pact stability.

Viability or Cohesion?
Poland and Limited Sovereignty,
1980–1981

6

Culmination of Crisis: Challenge to the Soviet Bloc

THE Polish crisis of 1980 differed from the crisis of the Prague Spring in two important ways. First, actions of the government in the CSR twelve years earlier had broad popular support. In Poland the situation was quite the reverse. The regime could not bring itself to institute reforms of even limited dimensions. This had the effect of exacerbating tensions between the regime and the masses. Second, and more important, the crises of Poland in 1980 and Czechoslovakia in 1968 were asymmetric in their points of inception. While reforms were initially instituted from above in Dubcek's regime, pressure for change came from below in Poland. The top of the party hierarchy ignored both pressures from the worker-intellectual coalition and the counsel of moderate elements within the party itself.

After the Eighth PUWP Congress in February 1980, it was clear that the party was not about to embark on a new course. Instead, it chose to deal with symptoms rather than to address the fundamental systemic problems that had been deepening the economic plight of Poland for more than five years. The extensive purge of managerial ranks in the spring of 1980 amply attested to this inertia, for such superficial actions were far from sufficient to meet the demands of economic realities and widespread public dissatisfaction.

The inexplicable inability of the PUWP to address even some revised form of the DiP analyses of both 1979 and 1980 only heightened the level of tension in the country. It was in this increasingly strained atmosphere that the announcement of price increases came at the end of June, almost exactly four years after the last attempts at changing prices.[1] This was the match that set off the powder-keg.

On 1–2 July work stoppages were reported at the Ursus Tractor Plant, encompassing some 40 percent of the work force. Both dailies *Zycie Warszawy* and *Trybuna Ludu* went to great lengths in explaining that these price hikes were "unavoidable." But the threat of spreading strikes forced the government to attempt somehow to appease the workers. A wage increase of 10 percent seemed to produce an end to the immediate crisis of strikes by pacifying the workers. Rakowski called for reforms while blaming "incompetent management" for the bad state of affairs, in contrast to continued citations by party organs of "natural calamities" plaguing Poland. An economic conference was quickly convened. Speaking to the PUWP Central Committee on 9 July, Gierek promised some relief for workers but held the line on meat prices.[2]

An uneasy quiet prevailed for several days as the events of 1970 and 1976 were recalled. Opinions differed widely as to the significance of the current developments. *Le Monde* reported that strikes were still continuing on 13–14 July, while Reuters saw the wage increases as effectively defusing the crisis. This led Reuters to predict rather confidently that "no threat of the repetition of the events of 1976" existed. The apparent confusion regarding the magnitude and significance of the situation was compounded by the continued silence of East European press organs on the developments in the PPR. Only by 17 July did it become apparent to the West that this was indeed a problem of large proportions, as "widespread" strikes in Lublin were reported.[3]

On 16 July a thinly veiled article in the Czechoslovak journal *Tribuna* cited the inherent dangers of "petty bourgeois ideology" and "individualism" and, at the same time, condemned ideas of liberalism in the socialist bloc. The only commentary from the Soviet Union was in the form of citations by Comrade Gierek blaming the economic problems of Poland upon rain and floods of the previous spring.[4]

Trybuna Ludu of 19–20 July carried long articles on the unrest and the need to resume work.[5] By this time, however, it was clear that the problems would not dissipate as quickly as the government had hoped. The Polish Politburo had met on 18 July only to conclude that workers should return to their jobs. Still, there was no talk of any reform.

On 19 July, almost three full weeks after the initial strikes, the Romanian news agency Scinteia became the first non-Polish East bloc media organization to report "work stoppages" in the PPR. Extremely cautious reportage of the explosive situation continued to characterize the communist "response" in the East bloc. *Bratislava Pravda,* the Slovak daily, announced its solidarity with the PUWP over the problems it faced and merely cited *Trybuna Ludu* on the need to get back to work.[6]

Western commentators were quick to identify the economic causes of the unrest in Poland, citing the gap between income and the rising cost of living. The Yugoslav press agency Tanjug also zeroed in on these economic indicators. Between 1976 and 1980, wages had risen by 33.4 percent while the cost of living had gone up 27.2 percent in the PPR. During the years 1970–1975, on the other hand, wages had gone up 56 percent while the cost of living had risen only 12.7 percent. The rising expectations of the Polish people had been dealt a severe blow by the failure of the modernization plans of the Gierek regime.[7]

The situation remained unresolved throughout July. Information seemed to be contradictory at times, as Polish radio depicted a return to normal in Lublin on 23 July. It was announced at the end of July that the issue of "better management" in economic policy was being discussed within the proper party organs. This facade of confidence was belied by PUWP's real fears of mounting workers' strikes. One week earlier it had been announced that strikes were affecting railway connections to the USSR, a situation that implicitly jeopardized the security of the Warsaw Pact.[8]

In the midst of these turbulent conditions, Edward Gierek made his yearly visit to the Crimea beginning 31 July to consult with Brezhnev.[9] Exactly what was discussed at this meeting is not known, but a rather rosy picture was projected of Soviet-Polish economic relations for the five-year period 1980–1985. They announced that Soviet-Polish trade was to increase by over one-third during this Five Year Plan and that huge joint ventures in the field of energy were also in the planning stages.[10] The PUWP emphasized the exclusively economic nature of these talks, possibly hoping the promise of expanded Soviet support for the Polish economy would offset general sentiment about Poland's gloomy economic prospects. In the meantime, it had already been revealed that the FRG had agreed to reschedule its share of the massive Polish debt to the West.[11] Both Gierek and Brezhnev probably hoped that the current crisis would blow over soon, as it had in 1976, with minimal effects on the PUWP.

Continued Soviet support of Gierek was reflected in the Soviet press, which praised the Gierek-Brezhnev friendship during the Crimea meeting and cited the Polish press on the secure nature of the Polish-Soviet relationship.[12] However, at the end of July increased attacks against "air subversion" by Radio Free Europe/Radio Liberty suggested heightened concern for threatening political developments in Poland.[13] The seriousness of the situation in the PPR was certainly recognized by both the CPSU and the PUWP leaderships, if not more explicitly portrayed in the party presses.

On 1 August anti-Soviet demonstrations were reported in Warsaw overtly resurrecting memories of the Katyn Forest massacre during one commemoration at the Powozki Military Cemetary.[14] On this same day strikes along the Baltic coast were announced, interrupting the normal work routine of several port cities.[15] The depiction of normalization had apparently been a vain hope, concocted to dissuade further unrest in the population. Announcement of forthcoming indictments against corrupt management in various enterprises did not seem to pacify strikers.[16] The situation was getting out of hand.

It was at this time that the goals of the worker-intellectual coalition were made public. Jacek Kuron, cofounder of KOR, rejected the notion that wage increases could resolve the current crisis and stressed that these measures would only increase inflationary pressures, not resolve the country's basic problems. In an interview with the West German journal *Der Spiegel* he claimed that Poland would need three years to change the society significantly to "make it" without provoking a Soviet intervention. Democracy and elections would be part of this three-year process of transformation.[17] The political aims of KOR were now boldly proclaimed – to change the societal and political structure of the PPR. Apparently KOR believed that its programs could be adopted by striking workers. What had been discussed at length both within and outside the party during the previous five years was now threatening to manifest itself completely outside the structure of the party.

The possibility of the Polish virus spreading to other WTO states was of noticeable concern after July. On 16 August it was reported that workers mounted a strike in the Romanian mining town of Tirgoviste, eighty kilometers northeast of Bucharest.[18] Restocking of meat supplies ended the threat shortly thereafter. But on the front page of its 23 and 25 August editions, *Rude Pravo* went out of its way to advise CPCz party groups to heed workers' suggestions and "discuss" production shortcomings with the workers.[19] The example of organized opposition to official union incompetence in Poland was sufficient inspiration for such prudent counsel, while the Romanian episode served to reinforce Czechoslovak apprehensions about party-worker relations.

A strongly worded article in *Pravda* on 15 August counterposed proletarian internationalism to nationalism and stated bluntly that a "national approach" inevitably slips into "narrow nationalist positions."

By analogy, it is not difficult to identify deteriorating events in Poland as the article's main object of attack. *Pravda* went on to accuse "bourgeois nationalist and revisionist concepts" of assaulting "socialist practice" and Marxism-Leninism. Four days later came the first direct acknowledgement in the Soviet media that the situation in the PPR was indeed serious, as TASS reported Gierek's 18 August television address to the Polish nation, citing events "disrupting normal rhythm" and blaming "mistakes in economic policy" for the crisis.[20]

Interestingly, *Pravda* had just days before intimated continued Soviet support of Gierek by announcing the publication of an anthology of Edward Gierek's speeches and works spanning the period 1975–1979. Gierek was still being portrayed as a sincere friend of the Soviet Union.[21]

The Fourth PUWP CC Plenum convening on 24 August not only announced leadership changes in the PUWP, but also promised free elections to the unions. TASS candidly cited Gierek on the readjustment to contemporary realities, stating that the PUWP was making "an essential turnabout" in state and party policies. This clear adoption of a compromise policy indicated the desire to avoid the pattern of turbulent confrontations of the past (1956, 1968, 1970) with the workers. Apparently no plans had been made for the use of force against such widespread social unrest – realizing that to attempt such action would risk a violent explosion in Poland.[22]

By this time it was becoming apparent that Gierek and the Kremlin were preparing for the worst. Gierek cancelled his long-planned trip to the FRG and gave no reasons.[23] *Rude Pravo* published in boldfaced type (to emphasize the point) an article calling for **"REAL SOCIALIST UNITY,"** in which loyalty to the Soviet Union on all fronts was stressed as the touchstone of true socialist convictions. This article attacked all "adversaries of socialism" and castigated those who:

1. falsify the terms "national sovereignty" and "national and state interests"
2. propagate concepts to prove the imminent disintegration of socialist countries' unity

Clearly, this was an intensification of the still veiled polemic against the course of events in Poland. Although no direct reference was yet made to the magnitude of the crisis within the PUWP, "contemporary revisionists" and followers of "national models" were said to be counterposing "national socialism" to Leninist "real socialism" in unnamed places. Linking both the elements in the international communist movement fostering such ideological revisionism and Western interference in the East bloc, the attack seemed to focus on current Polish developments *as a result* of contamination by reformist concepts from the West. Extensive citations are noteworthy and relevant:

> At the same time the bourgeois apologetics, social democratic theoreticians and opportunists of all colors are unable to cite any country in which the building of true socialism would have been accomplished according to the "models" suggested by them. **LIFE ITSELF AND THE PRACTICE OF THE CURRENT SOCIAL DEVELOPMENTS HAVE PROVEN THAT ALL THEIR NOTIONS ARE THEORETICALLY UNSUBSTANTIATED.**

Anti-Sovietism was claimed to be the main weapon of these efforts:

> **THE AIM OF IDEOLOGICAL BOURGEOIS ACTIVITIES IS TO DISRUPT THE UNITY OF THE SOCIALIST COMMUNITY, TO SEVER INDIVIDUAL COUNTRIES FROM REAL SOCIALISM AND TO RETURN THEM TO THE PATH OF CAPITALIST DEVELOPMENT. OUR OWN EXPERIENCE IN THIS IS MORE THAN INSTRUCTIVE . . . THEY START BY ATTACKING THE LEADING ROLE OF THE COMMUNIST PARTIES, ABOVE ALL THE SOVIET UNION, THE STRONGEST AND MOST POWERFUL COUNTRY OF REAL SOCIALISM.**

There was no evidence, at this point, that the CPSU was willing to accept a PUWP policy of compromise with the opposition based on the growing strength of opposition elements.[24]

By the last week in August, a full-scale propaganda offensive against the West was developing in response to the unresolved situation in Poland.[25] Coordinated attacks were launched by the Soviet and Czechoslovak media against West German interference in the internal affairs of socialist countries and against the West in general for exploiting Poland's "temporary" difficulties.[26] Resurrection of the image of a revanchist Germany, focusing on the issue of the 1971–1972 border agreements and treaties, also appeared in an apparent attempt to raise the spectre of the West German bogey once again before the Polish people.[27] Antisocialist elements in Poland were now, according to TASS, increasing subversive activity in the PPR and trying to push it from its "chosen path."[28] Soviet reservists were apparently mobilized, including those in the Trans-Carpathian Ukrainian region.[29] The entire array of attacks and criticism was becoming reminiscent of the offensive launched against the Prague Spring by the Polish and Soviet media beginning in May 1968.

Attacks sharpened against antisocialist elements after BBC interviewers posed some pointed questions to Lech Walesa, the Interfactory Committee representative of the strikers. Responding to the question "Is communism compatible with free trade-unions?" Walesa answered:

> The machine breaks down often – 1956, 1968, 1970, 1976, 1980. When it breaks down often enough there is little point in carrying out new repairs. We might as well buy a new machine.[30]

Such colorful metaphors published in the West could not have reassured the Kremlin about the status of the PUWP's leading role in the task of building "real socialism."

Rakowski, editor in chief of *Polityka,* had a more sophisticated, but nonetheless similar perspective, although it was couched in less vivid language. During an interview with *L'Unita* on 23 August he emphasized the need for a:

> . . . pact with society, between government and society. In this part of Europe, *society must change,* although some people believe that this is unnecessary. Many structures are no longer suited to the level of productive forces and the more modern and highly evolved awareness of society . . . . Poland has, despite everything, opened up to the world and managed to pay more attention to its national traditions . . . (but) *cannot express its de facto pluralism.*[31]

Obviously, the Polish party could not express the same sentiments to Moscow. On 29 August *Trybuna Ludu* reassured the Soviet Union that Poland still claimed allegiance to socialist foreign policy.[32] A heightened awareness of the age-old dilemma of Poland – existing between the powers of Russia and Germany – was noted during this time by a Polish writer.[33] The situation was fluid, but the prospects of trade unionism in Poland were, to be sure, viewed negatively by the Kremlin. The drama was just beginning.

A Historic Agreement and the Fall of Gierek

On 31 August 1980 an unprecedented agreement in the history of the Soviet bloc was signed between striking workers' representatives of the Interfactory Committee (Solidarity) and the government, which recognized and legalized workers' grievances and their right to form an independent union.[34] It was soon evident, however, that this agreement had not been accepted without serious reservations by both the PUWP and the CPSU, as the attack was stepped up by Soviet and Polish party organs on "antisocialist" elements who allegedly threatened anarchy in the PPR.[35]

More than a subtle message was issued by *Pravda* on 1 September in an editorial warning of attempts being made by "enemies of Poland" to change the status quo and also stressing the obligations Poland had to the bloc. A veiled threat was also included as the writer condemned those who ignore " . . . possible consequences for the state and the people." The counterrevolutionary aims of the opposition were trumpeted as the ground was apparently being prepared for any exigency. Despite these threats, there was no direct attack by the Soviet media on the agreement itself.[36]

Polish party spokesman, Jerzy Waszczuk, explained the necessity of the 31 August agreements, while admitting that the compromises with the opposition "could arouse some doubt in our country and other socialist countries." He stressed that these agreements had been "adopted in view that they will not be transformed into an opposition political force."[37] This possibility, of course, was the primary concern of Soviet leaders and other orthodox communist hierarchs in East Europe. Allowing economic reform and limited compromises with workers was one thing. Allowing the spillover of this process into the political arena was quite another matter. Any successful challenge to communist hegemony in Poland could provide an undesirable example for other East bloc members to emulate. The GDR joined in the chorus of denunciations, claiming that "real socialism" was being threatened by antisocialist forces in Poland.[38]

While the West watched apprehensively, a sophisticated analysis of the Polish situation appeared in the Yugoslav press immediately on the heels of the 31 August agreement. The crisis in Poland was carefully scrutinized; the final appraisal was that changes were of a positive nature as the "obsolete" model of Poland's socialism was being transformed.[39] Belgrade's *Politika* noted Soviet restraint in the current crisis as similar to the period of the 1970 disturbances in Poland; the Soviets were indeed applying pressure, but attempting to give the appearance that they were not influencing events.[40] This commentary included the reminder that $100 million of foreign exchange from Moscow was needed to alleviate the situation at that time and more would now be needed to assist Poland during the current crisis.[41] According to a Zagreb journal, the Soviets were indeed not satisfied with the 31 August agreement.[42]

Any references to the content of the accords between the Solidarity union and the Polish government were understandably absent in the Soviet press. Any admission by Soviet media that the Polish government had retreated in the face of opposition pressure, even regarding articles of the Gdansk agreement such as those reducing work hours and the guarantee of work-free Saturdays would have been embarrassing and potentially dangerous to the leaders of the world's first "workers' state." Rather, the event itself was reported without substantive explanation, while the propaganda assault on antisocialist forces continued.[43] At this time, it could be suggested that there was no need as yet to attack and criticize directly the nature of party leadership in Poland. The PUWP had not yet even suggested that it was prepared to concede crucial levers of power (for example, in the media) as the CPCz began to allow in Czechoslovakia twelve years earlier. *Trybuna Ludu* continued to describe a precarious situation in the country. *Izvestiia* of 2 September, citing *Trybuna Ludu,* noted that the political activity of antisocialist forces:

> ... has been well known since 1975, long before the June events (of 1976), they began creating their own program for penetrating the working class milieu.[44]

It was also claimed that since 1975 these forces had been trying to change completely Poland's political structure and promulgate a program for "Poland's retreat from socialism," making use of national slogans to achieve this result.[45] The implication that after the Helsinki Accords were finalized ("since 1975"), Poland had been experiencing difficulties of a *political* nature, was the first such exposition in the Soviet press. Criticism of the party itself was indirectly implied, for no firm response to these developments by the party was noted.

On 4 September *Rude Pravo* urgently echoed these Soviet views, counselling vigilance in the defense of the "gains of socialism." The firm promise of a "joint defense of gains of socialism" and "mutual fraternal assistance" harked back to the Czechoslovak crisis of 1968 and the Brezhnev Doctrine – the limited sovereignty of socialist states. It was clear by this darkening of tone in polemics that further deterioration of party control during the Polish crisis could lead to unfortunate but necessary consequences. *Rude Pravo* warned that "counterrevolution is not asleep" and that "socialism with a human face" was tantamount to antisocialism. Regarding Western sanction of Polish reform, the CPCz organ also warned that "when you are praised by your enemy, watch out!" Polemic was increasing on nearly all fronts. It was claimed that "enemies of socialism" were now trying to destroy Poland's link to the USSR and attempting to "infect" the entire international communist movement with "democratic-socialist revisionism."[46] The only charges that seemed to be lacking in these mounting attacks were direct charges against the party itself. Apparently, enough cadres within the PUWP were still loyal to the Kremlin that the situation was not yet critical enough to warrant either criticism of the failings of the Polish party or military action to "save socialism."

The importance of Poland to the Soviet security system was now openly stressed. TASS, citing the Polish military paper *Zolnierz Wolnosci,* explained:

> ... the morale and political unity of the people constitute the fundamental sources of the might of the Polish armed forces, and therefore, one can say without exaggeration that everything that undermines that unity aims at weakening our defense potential.[47]

This was a direct implication that the security of the WTO itself was considered as inextricably linked to Polish developments.

It was announced on 5 September that Edward Gierek, leader of the PUWP, had been released from his duties because of a "serious illness." Stanislaw Kania, Gierek's appointed successor, was cited by Moscow radio as saying there had been in Poland "a failure to observe Leninist norms in party life."[48] Although Kania's view of why Gierek was sacked was likely quite different, this mirrored the Soviet view. The admission that the PUWP had failed to observe these "norms" now put the entire nature of the development of Polish communism during the preceding five years into question.

Izvestiia of 6 September cited extensive portions of a long Czechoslovak analysis that clearly drew a parallel between the developments of Poland in 1980 and those of the Prague Spring in 1968:

> ... in 1968–69 international reaction planned to sever our country from the family of socialist community of states, break our ties with the Soviet Union ... rip our people's minds from the feeling of proletarian internationalism and socialist patriotism and replace them with bourgeois nationalism. ...
>
> We have seen for ourselves that counterrevolution does not slumber: it has dug itself in, camouflaged itself and is biding its time. Lacking the potential to eliminate socialism in a frontal attack, our opponents are attempting to destroy

socialism from within. . . . We will never forget the dangerous, reckless game played by anti-socialist forces in our
country. . . . They wanted to break up the socialist community and the unity of the Warsaw Pact and to weaken substantially the entire revolutionary workers' movement . . . these designs were not implemented and the initia-
tion of these pernicious plans exposed themselves.[49]

Clearly, Poland would not be allowed to succeed where Czechoslovakia
had failed.

During this time, the factor of intimidation came into play as well.
WTO maneuvers labelled "Brotherhood in Arms '80" were being conducted from 4 to 12 September in the Baltic Sea area, where strikes
were especially effective.[50] *Zolnierz Wolnosci* announced that Poles remained firm members of the Warsaw Pact, in an attempt to reassure
the Soviet Union that conditions would not necessitate intervention.

These assurances of loyalty to socialism and the WTO by Kania
and the Polish military in the face of obvious intimidation by maneu-
vering forces appeared to soothe Soviet anxieties during a very fluid
period of the crisis. Soviet media cautiously began to draw a portrait of
"normalization" beginning in Poland.[51] It was also claimed that workers
were *not* in fact taking a stand against socialism in Poland and that the
strikes were *not* antisocialist in content.[52] The clear implication that
the demands of workers contained some legitimacy did not, however,
diminish attacks against antisocialist forces. Workers' protests, it was
claimed, were not directed against socialism and the party, but against
"deformations which developed in socio-economic life."[53] This appeared to be an attempt to dissociate the workers from the intellectuals
in the opposition and to assure the workers that they would not be
blamed for the crisis.

On 10 September 1980 Polish Premier Mieczyslaw Jagielski journeyed to Moscow. It was later announced, as if in fulfillment of an
earlier Yugoslav prophecy, that Moscow was giving $150 million assist-
ance in foodstuffs, $260 million of credit postponement on previous
debts of the PPR, and $260 million of credits at a low ten-year rate of
repayment.[54] Although there is no evidence of direct Soviet pressure
on the Poles at this juncture, this subvention of the Polish economy no
doubt had many strings attached and probably included a promise of
future PUWP firmness against further concessions to the opposition.

Tensions continued through September, despite the official reference to "normalization" in Poland. It became increasingly apparent that
neither the PUWP nor the CPSU was eager to implement the accords
reached at Gdansk. Attacks against the leaders of Solidarity escalated

from the Czechoslovak side, including the assessment that Lech Walesa was "undeniably antisocialist." The trade-union movement as a whole was accused of "sabotage" of the Polish economy.[55]

The *political* demands of the trade union were now the target of orthodox communist assaults both from within the PPR and the Soviet Union. Polish antisocialist elements, it was claimed, had learned their lessons from the Prague Spring:

> In 1968 . . . explicit political demands . . . put their national-istic anti-Soviet card on the table. In the PPR, anti-socialist elements have been hiding from the very beginning behind the shield of social and economic demands.

The CPCz even made an overt attack on the papal role in the Polish crisis.[56] A purge and reevaluation of the PUWP had already been implied by *Trybuna Ludu,* while the Slovak daily, *Bratislava Pravda,* urged "intensified party work against non-socialist vestiges."[57]

A PUWP CC Plenum of 4–6 October did not, it can be concluded, adequately respond to increasing CPSU and CPCz criticism. While Kania guaranteed that:

> Poland is and shall be a member of the socialist community, the sincere ally of the Soviet Union, and an active supporter of peace and international cooperation. . .[58]

the agreements between Solidarity and the government were emphasized as the touchstone of *future* PUWP social policy as long as the social forces of trade unionism did not translate themselves into the political arena. "New and better" approaches to solving social and economic problems were touted by Kania as part of a PUWP strategy that one analyst has described as "acceptance of operational changes . . . combined with strong emphasis on institutional continuity."[59] However, the most important detail of this meeting was that no specific proposals or solutions were offered to address the ongoing crisis.[60]

Evidence of a purge of Gierek's lieutenants followed the plenum as: Edward Babiuch was announced to be among the important figures removed from the central committee.[61] The results of the plenum apparently did not hold great significance for the Soviet media, which merely reported Kania's address and did not bother to mention the changes in the PUWP CC.[62] The characterization of the PUWP as evidencing "political toughness, marginally mitigated by operational flexibility" vis-à-vis the workers' movement seems appropriate at this time.[63] However, it seems clear that the willingness to be "operationally flexible" did not satisfy the requirements of orthodox Marxist-Leninists. On 6 October Erich Honecker, GDR leader, stated unequivo-cally:

> Poland is our neighbor. It is our socialist brotherland and we
> cannot stand by and watch Poland's fate with indifference.[64]

The atmosphere surrounding the Polish problem became increas-ingly polarized in October. Eurocommunism was now being directly castigated by the CPCz for its part in poisoning Poland with tainted ideas:

> After all, the Polish anti-socialist forces and representatives
> of the so-called independent trade-union movement admit-
> ted frankly that the organized preparations for the gradual
> implementation of the plan — started as early as four years
> ago. . . . Revisionist and opportunist circles in some West
> European communist parties applaud Polish opposition and
> anti-socialist forces and claim that they strive to "combine
> democracy with socialism" and that Eurocommunist
> theories are being confirmed.[65]

Polemics had now spanned the entire spectrum of all those who were failing to reflect the Soviet perspective on Poland.

Calls for a new series of strikes were issued against Lech Walesa's advice.[66] By the third week in October, Silesian miners were striking for their own trade unions.[67] Serious splits within the opposition itself were appearing as some demanded more militance despite the possibil-ity of Soviet intervention. French commentary characterized this split as the difference between the positions of Adam Michnik (careful) and Jacek Kuron (violent).[68]

It seemed that the organized opposition was prepared to embark on a course of political change in Poland. The military paper, *Zolnierz Wolnosci,* cautioned the Polish nation against jeopardizing the socialist system in Poland:

> **OUR COUNTRY'S PARTICIPATION IN THE SYS-
> TEM OF SOCIALIST ALLIANCES IS AN IMPOR-
> TANT FACTOR OF THE POLISH RAISON D'ETAT.
> POLAND IS A PERMANENT FACTOR IN EURO-
> PEAN SECURITY AND IS SITUATED IN THE IM-
> MEDIATE SECURITY ZONE OF THE SOVIET UN-
> ION.**[69]

Former pleas for loyalty to socialism, couched in Leninist terms, were now giving way to direct appeals to national consciousness and reason of state. However, it should be noted that such warnings were not yet appearing in authoritative PUWP organs.

That this concern for Poland's immediate future was not without foundation became much more apparent in the weeks that followed. It was in this highly charged atmosphere of increasing apprehensions over the resolution of the Polish crisis (both within and outside the PUWP) that Stanislaw Kania and Jozef Pinkowski were called to the Kremlin.

7

From the Threat of Intervention to Martial Law

HE "working visit" of PUWP Secretaries Kania and Pinkowski to the Kremlin on 30 October 1980 could be seen as perhaps the turning point of the entire Polish crisis of 1980–1981. Despite the secretiveness surrounding the visit and its results, it was soon apparent that intensive instruction by the Soviet leadership on how to deal with continuing threats to Polish stability had been the central focus of the meeting.

Kania and Pinkowski were met at the airport by no less than four key members of the Soviet Politburo: L. I. Brezhnev, A. A. Gromyko, K. V. Rusakov, and N. A. Tikhonov. The two Polish leaders left Moscow that same day after what must have been several intense hours of deliberation with Soviet leaders. In the brief communiqué following the extraordinary visit, Kania and Brezhnev stressed the permanent nature of the ties binding the Soviet and Polish people. Czechoslovak radio, elaborating on the visit and the Soviet-Polish dialogue, described a "preparedness to strengthen and expand mutual relations—an outcome very topical for Poland's security and internal stability."[1] On the face of it, there was to be a redirection of efforts in building firmer Soviet-Polish relations at this critical juncture. However, subsequent events affirmed that this visit was more in the nature of a warning to the Polish party that further compromise with the opposition and further deterioration of the party's leading role would not be tolerated by the Kremlin.

The Soviet press continued its campaign against antisocialist forces in Poland and for the primacy of "socialist internationalism" in socialist norms of behavior.[2] While the Soviet leaders reaffirmed the Polish government's assertion that internal problems could be resolved without foreign assistance or interference, Soviet readiness to embark on any course necessary to protect its East European interests was apparent. On 9 November, a show of strength was made as joint Soviet-Polish exercises were staged near Warsaw at the Pomorze Military District training grounds.[3] More significantly, the Polish press went out of its way to give "unusual publicity" to these exercises, by way of a reminder that the situation in Poland was indeed precarious.[4] On 1 November *Bratislava Pravda* announced that the Soviet Union had given Poland $640 million in further assistance.[5] The Slovak daily went on to reject the "ultimatum" of demands by Solidarity that would, in its words, "put the trade-unions into opposition against the communist party."[6] Vasil Bilak, Slovak First Secretary, warned Poles that the search for elimination of errors in the formation of a socialist society must not:

> . . . lead to the dismantling of socialism, because no sensible person will wreck the foundation of a building or its roof when changing the windows.[7]

This message implied that a certain amount of reform was acceptable out of necessity, but that any measure of reform must take place within the prescribed framework of communist practice – and no challenge to the dictatorship of the party could be successful.

As other WTO leaders became more understanding and appreciative of the implications that political change in Poland held for communist hegemony in all of East Europe, the lack of public commentary supporting the Poles became conspicuous. A Yugoslav journal stressed two reasons why WTO members were now watching Poland very closely:

1. It was a dangerous example – transfer of which was to be prevented across borders
2. Polish events could stifle reform attempts in other socialist countries

The possibility of WTO intervention to thwart the spread of the virus was now being taken more seriously. Intervention would come, according to the Yugoslav analysis, if the party's monopoly of power were either destroyed or undermined, or if it were necessary to preserve the strategic equilibrium, or if the danger of contamination increased. A parallel was drawn with the events of 1968, when the Prague Spring affected workers in Southern Ukraine, where demands surfaced for soviets according to Lenin's formula—real workers' councils.[8]

Comparisons with the Czechoslovak events of 1968 were now commonplace in CPSU and CPCz organs. It was recalled that during the Prague Spring there were also calls for independent trade-unions.[9] But the issue of contamination was paramount at this time. An apparently greater unity among Warsaw Pact members regarding the increasingly dangerous Polish example reflected this fear. Nicolae Ceausescu, Romanian leader who was initially supportive of the Gierek regime's plotting of a separate road to socialism, now reappraised his stance:

> If appropriate action had been taken in time and a firm attitude had been adopted against anti-socialist elements and forces, the events we have witnessed would not have taken place.[10]

This direct criticism of the party's failure to control the situation in Poland was deleted in *Pravda*'s reprint of Ceausescu's comments, perhaps indicating that the CPSU did not wish to broach the topic of a wholesale reevaluation of both Gierek and Kania's efforts towards compromise with the opposition at this juncture.[11] Indeed, the entire Soviet emphasis was now on the struggle with the *current* problems facing the PUWP, not with evaluating *previous* errors and responsibility. There would be ample time for that later. For now, the problem remained one of negating the power of the opposition in Poland and restoring clear control of pro-Soviet forces in the PPR.

More evidence became available almost daily in early November of growing Soviet concern about the crisis in Poland and its possible effect on Poland's neighbors. Rail traffic between the GDR and Poland was interrupted on 8 November, the border between the two states was temporarily closed, and it was announced that visas for Poles to the GDR had been suspended.[12] The Soviet Army daily cited a Polish army discipline problem, implying that anarchy was growing in Poland within even traditionally staunchly pro-Soviet institutions. The PPR was being portrayed, by implication and analogy, as a potential counterrevolutionary flash point—a depiction that was the sine qua non in the event that intervention was deemed unavoidable.[13] PUWP policy was suddenly reversed, apparently in contravention of the Gdansk Accords of 31 August, as *Trybuna Ludu* announced that trade unions could not be independent of the party.[14] A showdown, inspired no doubt by the Kremlin during the Polish leaders' visit to Moscow on 30 October, seemed to be in the wind.

On 14 November the governor of Czestochowa District announced that he would use force if necessary against planned strikes, which were to be staged to protest the government's "lack of faith" in executing the full range of the 31 August agreements. Claiming these actions would be "anti-state," the governor was prepared to declare a "state of emergency and use force if local workers joined a nationwide strike planned."[15] Despite this threat of retaliation, strikes did indeed commence across the entire country, beginning on 19 November.

In a remarkable judicial decision, the Polish Supreme Court on 10 November had ruled favorably on the legality of Solidarity's registration, which had been debunked in the official press just after the 30 October visit to the Kremlin by Kania and Pinkowski. This prompted optimism among some observers that a "new democratic structure" had emerged in Poland. Despite this decision by the highest court in the PPR, tension mounted between the regime and the opposition. Yugoslav commentary hailed the "historic compromise" entailed in this legal decision, claiming that it created a "pluralist model" aimed at transforming socialism in Poland in a "democratic direction."[16] The Soviet media now counselled "urgent measures" for the "full restoration of the party to its leading role."[17]

TASS also claimed that railway strikes in Poland were affecting the security of the PPR. Warsaw Radio, on 24 November reiterated the TASS analysis of the problem, which appeared as a clear warning to the opposition regarding Soviet concern for lines of transit through Poland:

> In its report from Warsaw on the railroad warning strike, TASS quotes an opinion that this kind of strike could hit at national interests and interests of the national defense, as well as disrupt transit rail links through Poland.

This appeared to be a significant new development, as the same commentary was repeated over Polish radio a second time, emphasizing Soviet apprehensions about Poland.[18] The general strike was called off by Solidarity on 27 November.

Moscow again paraphrased *Trybuna Ludu,* claiming that the "socialist constitutional order" in Poland was irreversible and that European security itself was linked with the continued economic and political stabilization of the PPR.[19] On the same day (27 November), *Rude Pravo* warned the West that the ". . . present, essentially balanced correlation of world forces is unchangeable and irreversible."[20] These comments were part of a commemoration of the CPCz CC session of 1969 that reorganized the party leadership along staunchly pro-Soviet lines after Dubcek's failed experiment in Czechoslovakia. It was also implied that the leadership in Poland was not doing its job. Unnamed individuals were accused of:

> . . . striving for nothing else than to exhaust and paralyze socialist power and establish willfully or intentionally elements of petit bourgeois counter-revolution.[21]

A significant degree of retrenchment was also apparent in the PUWP after its seventh plenum, held 1–2 December. Politburo changes were made for the second time that autumn. Perhaps most important in the announced changes was the return of Mieczyslaw Moczar to the Politburo. His return signalled a firmer stance on the part of the PUWP against the opposition. Having helped Gierek in resolving the 1970 crisis and ousting Gomulka, he was now returning to the ruling circle to assist in a similar capacity ten years later. Now, only four members of the February 1980 Party Congress Politburo headed by Gierek remained. Party instability was behind the serious analysis of the political situation by the Military Council of the Ministry of Defense in Poland. At the council's 3 December meeting, "profound concern" was voiced over the state of affairs threatening social and economic order as well as the functioning of the state as a whole.[22] This was perhaps the most serious and sobering Polish evaluation of the situation thus far.

The Seventh PUWP Plenum also revealed that a "reconstruction of the party" was now in process in Poland. Kania announced that ". . . it is the highest time to sober up" in the face of "destabilization" of party and economic life. His words reflected the same "profound concern" the Ministry of Defense voiced:

> . . . the future of the nation is being decided. . . . Deep concern is being aroused by attempts to demand change in regional, state and political bodies of power . . . (and concerning Solidarity ultimatums) there cannot be a dual government in no [sic] state, also not in ours.[23]

It was at this session as well that both Gierek and Jaroszewicz were directly implicated in responsibility for the current state of affairs. "Serious errors" by both leaders were announced, including "ignoring" attempts to change socioeconomic policy during the seventies, which presumably would have alleviated Poland's problems. Polish radio announced on 3 December that there was an urgent need to return to "Leninist norms in party life," characterized by democratic centralism.[24]

There appeared to be serious divisions within the PUWP concerning the combination of restrengthening the party on the one hand, and proceeding with "renewal and democratization" of social life on the other. *Trybuna Ludu* published an appeal by Rakowski, editor in chief of *Polityka,* which counselled compromise while accepting the positive aspects of new elements in Polish politics represented by Solidarity.[25] Ten days prior to the seventh plenum, Jozef Klasa, PUWP CC Mass Media Unit Chief, admitted the possibility of a new crisis and upheavals engulfing the PPR and called for the real democratization of party life to complement the positive developments fostered by Solidarity in the previous months.[26] Despite publishing Rakowski's appeal for a conciliatory attitude from all factions, *Trybuna Ludu* also urged the party to adopt a more "forceful manner" in dealing with the broad array of political problems it faced.[27] This directly implied the inherent dangers of continued PUWP weakness. The entire spirit of the seventh plenum was encapsulated in this slogan, said to have been repeated at the meeting: "Renewal yes; anarchy no!"[28]

Between 2 and 4 December it was reported that two warnings were issued by the United States to the Soviet Union on the "unforeseeable consequences" of WTO intervention in the Polish Republic.[29] Rumors abounded of WTO troop movements around Poland and the blocking of Polish borders, possibly in preparation for such an action.[30] Polish radio of 3 December warned the people:

> Disturbances are bringing the fatherland to the brink of economic and moral devastation . . . the future of the nation is at stake. . . .[31]

All eyes were now upon the meeting of Warsaw Pact leaders in Moscow on 5 December.

It was at this key meeting that the firm Polish guarantee that the PPR would remain in the socialist camp was repeated to East bloc leaders in emphatic terms. The WTO strongly affirmed its intention to provide any assistance needed by the PPR in its struggle to remain on the socialist course of development. While it can only be conjectured as to precisely what transpired at the conference, it is eminently possible that hard-line WTO leaders indicated to their Polish comrades that a further deterioration of an already precarious PUWP position would not be tolerated. However, the communiqué issued from this meeting also indicated that the WTO did not *favor* the use of force in Poland, but that the Polish people could count on the "fraternal solidarity" of their allies in the Warsaw Pact during this time of difficulty.[32]

It was speculated that Nicolae Ceausescu of Romania had played a mediating role at the Moscow conference between the Poles and hard-line WTO representatives.[33] Yet, the exact nature of the discussion in Moscow remained unclear. European communists were split as well in their evaluation of the fruits of the meeting. The PCI appeared to interpret the events of the first week in December as ominous. On 6 December, *L'Unita,* the PCI organ, warned the Kremlin about the consequences of any military action against Poland.[34] This seemed to imply that the PCI was willing to risk a break in relations if the intervention took place. The PCF, on the other hand, bluntly asserted that there was no plan of Soviet intervention and that all talk of such an action was part of a "campaign of deception" in the West.[35] A climate of anxiety over the possibility of intervention prevailed.

Neither did the CPSU act to change this climate. The situation was soon portrayed in increasingly menacing tones by the Soviet media. On 8 December TASS reported that party activists in the PUWP were disappearing after confrontations with counterrevolutionary forces, citing specific examples. Open confrontations by the opposition with PUWP officials were described by *Rude Pravo* on 9 December. Apparently, these claims were either false or grossly exaggerated, as the Polish Ministry of Foreign Affairs in Warsaw made a formal "demarche" to the Soviet news agency TASS about its reportage of Polish events.[36] In contrast to this, at the end of November Foreign Minister Czyrek and PUWP Secretary Waszczuk had assessed "positively" the depiction of Polish developments in the Yugoslav press and thanked a visiting Yugoslav delegation from the LCY's Ministry of Information in this regard.[37]

Speculation on the state of Poland in the WTO increased. An especially perceptive analysis of Poland's future prospects appeared in the French press. A three-stage scenario was outlined:

1. Kania and Polish leaders would manage the situation
2. If not, the army would seize power and a state of emergency would be declared
3. Intervention by WTO countries was a last resort only if all else failed[38]

According to this analysis, the plan was concluded at the Moscow meeting with no apparent timetable visible for steps two and three.[39]

A CPSU delegation, headed by Vadim Zagladin, held talks with the PCI in Rome from 9 to 11 December. It seemed apparent that discussion at this meeting centered on Polish events and their effect on the international unity of communist parties, especially since the PCI had issued a warning to the Soviet party concerning the "irreparable consequences" of WTO action against Poland. Clearly, the Soviet leaders were attempting to discover the depth of the PCI's sensitivity to Soviet policy toward Poland and, at the same time, quell the Italians' fears. Zagladin also conducted an interview with an Italian paper about Poland's future.[40] Four days later, on 15 December, Valentin Falin, first deputy chairman of the CPSU's International Information Department and former ambassador to the FRG, gave an interview to the German journal, *Der Spiegel.* In both cases the topic was the same. Both high-level party figures, though cautious in their evaluations, portrayed a return to stability in the PPR and expressed confidence that Poland could work out its own problems without outside interference. Falin coolly offered the assessment that the situation in Poland would not result in anarchy, a condition which could dictate the use of "force."[41]

Soviet depiction of the dangerous situation had changed with the visit of Zagladin to Rome. *Pravda* of 15 December cited an address by the Hungarian leader Kadar to the Hungarian trade unions in which he affirmed the ability of the Poles to deal with their own problems. The crisis atmosphere was now abating somewhat. By 22 December Kania claimed that the public mood was "improving." TASS reaffirmed this evaluation on 25 December in a commentary stating, "trust in the Polish party is being restored."[42]

Polish Foreign Minister Czyrek visited Moscow on 25–26 December where he met with Brezhnev and Gromyko. Both sides now were approaching questions in an atmosphere of "mutual understanding." No hint of tension was present in a wholly positive depiction of the encounter in an official report by *Pravda* on 27 December.[43] The implication that relations were now returning to a more normal state of affairs indicated that the crisis of late November/early December had been defused, at least for the present.

But at the same time, *Pravda* made it unequivocally clear that the gains of Solidarity in Poland were not to be construed as a permanent structural feature in the socialist system. In a long article on 26 December, unions under socialism and capitalism were contrasted as to their raison d'être. *Pravda* bluntly asserted:

> The most important principle of structure in trade unions' activity has been and remains the Leninist principle of democratic centralism.

The overall purpose of trade unions was cited directly from Lenin:

> . . . an educational organization, an organization of involve-
> ment and training, that is a school of economic activity, a
> school of management, a school of communism.

No room was left for any initiative to negotiate with the state, the controllers of the means of production. Mensheviks and others who had worked for "autonomy and independence" of trade unions during the Russian revolution were directly condemned, while the role of unions in building a "new society" directed by the party was stressed. This was not merely a rhetorical counterpoint in the debate on systemic reforms in socialist society, but a prescriptive solution for the entire question of independent unions. The appearance of the article at this time in such an authoritative source left this in little doubt.[44]

Although attacks continued in the press on "ideological sabotage" by the West in Poland, the four-week period spanning the middle of December to the middle of January 1981 was characterized by noticeably less violent polemics over the situation in the PPR. Deputy Chairman of the Council of Ministers of the PPR, Mieczyslaw Jagielski, visited Moscow on 30 December 1980 for economic talks with his Soviet counterpart Nikolai Baybakov.[45] In *Krasnaya Zvezda*, Soviet Marshal Kulikov stressed the readiness and loyalty of the Polish armed forces, who were now permanently on alert.[46] Foreign Minister Czyrek publicly extolled the Soviet-Polish relationship.[47] The situation was apparently returning to "normalcy." Criticism was now directed to the past sins of Polish communism. *Rude Pravo* indicted Gierek for not having followed the "general laws and rules" of socialist development, the neglect of which "not only threatened the very foundations of socialism," but also slowed down the world revolutionary process.[48]

Although the threshold of tension had been considerably reduced, the struggle of the party to reassert itself against the opposition without the use of force was no easy task because of increasing pressure from the opposition for the government to adhere to the Gdansk agreements in full. The government was dragging its feet on the issue of accepting the registration of Rural Solidarity (a peasant-farmer union). Elimination of Saturdays from the normal work week was also at issue, while the entire question of reduction of total hours in the work week had not been satisfactorily addressed by the government. Solidarity warned that a general strike would be called if the government insisted on punitive action for workers not showing up on Saturday, 10 January. In the wake of the call for a new strike to begin on 23 January,

TASS charged that Solidarity was not interested in "normalization."[49]

Lech Walesa was in Rome during this time, meeting with the pope. *Rude Pravo* asked in ominous tones whether the pope had given his blessing to the new strikes. Unspecified "fifth columns" were also depicted as continuing to try to push Poland from its chosen path.[50] Upon Walesa's return from Rome, warning strikes were indeed announced, slated to begin 26 January. The demands of the opposition included registration of Rural Solidarity and more access to the mass media, along with negotiations for a shorter work week.[51]

A "partial compromise" was announced after negotiation between Solidarity and the government on 31 January over the points of contention. A crucial aspect of this compromise was the proviso to postpone further negotiation concerning perhaps the most sensitive point in Solidarity's demands—that of more access to the mass media.[52] Delaying negotiation on this point, the granting of which could signal to the Kremlin a serious retreat on the part of the PUWP (as it was construed in 1968 in the CSR), was the only victory the PUWP could claim in this series of talks.

Despite these tactical retreats in the face of broadening opposition in Poland, the prevailing mood in the government reflected a need for greater discipline and law and order in the country. The mandate given by WTO leaders in Moscow on 5 December to Kania—to reinvigorate the party and deal with Solidarity in a firmer manner—was not being successfully fulfilled.[53] One indication that the PUWP was indeed attempting to hold up its end of the bargain and "get tough" came at the PUWP CC Plenum of 10 February. Jozef Pinkowski was replaced as premier by General Wojciech Jaruzelski. The Polish general was known as a patriot who had also not been in a position of administrative responsibility in the tarnished Gierek regime. The Soviet media reported the appointment of Jaruzelski with no comment, but Moscow could not have been very disappointed with the change. The general represented the loyalty of the military, the sole constant of reliability for the Soviet Union in the entire crisis period of November–December 1980. The appointment of M. F. Rakowski, *Polityka* editor, as deputy premier was likely aimed at conciliating moderate and liberal elements in the party and indicated that the government and the party were not going to push aside these groups in the "renewal process." The new deputy premier had even dissociated himself several weeks earlier from what he termed "radicalism" and had cautioned a prudent path for Poland during the tension of early December.[54] Rakowski, long considered a representative of the more moderate elements in the PUWP, could assist in coopting some of these groups to a position of stronger support for the new regime.

On the same day the plenum announced these leadership changes, the Supreme Court of Poland rejected the application of Rural Solidarity for registration as an independent trade union. Yet a sudden improvement in the atmosphere of the strike-torn country was noted soon after the appointment of Jaruzelski as premier. Conflicts with miners and students were announced to be in process of resolution.[55] For the moment, tension seemed to abate. Jaruzelski called for a ninety-day social truce in his 12 February address to the *sejm* to allow the country to begin to recover from the effects of social upheaval. A "tough" course was announced for the party to insure that the "renewal process" would be successful. Interestingly, Soviet reservists were reported to be "demobilized" near the Polish border.[56]

Jiri Pelikan, former Czechoslovak leader, suggested in a Rome newspaper that Polish events were approaching a dangerous "turning point" because of three factors: the workers seemed split and lacking central control, the party leadership was "dead," and the CPSU Congress was just two weeks away.[57] Factionalism appeared to be growing in the opposition, yet the viability of the social truce Jaruzelski had called for was still uncertain. The CPSU's evaluation of the steps Poland had made in the preceding weeks was crucial to both PUWP and the Polish people.

The Twenty-Sixth CPSU Congress was convened on 23 February 1981. The absence of both Enrico Berlinguer and Santiago Carrillo, PCI and PCE leaders, was notable – Berlinguer's nonattendance represented the first time that a delegation from the PCI had not been to a CPSU Congress. The reasons for this absence stemmed from the confrontation between the PCI and CPSU over Poland the previous December. A harsh letter from the CPSU to Berlinguer condemning the PCI stance on Poland had been delivered to the PCI secretary before Christmas 1980. This "secret letter" was leaked to the Italian press by a PCI official prior to the CPSU Congress. In it, the PCI was chastised for operating

> . . . not in support of real socialism existing in Poland, but in its manifesting solidarity with those forces which have unleashed a proper offensive against socialism in Poland.[58]

With the absence of the PCI and PCE, as it happened, the appearance of international communist unity over the issue of Poland was much easier to create.

In his keynote address to the Congress, Soviet leader Brezhnev included significant references to the crisis in the PPR. Citing "complications" in the development of socialist countries, he affirmed the WTO's support for Polish communism, announcing "We will not abandon Socialist Poland . . . in its time of trouble—we will stand by it." The Soviet leader also referred to the difficult task the PUWP faced in its renewal, while also reminding all communist parties in power there were valuable lessons to be learned from the crisis:

> Events in Poland confirm anew how important it is for the party and for the strength of its leading role that it pay close attention to the voice of the masses, resolutely combat all manifestations of red-tape and voluntarism, actively develop socialist democracy and pursue a carefully considered and realistic policy in foreign-economic relations.

He went on to indict both domestic errors and foreign elements for Poland's position:

> . . . where opponents of socialism, with the support of outside forces, are creating anarchy and are seeking to turn the development of events into a counter-revolutionary course. As was noted at the recent plenary session of the PUWP CC, a threat to the foundations of the socialist state has arisen in Poland.

The strong implication that the crisis was still alive in Poland was not, however, reinforced with any mention of further Soviet action. Instead, the rejuvenation of the party and its leading role was stressed as the sine qua non for stability to return to the PPR. Referring to the Warsaw Pact meeting in Moscow on 5 December, Brezhnev reemphasized that the WTO members gave "important political support" to the Polish leaders. The entire section of his keynote address dealing with Poland was marked by an evident restraint in tone. While conditions "threatened" counterrevolution, Polish communists were "striving" to improve the situation. This speech, though reflecting apprehensions about Polish communism, evidenced a measure of confidence in the Polish party's ability to resolve its own problems. The Soviet leadership was still in a posture of "wait and see" regarding the success of the new regime.[59]

The crisis was by no means over, but the PUWP leadership had shown some signs that it was prepared to delineate more clearly the limits for Poland's opposition. For the CPSU, this was a step in the right direction. Vigilance was necessary, of course, but intervention could come only after there were clear indications that the party was losing control of the situation. This obviously had been the case in both Hungary in 1956 and Czechoslovakia in 1968. It was not yet the case in Poland. Whether or not Soviet leaders perceived such a critical situation in early December 1980 can never be unequivocally assessed, despite some suggestions that the Soviet Union was indeed ready to intervene at that time. However, after the appointment of Jaruzelski as premier and the announcement by the PUWP of a "get tough" policy, the Kremlin seemed willing to await the results of PUWP resolve to deal more firmly with the opposition.

Continued Party Disarray and Martial Law

The 10 February PUWP CC Plenum's "get tough" policy did not result in a substantial reversal of Solidarity's gains or in the reestablishment of a clear "leading role" for the party in Poland. The PPR moved from crisis to crisis in 1981 under constant Soviet pressure.

In March the Bydgoszcz incident, which saw the first use of police violence against the union movement since July 1980, seemed to backfire; confrontation deepened between the regime and the opposition. Jaruzelski's pleas for a three-month moratorium on confrontations rang hollow after Bydgoszcz. By April *Pravda* was again overtly comparing the PPR in 1981 to the CSR in 1968.[60]

A PUWP shake-up in March did not improve the situation. Rural Solidarity was recognized by the authorities on 6 May, with full legal rights coming shortly thereafter. A visit by chief CPSU ideologue, Mikhail Suslov, to Warsaw at the end of April failed to stem the renewed course of concessions by the PUWP to the opposition.[61] The announcement of an extraordinary PUWP Congress to be held from 14 to 18 July and a campaign to "get Gierek" for his mistakes (beginning in May) did little to appease the Soviet allies, who were again becoming apprehensive about the continued unrest in the PPR. The search for a public scapegoat was likely an attempt to divert the people's attention away from further challenges to the besieged regime. Serious divisions within the top levels of the PUWP, accentuated by the presence of a strong hard-line minority, suggested the difficulties the party faced in resolving the ongoing crisis.[62] There was no easy prescription to cure the Polish virus.

A tersely worded CPSU letter to the PUWP, delivered on 5 June 1981, increased apprehensions about possible action against Poland (see Appendix). The letter indicted the current PUWP leadership for bringing Poland once again to a "critical point" by making "endless concessions to the anti-socialist forces." It was also revealed that the course of Polish communism in the areas of ideology and economic policy had deeply concerned the CPSU "for a number of years."[63]

The CPSU also expressed reservations about the upcoming Extraordinary PUWP Congress, which might possibly undermine the party's position in the PPR.[64] Serious concern over the Polish situation was again evident in other WTO states as well. Romania remained the only bloc member not to step up criticism over the deterioration of party control in Poland; all other East bloc states reprinted the CPSU letter and criticized Poland in greater detail.[65]

Soviet Foreign Minister Gromyko paid a special visit to the PPR prior to the congress (3–5 July) to clarify CPSU concerns and exert further pressure upon the PUWP to put its house in order.[66] Results of this congress were ambiguous. First, only 4 members of the Politburo were reelected, leaving Kania and Jaruzelski in charge.[67] Second, only 18 of 143 central committee members were reelected. More significant than the figures themselves was the nature of the composition of the new central committee. Traditionally strong government and party representation was "reduced radically" from over 50 percent to some 8.5 percent of the body.[68] Yet the Soviet media prominently displayed Kania's loyalty to the Soviet Union and the bloc during the congress. Although the Kremlin might not have been optimally satisfied with Kania's selection to lead the PUWP in September 1980, the CPSU was sticking with him, still attempting to avoid the politically embarrassing alternative of placing the Polish military in charge of Polish politics.

However, Kania ultimately failed to fulfill the role the Kremlin had in mind for him. The announcement of Solidarity's First National Congress slated for September-October brought with it an escalation of polemics. Soviet military maneuvers along Poland's eastern border were noted as the first part of the congress got under way (4–12 September).[69] On 9 September, during the first part of the congress, a bold message was communicated by the Solidarity delegates to workers in the Soviet bloc. The message conveyed

> . . . greetings and support to the workers of Albania, Bulgaria, Czechoslovakia, the German Democratic Republic, Romania, Hungary, as well as [to the workers] of all nationalities in the Soviet Union. As the First independent labor union in Poland's post-war history, we deeply feel a sense of community [with you] through our common experiences. We assure you that contrary to the lies spread [about us] in your countries, we are an Authentic 10 million-strong representative of the working people, [an organization] created as a result of the workers' strikes. Our goal is to struggle for an

improvement in life for all working people. We support those of you who have decided to enter the difficult road of struggle for a free and independent labor movement. We trust that our and your representatives will be able to meet soon to compare union experiences.[70]

TASS denounced this congress as an "anti-Soviet orgy," which was leading the country closer to capitalism.[71] The message to East bloc workers evidenced Solidarity's confidence that it had achieved a position that could not be rolled back, but on the contrary, could influence the rest of the bloc's social development. Deputy Premier Rakowski now lined up in complete opposition to the union:

The programmatic objectives outlined in the documents already adopted in Gdansk annihilate the spirit of partnership, which has been replaced with a spirit of struggle with the government, or, to put it more precisely, with the PUWP and the people's power above all.[72]

This analysis was from the man who was a close ally of Gierek and proponent of greater "socialist democracy" in Poland just one year prior to the first Solidarity congress. The increasingly polarized atmosphere in Poland could not continue indefinitely.

In retrospect, it seems clear that the uninterrupted course of the Solidarity Congress, with its visibly anti-Soviet statements and call to the workers of the bloc to "unite," sealed the fate of the Kania regime. On 18 October 1981 Stanislaw Kania resigned as first secretary of the PUWP (overwhelmingly elected just four months earlier by secret ballot) and General Wojciech Jaruzelski took his place, at the same time announcing the rekindling of a "front of national unity." Brezhnev's letter of congratulation to Jaruzelski expressed confidence that the general would be able to rally the party behind him and defend the "gains of socialism in Poland."[73] The Soviet leaders were counting on this "last chance" government to reverse the trend of developments in the PPR. It was up to Jaruzelski to succeed where Kania (and Gierek) had failed.

The commencement of a new series of strikes just after Jaruzelski's assumption of power in Poland and the increasing disillusionment of more Poles with the prospects of continued turmoil through another hard winter led to a "political summit" composed of government, church, and Solidarity leaders on 4 November.[74] Nothing was resolved at these meetings. Their inability to reach consensus on how to resolve the new crisis forced a 28 November resolution by the Central Committee of the PUWP to provide the government with special powers in "contingency legislation"—a state of emergency could now be declared. All the government needed now was an appropriate action on the part of the opposition.

Such an opportunity occurred during a Solidarity meeting in Radom on 3 December 1981. At this meeting the prevailing mood indicated an increase of confrontational behavior in response to the perceived threat of martial law.[75] Street demonstrations were to be part of the plan to rekindle public support.[76] Later, after the declaration of martial law on 13 December 1981, Deputy Prime Minister Rakowski declared, "Radom simply scared us."[77] It has been suggested that Solidarity's support eroded with calls for more confrontations because "Solidarity was overly self-confident and tactically out of touch by the end of 1981."[78] Poland was simply worn out by a year and a half of crisis after crisis. The announcement of martial law on 13 December was not openly contested by the Polish people. The process of attrition had taken its toll on the PPR and the reversal of the gains of Solidarity was now the main focus of the PUWP. Kremlin leaders had been successful, at least in the short run, in "saving socialism" in yet another Warsaw Pact country.

The strikes of summer 1980, which culminated in the Gdansk Agreement at the end of August, forced the CPSU to abandon its official silence on Polish developments in the latter half of the 1970s. CPSU criticism of the course of Polish communism began with the recognition of certain "mistakes" of the Gierek regime in economic policy but eventually spanned as well the broad spectrum of political errors that contributed to the deterioration of the PUWP's leading role in Polish society.

The belated infusion of Soviet economic assistance in 1980 did not help to defuse the new crisis, as had been the case in both 1971 and 1976. Lack of any direct Soviet recognition of the seriousness of the crisis (up until Gdansk), along with continued Soviet support of Gierek right up through August, suggested that Soviet leaders were perhaps not anticipating a dangerous confrontation between the opposition and the regime. Moreover, the CPSU failed to anticipate the strength of the new worker-intellectual coalition and the extent of the disunity in the party.

It seems clear that Soviet leaders at least considered the option of military intervention to stem the tide of continuing concessions to the opposition by the regime. However, both Soviet concern for the course of the Kremlin's relations with West European governments (the Helsinki process) and with West European communists (the PCI in particular) acted, to some extent, as a constraint upon the decision to take this option.

The most critical time frame for the Kremlin in this regard was the first week of December 1980. It had already been made clear to Kania and Pinkowski at the end of October that further concessions to the opposition were unacceptable to the CPSU. Continued turmoil in Poland and the inability of the PUWP to thwart Solidarity's progress in November precipitated a serious escalation of polemics and threatening innuendo. Yet the risks of intervention were underscored by PCI warnings to the CPSU as well as serious concerns voiced by Washington. Embarkation on a military course could have derailed Soviet West European policies, not to mention also risking the possibility of overt Polish resistance to a Czechoslovak-style intervention.

The passing of the intervention scare in December into a "patience with firmness" posture by the Kremlin indicated Soviet willingness to rely on hard-line Polish cadres to restore the leading role of the PUWP over the long term. Jaruzelski's appointment to the PUWP leadership in early 1981 likely reassured Soviet leaders that the Poles were not embarking on a course of political reform "from above." The repetition of the pattern of Soviet pressure and veiled threats, set in the autumn of 1980 and reappearing in the spring of 1981, indicated Soviet impatience with the lack of PUWP resolve to "get tough." The June letter of the CPSU to the Polish party clearly showed this impatience.

However, the many months of Solidarity's intransigence, characterized by continued strikes and a deepening of economic problems, eroded the initially broad-based support of the movement among the population. This was, perhaps, something which Soviet leaders hoped would occur. The lack of any reaction to the imposition of martial law by the Polish people suggested the extent of their disenchantment with the state of affairs and hence the success of the CPSU's waiting game.

As suggested earlier, two important factors in the Soviet decision to resolve the Polish crisis by means other than direct intervention were the damage such action would incur on the Soviet political agenda in West Europe and the danger of an open rupture occurring with Western Communists. Several other factors were important as well. First, intervention could mean bloody Polish resistance and the taking over of the huge Polish economic burden by the Soviet Union. It is clear that the costs of military occupation by Soviet and/or Warsaw Pact forces would be substantial. Second, the possibility that other WTO members would not cooperate in such an action was also a risk. It will be recalled that Romania declined to participate in the Czechoslovak intervention in 1968 and appeared somewhat cool to the escalating Soviet polemics against Poland in the spring of 1981. Third, the developing succession question in the CPSU likely formed part of the backdrop for the decision not to intervene. An orderly transition of leadership could have been hampered by such a high-risk venture as intervention seemed to suggest in the Polish case. Last, but not least, the presence of Soviet forces in Afghanistan (by this time with no quick victory at hand) compounded the problems of deciding upon a course that could, in the long run, prove to be an extended occupation as well.

By riding out the storm and having Solidarity burn itself out, the Soviet Union had an excellent example in Poland of counterrevolution being defeated from within by indigenous communists, vindicating CPSU strategy. The implications this last point has for the relevance of the Brezhnev Doctrine and the dual notion of cohesion and viability in Soviet policy towards East Europe will be addressed in the concluding chapter.

Conclusions

THIS study has attempted to clarify Soviet interests and concerns in East Europe as they evolved in the 1970s by examining Polish communism and Warsaw Pact politics during that decade. Regime stability in the WTO was then and continues to be the indispensable precondition for the fulfillment of Soviet security needs, both strategic and ideological, as these are perceived from Moscow. Thus the deterioration of the PUWP in the latter half of the 1970s as the "leading force" in Polish society was the major concern of Soviet policy vis-à-vis the Polish People's Republic.

The conspicuous lack of any clear indication that Soviet leaders were vitally concerned with the disastrous course of the Gierek regime's economic policies suggests that the critical questions for the CPSU in East Europe were of a *political* and not of an *economic* nature as they worked to retain Soviet dominance in the East European periphery. It is nevertheless ironic that Soviet willingness to allow the Polish leadership to pursue economic policies conducive only to short-term gains brought the very thing the Kremlin feared most—the deterioration of the party and, in the case of Poland in 1980, the consolidation of opposition to the regime in a dramatic way. Short-term Soviet concerns to improve declining East European economic performance with infusions of Western capital seem to have taken precedence over the potential dangers that expansion of economic relations posed for political stability in Poland.

Perhaps Soviet leaders were confident that their previous success in reversing moves towards pluralism in East Europe (Hungary 1956 and Czechoslovakia 1968) would be enough to dissuade future challenges to Soviet-sponsored communist dictatorships in the region. The "lessons" of Czechoslovakia perhaps influenced CPSU leaders to perceive the real threat to Soviet hegemony as coming "from above," that is, from the PUWP itself relinquishing its "leading role" and redefining Marxist-Leninist tenets. But the threat in Poland in 1980 came "from below," presenting the Kremlin with an altogether different political situation.

A new factor, however, was present in Polish developments of the 1970s, one which gave sufficient cause for Soviet concern over the course of Polish communism, perhaps even more than was evidenced. Growing Eurocommunist opposition to Soviet international positions included a stinging critique of the Soviet model of communism in East Europe. This criticism had adherents within the Polish party as well as among leading elements in the opposition. The willingness of important figures in the PUWP (most notably, Gierek and Kania) to promote good relations with the PCI and to deal rather leniently with opposition elements (directly or indirectly due to PCI requests) indicated that the Poles were not simply taking orders from the CPSU on domestic and international issues. Rather, they were attempting to forge a new position for Poland within the Soviet bloc, the character of which was unclear. By the late 1970s, why the PUWP leadership continued to maintain close ties with the PCI became less and less apparent, especially in light of increased CPCz and CPSU polemics against the doctrines of pluralism and reformism in socialism purveyed principally by the Italian party.

That the Gierek regime failed or was unwilling to initiate economic reforms of even limited scope, just as the internal crisis came to a head in the summer of 1980, suggested not only a split within the PUWP between vested interests in the continuation of highly centralized economic administration and those seeking some changes, but also a realistic appraisal for the limits of Soviet toleration.[1] Gierek could play the role of self-pronounced "mediator" between East and West in the game of detente *and* take a stance on Eurocommunism unpopular with the Kremlin, but he could not play these parts and also become a "reformer" on the domestic stage. Romania and Hungary are instructive examples in this regard. Both were able to decouple foreign and domestic policies to an extent, but only by retaining orthodoxy in either one or the other.

Although it is unclear to what extent "cross-fertilization" of both

East and West European communist ideas on socialism and the issue of pluralism took place in the Polish case, it is clear that some of these notions were influential within the party and among the opposition by the end of the 1970s.[2] Whether this was the case because of a true congruence of political and theoretical concerns or merely because the Poles (both in the party and among the opposition) saw it to their advantage to emphasize parallel concerns is difficult to determine. However, it is interesting to note that after the strikes of August 1980 and the initial concessions by the regime to the opposition, esteem for the pluralist ideas of the PCI receded into the background. During this time the attention of Poles turned inward. But as factionalism grew within the party and among the opposition, it appeared that Poles themselves did not know how to deal with the questions of reform and budding pluralism. Something new was being born, but there was no clear consensus as to what exactly it was.

Gradualism seemed to be the course of Solidarity (and certainly of the PUWP after Gdansk). This was born of the knowledge that to move too rapidly could create an atmosphere of desperation among orthodox pro-Soviet elements within the PUWP and lead to WTO intervention. The critique of the Soviet model of communism in East Europe by the Eurocommunists (especially in *Eurocommunism and the State*) offered no plan for resolving the problems of the model. The Poles could neither rely on the Eurocommunists for details about what was to be done, nor forge any consensus on what to do themselves over the long haul. Ironically, it is this same gradualism that contributed to the demise of Solidarity itself. The intimidation factor of the Soviet trump card – military intervention – proved successful over the long term. Broad-based support for the trade-union movement declined by autumn of 1981, and the aftermath of martial law sapped the strength of the opposition.[3]

Did the Soviet leaders fail to anticipate the direction in which Poland was heading in the last half of the 1970s? Organizational and ideological problems in the PUWP were recognized by the Kremlin and attempts to address these problems were visible in high-level party-to-party contacts and interparty conferences on these topics from 1975 on. This indicates that there was indeed CPSU concern for the PUWP apparatus and the regime's dealings with the opposition. However, Soviet leaders were unable to anticipate the implications *both* factionalism and economic mismanagement had for stability in the PPR. Neither did the Kremlin properly gauge the strength the increasingly organized opposition would be able to draw from such a situation. It appears that neither the CPSU nor the PUWP recognized the unique situation facing Polish communism entering the 1980s. This situation presented a challenge demanding new efforts to develop a particularly Polish brand of "national communism." This was the same challenge that Gomulka, Gierek's predecessor, had failed to meet after the 1956 "revolution."

Poland of the 1970s is the quintessential example of the Soviet failure to create a more viable "socialist internationalism" and the continued dangers of national communism to the Soviet position in the East bloc. The dilemma of national communism in Poland goes beyond questions of political form and economic performance. It is deeply rooted in the particular experience of Poland as a national state and in the history of Russo-Polish relations – a history that sets Poland apart from the rest of the bloc.

Spillover of economic problems into the political arena has threatened directly party dictatorships several times. Certainly, economic performance was a salient factor in the demise of both Gomulka and Gierek. However, the dilemma posed by successful national communism in Poland is also linked to Poland's national identity, including its strong Catholic heritage. These factors in effect question the possibility of a viable national communism ever developing in Poland that would not threaten Soviet hegemony in the region.

What can we learn from the cohesion-viability model when applied to Soviet policy towards Poland in the 1970s? This model is a simplification of the Soviet dilemma in East Europe insofar as it suggests that the search for viability leads to numerous problems for the Kremlin in promoting greater cohesion in this vital security zone. Even before the crisis came to a head in 1980, it is unlikely that the promotion of greater viability via economic reforms was seriously entertained by either Gierek or the CPSU leadership, especially after the food riots of 1976. After embarking on a path of concessions to the opposition (however minor at first), reforms could have posed a mortal danger to the Polish regime or at least accelerated dangerously the activities of the opposition.

At the time of the Eighth PUWP Congress (February 1980), a move toward reform could have defused (at least in the short run) the imminent crisis. But the Soviet leaders themselves had been promoting greater cohesion in the bloc since at least the time of the Berlin Conference of Communist Parties in 1976, faced as they were with the challenge of Eurocommunism's attractiveness to East Europeans. *After* the crisis came to a head, there is little likelihood that promotion of the viability option was seriously considered by either the PUWP or the CPSU. It was time to stand firm against the opposition.

It has been shown, in the case of Poland from 1975–1981, that although the failure of a regime's viability can threaten security and cohesion of the bloc, the Kremlin is not faced immediately with an "either-or" choice—to intervene or not. Soviet leaders may be willing (or even forced), as the example of Poland suggests, to dispense with the notion of viability in East Europe when the crucial element of cohesion is at risk. The Kremlin leadership has shown a degree of flexibility (whether out of choice or necessity) in recognizing a broader range of options other than intervention to guarantee cohesion.

This brings us to the question of whether or not the Brezhnev Doctrine has a "bottom line." The Soviet Union intervened in order to "save socialism" in both Hungary in 1956 and in Czechoslovakia in 1968. The example of Afghanistan in 1979 could possibly be added here as well. In Poland of 1980–1981, the domestic situation paralleled none of these, although it threatened to do so given more time. The Polish party was neither instituting changes "from above" (Czechoslovakia 1968) nor threatening to withdraw from the Warsaw Pact (Hungary 1956). Open conflict between the regime and the opposition "in the streets" had not broken out (Afghanistan 1979). The success of General Jaruzelski's "last-chance" regime defused the incipient threat after Solidarity's First National Congress in October 1981 and eased Soviet concerns following the unsatisfactory course of the PUWP Congress in July 1981. Jaruzelski's success made it unnecessary to invoke the Brezhnev Doctrine to restore the party to its leading role in Poland.

The Brezhnev Doctrine—proclaiming the limited sovereignty of socialist states—was formally announced within six weeks of the Czechoslovak intervention of 1968 and seems to have been at least initially a response to the dangers inherent in reformism "from above." The Polish situation in the late 1970s and up to Jaruzelski's declaration of martial law was, as we have seen, quite different. It would seem that the Kremlin was put in a difficult position, especially given the party's weakness on almost all fronts. However, in whom could the Soviet leaders repose trust and confidence to reverse the disastrous course of events? They had already, in effect, established a policy of nonintervention in questions of leadership succession in Eastern Europe (especially visible in Poland since 1956). The selection of Kania was probably made palatable to the Soviet leaders only after Jaruzelski's inclusion in the top ranks of party leadership in early 1981. One conclusion that could be drawn from the extended chaos in the PUWP and the Soviet willingness to let it continue so long (sixteen months) is that there was no alternative to the Kania transition beyond intervention.

If the Soviet leaders were not particularly anxious to invoke the

Brezhnev Doctrine, as was suggested in Chapter 7, it is likely that the vehement protestations of the Kania-Pinkowski leadership after Gdansk further constrained those voices in the Kremlin calling for intervention.[4]

It is not too much to assume that the Kania-Pinkowski leadership was doing all that it could to hold the line against the swelling tide of domestic unrest. After all, what more could they have done? The question remains: can the Kremlin leadership dictate what the precise "limits of sovereignty" are in ambiguous situations in which the party has not clearly abandoned dictatorship on its own? It seems doubtful.

Of course, if the Jaruzelski regime had failed to reverse the opposition's successes, the situation would have been viewed differently. Such a result would have meant the complete collapse of the party, a condition that would have spelled catastrophe for Poland. It is unlikely that a "Finlandization" of Poland would have been allowed in such an event. The dangers inherent in the emergence of an overtly anti-Russian character to Polish politics were no doubt quite clear to Soviet leaders. Historically, the Russians have been acutely sensitive to Polish tendencies toward anti-Russian sentiments. Yet it is ironic that this same factor of historic animosity played its own role in the Soviet decision *not* to intervene militarily, since the risk of Polish resistance was likely much greater than in the CSR in 1968.

Another reason why the Finlandization of Poland would not be allowed lies in the attractiveness such an experiment would have for other bloc states. This was understood in Czechoslovakia twelve years earlier as well. The spillover effect of a successful challenge to Soviet hegemony in other WTO states could not be discounted by the CPSU leaders. A weakening of Soviet will in this regard could have many unwelcome ramifications. After autumn 1980, other WTO leaders also seemed to recognize the inherent dangers more clearly.

What does the future hold for Soviet-Polish relations? The period since the imposition of martial law by the Jaruzelski regime has not provided unambiguous signals. Martial law has been rescinded and many members of the opposition have been released from internment. It appears that the regime sees the necessity for reform but has not seemed anxious to incur the wrath of Moscow by embarking on a path of significant economic reform. If the PUWP is able to accomplish meaningful reform in the future, it would follow the example of Janos Kadar in Hungary—being able to achieve such reform only *after* the defeat of the enemy.[5]

In the short term, the Soviet leaders may be reassured by the "lessons" that the International Department of the CPSU's Central

Committee is able to draw from the Polish crisis of 1980–1981. After all, the threat was ultimately defeated by Poles themselves. Furthermore, the military control of a Soviet bloc state the Jaruzelski regime represents has not yet proved to be a significant liability to the Soviet Union, despite the considerable damage that the Polish image has suffered in Western eyes.

The restabilization of Poland has not resolved the fundamental economic and political problems that were manifested in the late 1970s. The opposition survives, albeit sapped of its former strength and underground for the time being; the Polish economy remains under great stress.[6] Faced with these profound problems, the Soviet leaders have little reason to be overconfident about the future of Polish communism or East bloc communism in general. Perhaps cohesion cannot ultimately be maintained and promoted without allowing for significantly greater viability.[7]

The new Kremlin leadership has stated forcefully its resolve not to tolerate any developments reminiscent of Poland in the 1970s. Thinly veiled warnings were issued to the bloc regimes not long after Mikhail S. Gorbachev's rise to the leadership of the CPSU. Flirtation with the "propaganda" of political pluralism was condemned along with the concept of "national communism."[8] Criticism was also made of the idea that bloc states could play a "go-between" role between the superpowers in the future.[9] Moreover, notice was given at the Fortieth CMEA Session in Warsaw in mid-1985 that bloc members encountering difficulties in economic relations with the West would not necessarily be able to rely on Soviet assistance in the future.[10]

Gorbachev not only gave Soviet blessing to the continued militarization of Polish communism in his strong support of General Jaruzelski at the opening session of the Tenth PUWP Congress (29 June to 3 July 1986), but also reiterated Soviet readiness to defend socialist gains in East Europe. His comments preceded a substantial reshuffling of the PUWP Central Committee that included the retirement of both Stanislaw Kania and Stefan Olszowski from Polish politics. Three generals were added to the Polish politburo as well.[11] All this represented the strengthening of Jaruzelski's position and an attempt to erase lingering memories of the PUWP's turbulent days in 1980–1981 before the imposition of martial law.

Such a forcefully reiterated hard line against disruptive external influences in the bloc serves to underscore Soviet wariness concerning the pull exerted on the East by the West. The CPSU has not been capable of insulating completely the bloc from dangerous Western ideas, nor has it been able to reverse centrifugal tendencies in the international communist movement that were accelerated by the "different roads to socialism" thesis in 1956. This continues to be true despite the waning influence of Eurocommunism in the 1980s and the passing of the charismatic PCI leader Enrico Berlinguer in 1984. Polycentrism and doctrinal disputes continue to present the CPSU leadership with formidable obstacles to the more complete "socialist integration" of the Warsaw Pact nations in East Europe. Under these conditions, it remains to be seen if Soviet leaders will be able to maintain the necessary level of scrutiny in oversight of East Europe to avert a future challenge to their hegemonic position. If the new Kremlin leadership is incapable of so doing, the next crisis in Poland or elsewhere may require a resolution on the basis of one of the more Draconian options suggested by Machiavelli to the Prince in the epigraph that begins this study.

Appendix

"To the Polish United Workers' Party Central Committee."
Pravda, 12 June 1981, 2.

Dear Comrades! The CC of the CPSU, out of a feeling of deep anxiety for the fate of socialism in Poland and for Poland as a free and independent state, addresses this letter to you.

Our appeal is dictated by comradely interest in the affairs of the party of Polish Communists, the entire fraternal Polish people and socialist Poland as a member of the Warsaw Treaty and the Council for Mutual Economic Aid. Soviet and Polish Communists stood shoulder to shoulder in the battle against fascism and have been together throughout the post-war years. Our Party and the Soviet People helped their Polish comrades to build a new life. And we cannot but be alarmed at the mortal danger that hangs over the Polish people's revolutionary gains today.

Let us say frankly that some tendencies in the development of the Polish People's Republic, especially in the fields of ideology and economic policy of its former leadership, have given us concern for a number of years. In full accordance with the spirit of the relations that have evolved between the CPSU and the PUWP, the Polish leaders were told about this during summit talks and at other meetings. Unfortunately, these friendly warnings, like the sharply critical statements made within the PUWP itself, were not taken into consideration and were even ignored. As a result, a profound crisis has broken out in Poland, one that has extended to all political and economic life in the country.

The change in the PUWP's leadership and the endeavor to overcome the flagrant errors related to violations of the laws governing the construction of socialism, to restore the confidence of the masses – of the working class first of all – in the party, and to strengthen socialist democracy met with our full understanding. From the first days of the crisis, we considered it important that the party administer a resolute rebuff to attempts by the enemies of socialism to take advantage of the difficulties that arose for their own far-reaching aims. However, this has not been done. Endless concessions to the antisocialist forces and their importunities have led us to a situation in which the PUWP has retreated step by step under the onslaught of internal counterrevolution, which relies on the support of imperialist subversion centers abroad.

135

Today the situation is not simply dangerous, it has brought the country to a critical point—no other evaluation is possible. The enemies of socialist Poland are making no special effort to hide their intentions; they are waging a struggle for power, and are already seizing it. One position after another is falling under their control. The counterrevolution is using the extremist wing of Solidarity as its strike force, employing deception to draw the workers who have joined this trade union association into a criminal conspiracy against the people's power. A wave of anticommunism and anti-Sovietism is mounting. The imperialist forces are making increasingly brazen attempts to interfere in Polish affairs.

The extremely serious danger that hangs over socialism in Poland is also a threat to the very existence of the independent Polish state. If the worst happened and the enemies of socialism came to power, if Poland was deprived of the protection of the socialist commonwealth, the imperialists' greedy hands would at once reach out for it. And who then could guarantee the independence, sovereignty and borders of Poland as a state? No one.

Comrades, you know about the December 5, 1980 meeting in Moscow of leaders of the fraternal parties of the countries of the socialist commonwealth. On March 4, 1981, the Soviet leadership held talks with the PUWP delegation to the 26th CPSU Congress. On April 23, 1981, a CPSU delegation met with the entire Polish leadership. During all these meetings, and also in other contacts, our side emphasized its growing concern in connection with the intrigues of counterrevolutionary forces in Poland. We spoke about the need to overcome the confusion in the PUWP's ranks, to firmly defend its cadres against enemy attacks, and to stand up staunchly in defense of the people's power.

Special attention was called to the fact that the enemy had virtually taken control of the mass news media, the overwhelming majority of which have become tools of anti-socialist activity used to undermine socialism and to demoralize the party. It was noted that it is impossible to win the battle for the party as long as the press, radio and television are working not for the PUWP but for its enemies.

The pointed question was raised of the need to strengthen the prestige in the country of agencies of public order and the army and to protect them from encroachments by counterrevolutionary forces. To permit attempts to defame and demoralize the security agencies, the police and then the army to be crowned with success would mean, in effect, to disarm the socialist state, to put it at the mercy of the class enemy.

We want to emphasize that S. Kania, W. Jaruzelski, and other Polish comrades voiced agreement with our opinions on all the questions raised. But in fact everything remains as it was, and no corrections have been made in the policy of concessions and compromises. One position made after another is being surrendered. Despite the fact that the materials of the recent plenary sessions of the PUWP CC recognize the fact of the counterrevolutionary threat, no actual steps to combat it have been taken so far, and the counterrevolution's organizers are not even being named directly.

The situation within the PUWP itself has recently become a matter of special concern. A little over a month remains before the congress. However, the tone of the election campaign is increasingly being set by forces that are hostile to socialism. The fact that frequently casual people who openly profess opportunistic views become the leaders of local party organizations and are among the delegates to conferences and the congress can only cause concern. As a result of various manipulations by the PUWP's enemies and by revisionists and opportunists, experienced personnel who are devoted to the party's cause and have unblemished reputation and moral qualifications are being shunted aside.

The fact that, among the delegates to the forthcoming congress, the number of Communists with a worker's background is extremely small is also alarming. The course of preparations for the congress is complicated by the so-called movement of horizontal structures—a tool for splitting the party that is being used by opportunists to get people they want picked for the congress and to divert its work into a channel advantageous to them. One cannot exclude the possibility that an attempt may be made at the congress itself to decisively defeat the Marxist-Leninist forces of the party in order to liquidate it.

We would like to make special mention of the fact that in recent months counterrevolutionary forces have been actively spreading all kinds of anti-Soviet fabrications designed to nullify the fruits of the work done by our parties and to revive nationalistic, anti-Soviet sentiments in various strata of Polish society. These slanderers and liars stop at nothing. They even claim that the Soviet Union is "plundering" Poland. They say this, despite the fact that the Soviet Union has given and is continuing to give enormous additional material assistance to Poland in this difficult time. They say this about a country that, with its deliveries of petroleum, gas, ore and cotton at prices one-third to one-half lower than world prices, is to all intents and purposes provisioning the main branches of Polish industry.

Esteemed Comrades! In addressing this letter to you, we proceed not only from our concern over the situation in fraternal Poland and over the conditions of and prospects for further Soviet-Polish cooperation. We, as well as the fraternal parties, are no less concerned about the fact that the offensive of hostile anti-socialist forces in the PPR threatens the interests of our entire commonwealth, its cohesion, its integrity, and the security of its borders. Yes, our common security. Imperialist reaction, which supports and encourages the Polish counterrevolution, does not conceal its hope of thus sharply changing in its favor the alignment of forces in Europe and in the world.

Imperialism is actively using the crisis in Poland to discredit the socialist system and the ideals and principles of socialism and to make new attacks against the international communist movement.

Thus, the PUWP bears a historic responsibility not only for the fate of its homeland, its independence and progress and the cause of socialism in Poland. Comrades, you also bear an enormous responsibility for the common interests of the socialist commonwealth.

We believe that there is still a possibility of staving off the worst, of preventing national catastrophe. There are in the PUWP many honest and steadfast Communists who are in fact ready to struggle for the ideals of Marxism-Leninism, for an independent Poland. There are many people in Poland who are devoted to the cause of socialism. The country's working class and working people, even those who are being drawn by deception into the enemies machinations, will ultimately follow the party.

The question is to mobilize all the healthy forces of society to repulse the class enemy, to combat the counterrevolution. This requires, first of all, revolutionary determination on the part of the party itself, its aktiv and its leadership. Yes, leadership. There's no time to be lost. The party can and must find in itself the strength to change the course of events and, even before the Ninth PUWP Congress, direct them into the proper channel.

We would like to be confident that the CC of the fraternal Polish party of Communists will measure up to its historic responsibility!

We want to assure you, dear comrades, that in these difficult days, as always in the past, the CPSU CC, all Soviet Communists and the entire Soviet people are in sympathy with your struggle. Our position was clearly expressed in Comrade L. I. Brezhnev's statement at the 26th CPSU Congress: "We will not abandon socialist Poland, fraternal Poland in its time of trouble—we will stand by it!"

Signed: THE CC OF THE CPSU.

Source of translation: *Soviet Foreign Policy Today* (Selections from the *Current Digest of the Soviet Press*), (Columbus, Ohio: 1983), 149–50.

Notes

Introduction

1. Niccolo Machiavelli, *The Prince*. Ed. T. G. Bergin. (New York: Appleton-Century Crofts, 1947), 12.

2. Alfred G. Meyer, *Marxism: The Unity of Theory and Practice* (Ann Arbor: Univ. of Michigan Press, 1963), 4; *kto-kogo* is the Russian term for "who gets whom," or the characterization of the life-death struggle in politics. See Carl Linden, *Khrushchev and the Soviet Leadership, 1957–1964* (Baltimore: Johns Hopkins Univ. Press, 1966), 11–12 ff.

3. See Nish Jamgotch, Jr., *Soviet-East European Dialogue: International Relations of a New Type?* (Stanford: Hoover Institution, 1968), especially 89; also see Teresa Rakowska-Harmstone, "Socialist Internationalism and East Europe: A New Stage," *Survey* 22(Winter 1976):38–40.

4. For full treatment of the viability-cohesion dilemma, see J. F. Brown, *Relations between the Soviet Union and Its East European Allies: A Survey* (Santa Monica: Rand Corporation R-1742PR, 1975), vi, ff.

5. See Andrzej Korbonski, "Eastern Europe as an Internal Determinant of Soviet Foreign Policy," in *The Domestic Context of Soviet Foreign Policy*, ed. Seweryn Bialer (Boulder, Westview, 1981), 313.

6. For example, the bureaucratic paradigm has been adapted and applied to the Soviet decision to intervene in Czechoslovakia by Jiri Valenta in his, *Soviet Intervention in Czechoslovakia: Anatomy of a Decision* (Baltimore: Johns Hopkins Univ. Press, 1979).

7. Soviet behavior and Kremlin crisis management during the deepening crisis of the Prague Spring have been analyzed in Karen Dawisha, *The Kremlin and the Prague Spring* (Berkeley: Univ. of California Press, 1984); these sources include the eyewitness accounts of former leaders of the Prague Spring. As Karen Dawisha writes (8):

> The data base available on Soviet behavior in the 1968 Czechoslovak crisis is better than that for many other Soviet crises, mainly because a wealth of information from Czechoslovak sources exists and the Soviet press and leadership were involved in an open and lengthy dialogue with their counterparts in Prague in the months preceding and following the crisis ... therefore, it is possible to present a fuller picture of Soviet perceptions and actions than might otherwise be possible.

Professor Dawisha also points out the difficulty (even amidst a great deal of information) of determining elite differences over issue areas in the Soviet case and " . . . drawing inferences about the positions of top leaders from views expressed in the editorial columns of certain newspapers." (See Dawisha, 7.)

8. Some of the more interesting interpretations of the available data on the crisis after Gdansk include Richard D. Anderson, Jr., "Soviet Decision-Making and Poland," *Problems of Communism* 31(Mar.–Apr. 1982):22–36, and Jan B. de Weydenthal et al., *Poland 1980–1982: The Making of the Revolution* (Lexington, Mass.: Lexington Books, 1982).

Chapter 1

1. For a general historical background on Polish history and Russo-Polish relations, see W. F. Reddaway et al., *The Cambridge History of Poland* 2 vols. (Cambridge: Cambridge Univ. Press, 1951). More recently, see Norman Davies, *Heart of Europe: A Short History of Poland* (Oxford: Oxford Univ. Press, 1984) for a lucid and provocative interpretation. For a standard Polish (socialist) account, see A. Gieysztor et al., *History of Poland* (Warsaw: Polish Scientific Publishers, 1969), especially 300–423. Other relevant general works covering various periods of Russo-Polish and Soviet-Polish relations include Nicholas Riasanovsky, *A History of Russia* (New York: Oxford Univ. Press, 1969), R. F. Leslie et al., *History of Poland Since 1863* (Cambridge: Cambridge Univ. Press, 1983), R. F. Leslie, *Reform and Insurrection in Russian Poland, 1856–1865* (Westport: Greenwood, 1969), and Adam Ulam, *Expansion and Coexistence: Soviet Foreign Policy, 1917–1973* (New York: Praeger, 1974). An in-depth account of Polish communism and relations between the CPSU and PUWP is provided by M. K. Dziewanowski, *The Communist Party of Poland*, 2d ed. (Cambridge: Harvard Univ. Press, 1976), Adam Bromke, *Poland's Politics: Idealism vs. Realism* (Cambridge: Harvard Univ. Press, 1967), and Zbigniew Brzezinski, *The Soviet Bloc: Unity and Conflict* (New York: Praeger, 1961).

2. Piotr Wandycz, "Polish Federalism, 1919–20 and Its Historical Antecedents," *East European Quarterly* 4(Mar. 1970):25, 26.

3. Nikolai Karamzin, *Istoria gosudarstva rossiiskogo* (St. Petersburg: 1892), cited in Wandycz, "Polish Federalism," 26.

4. For aspects of Polish political culture that contributed to this state of affairs, see Daniel Stone, "The Cultural Life of Conservative Polish Nobles in the Late Eighteenth Century," *East European Quarterly* 9(Fall 1975):271–72. See also Davies, *Heart of Europe*, 296–311.

5. I have chosen to use the terms "opposition" and "collaboration" to refer to two important strands of continuity in Polish relations with the imperial Russian and Soviet powers. There are other rough equivalents to these terms such as "idealism and realism," "Romanticism and Positivism," and "resistance and loyalism." These other pairs have been used by various observers of Poland to describe the historical tension and dilemmas of Polish politics. See for example, Bromke, *Poland's Politics*, and Davies, *Heart of Europe*, especially 179–92.

6. This saw the end of the so-called Confederation of Bar. See Redda-

way et al., *Cambridge History of Poland,* 35–41. See also Davies, *Heart of Europe,* 308–11.

7. See Stone, "Cultural Life," 272. The nobles who sided with Catherine in this coup met in the town of Targowica. It is interesting that the term *targowica* later became synonymous with treason in Poland. See Jan Tomasz Gross, "In Search of History," in *Poland: Genesis of a Revolution,* ed. A. Brumberg (New York: Random House, 1893), 3–6, 299.

8. Cited in Walter Leitsch, "Russians and Poles in the Nineteenth Century," *East European Quarterly* 8(Fall 1974):285 (emphasis added).

9. See Julia Brun-Zejmis, "The Russian Idea and the Polish Question: Some Russian Views on the Polish Insurrection of 1830," *East European Quarterly* 14(Fall 1980), 315–26; also see Leitsch, "Russians and Poles," 289–90, 293.

10. Leitsch, "Russians and Poles," 291.

11. Leitsch, "Russians and Poles," 291; Brun-Zejmis, "Russian Idea."

12. Brun-Zejmis, "Russian Idea," 325, citing M. S. Lunin.

13. N. Naimark, "Problems in the Historiography of the 'Proletariat': Poland's First Marxist Party," *East European Quarterly* 12(Summer 1978):244–45.

14. See Hans Roos, *A History of Modern Poland* (London: Eyre and Spottiswoode, 1966), 9. As Professor Roos writes, " . . . reactionary tendencies . . . gained the upper hand in Russia, the hoped-for autonomy failed to materialize."

15. M. K. Dziewanowski, "Jozef Pilsudski, 1867–1967," *East European Quarterly* 2(Jan. 1969), especially 366–68.

16. See Wandycz, "Polish Federalism," 28–29.

17. For an in-depth discussion of Dmowski's ideas, see Alvin Fountain, *Roman Dmowski: Party, Tactics, Ideology, 1895–1907* (Boulder: East European Monographs/Columbia Univ. Press, 1980). Also see Roos, *A History,* 6–7, 8.

18. Dziewanowski, "Jozef Pilsudski," 368.

19. See Norman Davies, *White Eagle-Red Star: The Polish-Soviet War 1919–1920* (New York: St. Martin's, 1972), 100–104.

20. Cited by E. H. Carr, *The Bolshevik Revolution, 1917–1923,* vol. 3 (London: Penguin, 1953), 192.

21. Dziewanowski, "Jozef Pilsudski," 379.

22. See Jane Degras, *The Communist International, 1919–1943: Documents,* vol. 1 (London: Oxford Univ. Press, 1960), 166–72.

23. See Dziewanowski, "Jozef Pilsudski," 375; see also Dziewanowski, *The Communist Party of Poland,* 2d ed. (Cambridge: Harvard Univ. Press, 1976), 123–25.

24. See Khrushchev's remarks on the destruction of the Polish communist party in *Khrushchev Remembers: The Last Testament,* ed. and trans. Strobe Talcott (Boston: Little-Brown, 1970), 107. See also Dziewanowski, *Communist Party,* 147–51.

25. Cited in Joseph Korbel, *Poland between East and West: Soviet and German Diplomacy towards Poland, 1919–33* (Princeton: Princeton Univ. Press, 1963), 273. My discussion of the nonaggression pact is condensed from Korbel, 266–72.

26. See Jozef Beck, *Final Report* (New York: Speller, 1957), 60–66, 171–72. Also see R. Buell, *Poland: Key to Europe* (New York: Knopf, 1939), 348–49.

27. Korbel, *Poland,* 273.

28. See Adam Ulam, *Expansion and Coexistence: Soviet Foreign Policy 1917-73* (New York: Praeger, 1974), 260–84, and especially 278 for Stalin's perspectives on Poland. There are, of course, other views apart from Professor Ulam's interesting speculation. For a more cautious evaluation of Stalin's goals as "evolving rather than as a design firmly fixed and single-mindedly pursued," see Vojtech Mastny, *Russia's Road to the Cold War: Diplomacy, Warfare, and the Politics of Communism, 1941-1945* (New York: Columbia Univ. Press, 1979), xvii–xviii, 23–29.

29. See Alvin Z. Rubinstein, *The Foreign Policy of the Soviet Union* (New York: Random House, 1972), 152.

30. On the Katyn story see J. K. Zawodny, *Death in the Forest: The Story of the Katyn Forest Massacre* (Notre Dame: Univ. of Notre Dame Press, 1962), especially 169–78.

31. A. Bliss Lane, *I Saw Poland Betrayed* (Indianapolis: Bobbs-Merrill, 1948), 304, also cited by Dziewanowski, *Communist Party,* 182. For standard accounts of the Warsaw Uprising, see Ulam, *Expansion,* 361–63, and Dziewanowski, *Communist Party,* 179–80. Also see J. K. Zawodny, *Nothing but Honour: The Story of the Warsaw Uprising, 1944* (Stanford: Hoover Institution, 1978), especially 232.

32. See Dziewanowski, *Communist Party,* 201–5 for the standard discussion.

33. Ibid., 187.

34. See ibid., 218–20.

35. Cited in ibid., 214.

36. This has been estimated at $14 billion. See Paul Marer, "Has Eastern Europe Become a Liability to the Soviet Union? The Economic Aspect," in *The International Politics of Eastern Europe,* ed. Charles Gati (New York: Praeger, 1976), 61.

Chapter 2

1. See Wolfgang Kraus, "Crisis and Revolt in a Satellite: The East German Case in Retrospect," in *East Europe in Transition,* ed. Kurt London (Baltimore: Johns Hopkins Univ. Press, 1966), 41–65.

2. See Carl Linden, *Khrushchev and the Soviet Leadership, 1957-1964* (Baltimore: Johns Hopkins Univ. Press, 1966), 34–35; Zbigniew Brzezinski's comment on communist dogma, cited in M. K. Dziewanowski, *The Communist Party of Poland,* 2d ed. (Cambridge: Harvard Univ. Press, 1976), 266, 255.

3. See Zbigniew Brzezinski, *The Soviet Bloc: Unity and Conflict* (New York: Praeger, 1961), 243, 237–52, and Dziewanowski, *Communist Party,* 256–76, for Gomulka's return to power.

4. Kraus, "Crisis," 61.

5. Dziewanowski, *Communist Party,* 311.

6. The preceding remarks on Gomulka are drawn from Adam Bromke, "Poland's Role in the Loosening of the Communist Bloc," in *East Europe in Transition,* ed. Kurt London (Baltimore: Johns Hopkins Univ. Press, 1966), 77.

7. See ibid., 78, 88–89. Also see Dziewanowski, *Communist Party,* 283–93.

8. Bromke, "Poland's Role," 78–79.

9. Ibid., 79, 85.

10. See Dziewanowski, *Communist Party,* 303–4.

11. On the issue of borders, see Sarah M. Terry, *Poland's Place in Europe* (Princeton: Princeton Univ. Press, 1983); see Nikita S. Khrushchev, *The Soviet Stand on Germany* (New York: Crosscurrents, 1961) on the importance of the German question at this time.

12. See H. Gordon Skilling, *Czechoslovakia's Interrupted Revolution* (Princeton: Princeton Univ. Press, 1976), and Galia Golan, *Reform Rule in Czechoslovakia: The Dubcek Era, 1968–69* (Cambridge: Cambridge Univ. Press, 1973) for the process of the Prague Spring's development and immediate aftermath. Also see Jiri Valenta, *Soviet Intervention in Czechoslovakia, 1968: Anatomy of a Decision* (Baltimore: Johns Hopkins Press, 1979), for analysis of the Soviet decision to intervene.

13. *Rude Pravo,* 24 Apr. 1968, cited in Robin Remington, "Czechoslovakia and the Warsaw Pact," *East European Quarterly* 3(Sept. 1969):320.

14. Remington, "Czechoslovakia," 320–21; also see Dziewanowski, *Communist Party,* 296–302.

15. See *Radio Free Europe Research* (henceforth referred to as *RFER*), Polish Situation Report/14, 20 May 1968.

16. See Remington, "Czechoslovakia," 323.

17. Cited in *RFER,* Polish Situation Report/56, 19 July 1968.

18. Remington, "Czechoslovakia," 323 cites *Krasnaya Zvezda,* the Soviet Army paper, as reiterating this line continually.

19. See Peter Potichnyj, *The Ukraine and the Czechoslovak Crisis* (Australia: Canberra National Univ. Press, 1970), 77–79 and ff, whose analyses of Ukraine's relation to the crisis I have drawn upon extensively.

20. See Remington, *The Warsaw Pact* (Cambridge: MIT Press, 1971), 107.

21. See various issues of *L'Unita,* the PCI's organ, from 22 Aug. through Oct. 1968. Also see Joan Urban, "The West European Communist Challenge to Soviet Foreign Policy," in *Soviet Foreign Policy in the 1980's,* ed. Roger Kanet (New York: Praeger, 1982), 178–79.

22. See S. Kovalev, "Sovereignty and International Obligations of Socialist Countries," *Pravda,* 26 Sept. 1968, 4, for the enunciation of the Brezhnev Doctrine.

23. See Rakowski's article, "The Commonwealth Yesterday and Today," in *Polityka,* 7 Sept. 1968.

24. See *RFER,* Polish Situation Report/63, 6 Sept. 1968.

25. See A. Ross Johnson, "Polish Perspectives, Past and Present," *Problems of Communism* 20(July–Aug. 1971):65–66.

26. Konstantin Zarodov, *Leninism and Contemporary Problems of Transition from Capitalism to Socialism* (Moscow: Progress, 1972), 49–50.

27. See Skilling, *Czechoslovakia,* for the process of the purge of the Dubcek leadership.

28. This denunciation came at the planning sessions of the Twelfth PCI Congress. See *L'Unita,* 26 Oct. 1968, suppl., sec. 4, as cited in Kevin Devlin, "The New Crisis in European Communism," *Problems of Communism* 17(Nov.–Dec. 1968):68.

29. Kevin Devlin, "The Inter-Party Drama," *Problems of Communism* 24(July–Aug. 1975):33.

30. Ibid., 33, 22.

31. See *Review of International Affairs* (Belgrade), 20 June 1970, 23–24.
32. Ibid.
33. *Trybuna Ludu,* 18 May 1969, 4.
34. See Johnson, "Polish Perspectives," 68–70, and Dziewanowski, *Communist Party,* 306–8.
35. *Zycie Warszawy,* 4 June 1970, cited in Johnson, "Polish Perspectives," 61.
36. Ibid., 65–67. The "partisans" were veterans of the Polish underground during World War II. Communist and nationalist at the same time, their strength lay in the army and security forces. See A. Bromke, *Poland's Politics: Idealism vs. Realism* (Cambridge: Harvard Univ. Press, 1967), 198–200.

Chapter 3

1. On legitimacy in Eastern Europe see, Bogdan Denitch, "The Domestic Roots of Foreign Policy in Eastern Europe," in *The International Politics of Eastern Europe,* ed. Charles Gati (New York: Praeger, 1976), especially 244–45, 251.
2. J. F. Brown, *Relations between the Soviet Union and Its East European Allies: A Survey* (Santa Monica: Rand Corporation, 1975), 2. See also Andrzej Korbonski's comments on the Kremlin and East European leaders' legitimacy in "Eastern Europe as an Internal Determinant of Soviet Foreign Policy," in *The Domestic Context of Soviet Foreign Policy,* ed. S. Bialer (Boulder: Westview, 1981), especially 325. Also, see Karen Dawisha, *The Kremlin and the Prague Spring* (Berkeley: Univ. of California Press, 1984), 16–19, for the initial Soviet reactions to Alexander Dubcek's ascension to the CPCz leadership.
3. See *Zycie Warszawy,* 16 Apr. 1971 and A. Ross Johnson, "Polish Perspectives, Past and Present," *Problems of Communism* 20(July–Aug. 1971):68–70. Also see *Radio Liberty Reports/49,* 2 Feb. 1981.
4. Johnson, "Polish Perspectives," 68–70.
5. Ibid., 61, citing Edward Gierek, Warsaw Radio, 7 February 1971.
6. *Zycie Warszawy,* 27 Dec. 1970, 3–4. Also see Johnson, "Polish Perspectives," 72.
7. *Zycie Warszawy,* 27 Dec. 1970, 4.
8. See Johnson, "Polish Perspectives," 69–70; *Trybuna Ludu,* 22 Dec. 1970, cited in Johnson, "Polish Perspectives," 69.
9. Cited by Franklyn Griffiths, "Ideological Development and Foreign Policy," in *The Domestic Context of Soviet Foreign Policy,* ed. S. Bialer (Boulder: Westview, 1981), 23.
10. Ibid., 27.
11. For more on this process, see Morris Bornstein, "Soviet Economic Growth and Foreign Policy," and Paul Marer, "Economies of East Europe and Soviet Foreign Policy," both in *Domestic Context,* ed. S. Bialer. For this process in Poland under Gierek, see Zbigniew Fallenbuchl, "The Strategy of Development and Gierek's Economic Manoeuvre," in *Gierek's Poland,* ed. A. Bromke and J. W. Strong (New York: Praeger, 1973), 52–70.
12. Marer, "Economics," 279.
13. Ibid., 280.

14. *Pravda,* 31 Dec. 1974, 4; *Izvestiia,* 28 Dec. 1974, 1.

15. For trends in trade, see M. K. Dziewanowski, *The Communist Party of Poland,* 2d ed. (Cambridge: Harvard Univ. Press, 1976), 314; on the press campaign, even a cursory examination of *Pravda* and *Izvestiia* during the latter half of 1974 and the period leading up to Helsinki's Final Act in summer 1975 reveals as much.

16. *Trybuna Ludu,* 5 Dec. 1974, 7. Also in translation in *Foreign Broadcast Information Service (FBIS),* East Europe, Daily Report, 9 Dec. 1974, A1–A3.

17. Griffiths, "Ideological Development," 32–33.

18. See Longin Pastusiak, "East-West Relations and Arms Control: Achievement and Prospects," *East European Quarterly* 9(Spring 1975), 1–13, and Mieczyslaw Rakowski, *Polityka Zagraniczna PRL* (Warsaw: Interpress, 1974). This enhanced prestige is also reflected in *Zycie Warszawy* and *Trybuna Ludu* in the period of early to mid-1975 before Helsinki. See also Dziewanowski, *Communist Party,* 323–24.

19. Paul Marer writes that Soviet criticism of East European countries "turning to the West is probably constrained by the Soviets' own rapid trade expansion with the West." The figures he offers are $6 billion in 1975 augmented by $5 billion more in 1976. See Marer, "Economics," 301.

20. See Bennet Kovrig, "The US: Peaceful Engagement Revisited," in *The International Politics of East Europe,"* ed. Charles Gati (New York: Praeger, 1976), 135.

21. PAP (Warsaw), 20 June 1975, as reported in *FBIS,* Daily Report, East Europe, 23 June 1975, G4–G5.

22. Adam Bromke, "A New Juncture in Poland," *Problems of Communism* 25(Sept.–Oct. 1976), 17; *Izvestiia,* 5 Jan. 1976, 2. This praise was on the occasion of the thirtieth anniversary of the PPR's diplomatic relations with the USSR.

23. See *RFER,* Polish Situation Report/2, 16 Jan. 1976.

24. See Vincent Chrypinski, "Church and State in Gierek's Poland," in *Background to Crisis: Poland,* ed. Roger Kanet and Maurice Simon (Boulder: Westview, 1981), 255–57.

25. See Wojciech Sokolewicz, *Konstytucja PRL po zmianiach z 1976 r.* (Warsaw: Panstwowe Wydawnictwo Naukowe, 1978), 242–46, also 47–49 and 64–65. See also *RFER,* Polish Situation Report/4, 30 Jan. 1976.

26. See *RFER,* Polish Situation Report/4, 30 Jan. 1976, and *RFER,* Polish Situation Report/6, 20 Feb. 1976; *RFER,* Polish Situation Report/4, 30 Jan. 1976; Chrypinski, "Church and State," 256.

27. *RFER,* Polish Situation Report/4, 30 Jan. 1976.

28. See Chap. 2, pt. 1.

29. Brezhnev's address to the Twenty-Fifth CPSU Congress is in *Pravda,* 25 Feb. 1976, 2–9. For this citation see *Current Digest of the Soviet Press (CDSP)* 28, no. 8(24 Mar. 1976):14. Also cited in Griffiths, "Ideological Development," 36; *CDSP,* 4, and Griffiths, "Ideological Development," 37.

30. See *L'Humanité,* 7 May 1976, as reported in *RFER,* Polish Situation Report/16, 14 May 1976.

31. TASS, 29 June 1976, as reported in *FBIS,* Daily Report, Soviet Union, 30 June 1976, CC15.

32. ANSA (Rome), 29 June 1976, as reported in *FBIS,* Daily Report, Eastern Europe, 30 June 1976, CCI.

33. To compare the tenor of the leaders' speeches, see *FBIS*, 30 June 1976, Daily Reports from the Soviet Union, Eastern Europe and Western Europe, under the category heading of "the East Berlin Conference of Communist Parties."

34. Bucharest Radio, 29 June 1976, as reported in *FBIS*, Daily Report, Eastern Europe, 30 June 1976, CC15.

35. *Le Monde*, 3 July 1976, 3.

36. *L'Unita*, 4 July 1976, as reported in *FBIS*, Daily Report, Western Europe, 7 July 1976, L4–L5. For truncated versions of some of the speeches, see *Pravda*, 2, 3 July 1976, 3, also cited in *FBIS*, Daily Report, Soviet Union, 7 July 1976, CC13–CC19.

37. See the excellent analysis of these comments in *RFER*, Polish Situation Report/23, 13 July 1976. Also note Ceausescu's remarks that ". . . an international center of Communist and Workers' Parties has become impossible and is not necessary," were also part of *Trybuna Ludu*'s coverage of the conference.

38. Prague Radio, 14 Jan. 1976, as reported in *FBIS*, Daily Report, Eastern Europe, 16 Jan. 1976, AA1.

39. For example, see *Pravda*, 17 Dec. 1975, 5 ("Questions of U.S.-Soviet Trade"); *Pravda*, 6 Jan. 1976, 4, ("The Materialization of Detente"); and regarding greater cohesion and integration: *Krasnaya Zvezda*, 8 Jan. 1976, as reported in *FBIS*, Soviet Union, Daily Report, 12 Jan. 1976, D3, and *Pravda*, 15 Jan. 1976, 5 ("The Strength of Our Cooperation").

40. Cited by TASS, 16 Apr. 1976, as reported in *FBIS*, Daily Report, Soviet Union, 27 Apr. 1976, A12.

41. *Trybuna Ludu*, 30 June 1976, 1 (emphasis added). Gierek's comments were made on June 30. *RFER*, Polish Situation Report/23, 13 July 1976 cites them as well.

42. For example, see *Sovetskaya Belorossia*, 29 June 1976, as reported in *FBIS*, Daily Report, Soviet Union, 23 July 1976, A12.

Chapter 4

1. Adam Bromke, "The Opposition in Poland," *Problems of Communism* 27(Sept.–Oct. 1978):37.

2. *Pravda*, 21 July 1976, 4.

3. See *RFER*, Polish Situation Report/23, 23 July 1976, for trial details and *RFER*, Polish Situation Report/34, 8 Oct. 1976 for more information on sentence reductions.

4. See Konstantin Zarodov, *Tri revoliutsii v Rossii i nashe vremya* (Moscow: Mysl', 1977), 446–47, 496–500, and 596–99. The *Pravda* review of this book is in the 17 July 1976 issue, 3, under the title of "Priceless Experience." *L'Unita*, 20 July 1976 takes issue with the Soviet review. See *FBIS*, Daily Report, Western Europe, 23 July 1976, L3.

5. The following succinct summary of Soviet perceptions of Eurocommunism's threat is given by Paul Marer:

> Soviet attitude toward the Eurocommunist movement . . . is probably shaped in part by Soviet concern over Eurocommunism's impact on Eastern Europe. Eurocommunism differs from Soviet com-

munism in that the former rejects the dictatorship of the proletariat, formulates a national road to socialism, and criticizes Soviet policies in Eastern Europe. The more the Soviet leadership is concerned with centrifugal political tendencies in the region–to which independent economic policies tend to contribute–the more it is forced to take a hard-line attitude toward Eurocommunist movements. How can it appear to sanction "revisionist" views of the CP of one country and condemn similar views of the CP of another East European country?

See Paul Marer, "The Economies of Eastern Europe and Soviet Foreign Policy," in *The Domestic Context of Soviet Foreign Policy*, ed. S. Bialer (Boulder: Westview, 1981), 307 ff.

6. N. Inozemtsev, "O Leninskom metodologii analiza mirovogo obshchesvennego razvitiia," and S. Trapeznikov, "Obshchestvennaia nauka, ideinoe bogatstvo partii i naroda," 66–77 and 19–31 respectively, in *Kommunist* 12(Aug. 1976). It is interesting to note that *L'Unita* took issue with the refusal of these articles to identify the parties to which they were referring, as well as the general methods of Soviet polemics in an article entitled "Pointless Polemics." See *FBIS*, Daily Report, Western Europe, 27 Aug. 1976, L4.

7. See *New Times*, (Moscow) 37(Sept. 1976):30–31.

8. General Wojciech Jaruzelski met with Marshal Dmitri F. Ustinov on 18 Aug. See *FBIS*, Daily Report, Soviet Union, 18 Aug. 1976, D1.

9. See *Pravda*, 10 Aug. 1976, 4.

10. *RFER*, Polish Situation Report/34, 8 Oct. 1976.

11. Communiqué issued by *Trybuna Ludu*, 20 Oct. 1976, as reported by *RFER*, Polish Situation Report/37, 8 Nov. 1976. It was reported that from 12 to 19 October a CPSU CC Organizational Department delegation visited Warsaw and also 21–22 October Deputy Foreign Minister Nikolai Rodionov led a delegation to Poland: see *Trybuna Ludu*, 24 Oct. 1976.

12. *RFER*, Polish Situation Report/38, 12 Nov. 1976.

13. *Stuttgarter Zeitung*, 10 Nov. 1976, cited in *RFER*, Polish Situation Report/38, 12 Nov. 1976; *RFER*, Polish Situation Report/1, 14 Jan. 1977.

14. The communiqué, Brezhnev's comment, and the visit by Zimyanin are all reported in ibid.

15. For Bilak's comments see *Rude Pravo*, 9 Feb. 1977, as reported in *FBIS*, Daily Report, Eastern Europe, 10 Feb. 1977, D1–D4, and TASS, 12 Jan. 1977, as reported in *FBIS*, Daily Report, Soviet Union, 14 Jan. 1977, D1; the Soviet reaction to Carter's human rights emphasis is in *Pravda*, 20 Jan. 1977, 4.

16. See, for example, TASS, 14 Feb. 1977, citing *Trybuna Ludu*, as reported in *FBIS*, Daily Report, Soviet Union, 16 Feb. 1977, D3; TASS, 14 Feb. 1977, citing *Rude Pravo;* and *Rude Pravo*, 12 Feb. 1977, as reported in *FBIS*, Daily Report, Eastern Europe, 15 Feb. 1977, D4.

17. See TASS (in English), 23 Feb. 1977, as reported in *FBIS*, Daily Report, Soviet Union, 24 Feb. 1977, D3–D4. The Polish source of this Soviet account is *Trybuna Ludu*, 21 Feb. 1977, 7.

18. Cited by TASS (in English), 12 Mar. 1977, as reported in *FBIS*, Daily Report, Soviet Union, 14 Mar. 1977, D1. It is curious to note that I could not, after reviewing *Zycie Warszawy* during the period, find the article to which TASS was referring. This could be my own oversight or perhaps the Soviet misrepresentation of *Zycie Warszawy*'s statements.

19. For example, see *Trybuna Ludu*, 31 Dec. 1976 and 2 Jan. 1977, as reported in *FBIS*, Daily Report, Eastern Europe, 4 Jan. 1977, G1, and *Słowo Powszechne*, 29 Dec. 1976, as reported in *FBIS*, Daily Report, Eastern Europe, 3 Jan. 1977, G1–G2.

20. See *L'Unita*'s statement as reported by *FBIS*, Daily Report, Eastern Europe, 27 Jan. 1977; also see *The Times* (London), 18 Jan. 1977, 6.

21. See *RFER*, RAD Background Report/11, 18 Jan. 1977.

22. See Kevin Devlin's comments on this "coalition" in *RFER*, RAD Background Report/26, 4 Feb. 1977; on the Yugoslav response see *RFER*, RAD Background Report/64, 24 Mar. 1977 and *RFER*, RAD Background Report/51, 4 Mar. 1977.

23. Tanjug, as reported in *FBIS*, Daily Report, Eastern Europe, 13 Jan. 1977, 117–18.

24. Warsaw Television, 3 Feb. 1977, as reported in *FBIS*, Daily Report, Eastern Europe, 4 Feb. 1977, G2.

25. My thanks to Paul Shoup for suggesting this possibility.

26. *Le Monde*, 29 Jan. 1977, 2.

27. Interview in *L'Espresso* (Rome), 5 Dec. 1976, as reported in *FBIS*, Daily Report, Eastern Europe, 29 Dec. 1976, G1–G4.

28. See for example, Moscow Radio broadcast, 17 May 1977, as reported in *FBIS*, Daily Report, Soviet Union, 19 May 1977, A7. Also see *Trybuna Ludu*, 11 Feb. 1977, 7.

29. For one analyst's views on this meeting, see Kevin Devlin's comments in *RFER*, RAD Background Report/85, 26 Apr. 1977.

30. For the suggestion that the Soviets were outmaneuvered see *Frankfurter Allgemeine Zeitung*, as reported in *FBIS*, Daily Report, Eastern Europe, 3 May 1977, D1; for Bilak's comment on dissent see *Rude Pravo*, 26 Mar. 1977, as reported in *FBIS*, Daily Report, Eastern Europe, 31 Mar. 1977, D1; Bilak's "traitors" comment is cited by *Le Monde*, 1 Apr. 1977, 13.

31. See interview in *L'Espresso* (Rome), 3 Apr. 1977, 39, 41, 43, where Pelikan and Michnik both expand on their views, as reported in *FBIS*, Daily Report, Eastern Europe, 22 Apr. 1977, D1–D4.

32. On the arrests see *Le Monde*, 11 May 1977, 5; on amnesty see *L'Unita*, 24 July 1977, as reported in *FBIS*, Daily Report, Eastern Europe, 29 July 1977, G2; *Le Monde*, 1 Apr. 1977, 13 has some interesting observations about Czechoslovak dissent at this time.

33. *RFER*, Polish Situation Report/11, 29 Apr. 1977.

34. Ibid.

35. *RFER*, RAD Background Report/151, 26 July 1977.

36. See M. F. Rakowski, "The Image of Democracy," *Contemporary Poland* (Warsaw) 11(Apr. 1977):1–3. (Emphasis added). Rakowski's ideas are sufficiently vague to suggest numerous things and yet imply changes. One observer has called the idea of "socialist democracy" *a la* Gierek and Rakowski, ". . . a vague concept which encompasses party-people consultations, increased responsibility for local authorities, and a more open and critical approach in the press." See *RFER*, RAD Background Report/151, 26 July 1977.

37. *RFER*, RAD Background Report/151, 26 July 1977.

38. See *RFER*, RAD Background Report/92, 3 May 1977.

39. See Santiago Carrillo, *Eurocommunism and the State* (Westport: Lawrence Hill, 1978), especially 153–69.

40. See *Voprosy istorii KPSS* (Moscow) 5(May 1977):9-18.

41. See *New Times* (Moscow) 26(June 1977):9-13, for the attack. The notion that this was directed at the PCI is a generally accepted thesis.

42. *New Times* (Moscow) 28(July 1977):16-17 and 29(July 1977):30-31, for the retreat in polemics.

43. *Trybuna Ludu,* 3 Aug. 1977, 7.

44. *Le Monde,* 13 Sept. 1977, 3.

45. See the translated interview in *FBIS,* Daily Report, Eastern Europe, 14 Sept. 1977, G4-G7, and *Le Monde,* 13 Sept. 1977, 3.

46. See *L'Express* (Paris), 2 May 1977, as reported in *RFER,* Polish Situation Report/16, 15 June 1977.

47. *Daily Telegraph* (London), 30 Sept. 1977, as reported in *FBIS,* Daily Report, Eastern Europe, 30 Sept. 1977, G1-G2.

48. Vatican Radio Broadcast, as reported in *FBIS,* Daily Report, East Europe, 20 Sept. 1977, G2.

49. *Polityka,* 29 Oct. 1977, and *Polityka,* 19 Nov. 1977. (For translated texts of these important articles, see *FBIS,* Daily Report, Eastern Europe, 10 and 23 Nov. 1977, G1-G3 and G13-G19 respectively.)

50. Ibid. Also see *RFER,* Polish Situation Report/27 and 28, 9 Nov. and 2 Dec. 1977, for further analysis of these polemics.

51. Warsaw Radio, 1 Dec. 1977, as reported in *FBIS,* Daily Report, Eastern Europe, 2 Dec. 1977, G1-G3.

52. See *Trybuna Ludu,* 7 Dec. 1977, 2. It is interesting that this analysis of the PCI-Gierek meeting by Ryszard Wojna amended the radio comments broadcast several days earlier. Reference to the "Berlin Conference" (PUWP-PCI planned) was deleted, perhaps in the growing realization that this was becoming an embarrassing reference to hard-liners and the Soviet party.

It is also interesting to note that Polish primate Cardinal Wyszynski was at the Vatican during the course of Gierek's visit. He had been there for a month on an "extended visit" and left just after Gierek did. See Vatican Radio Broadcast, 6 Dec. 1977, as reported in *FBIS,* Daily Report, Eastern Europe, 9 Dec. 1977, G1.

53. Vatican Radio Broadcast, 16 Dec. 1977, as reported in *FBIS,* Daily Report, Eastern Europe, 29 Dec. 1977, G1.

Chapter 5

1. *L'Espresso* (Rome), 15 Jan. 1978, 33-34, as reported in *FBIS,* Daily Report, Eastern Europe, 24 Jan. 1978, G1.

2. See *Rude Pravo,* 16 Jan. 1978, as reported in *FBIS,* Daily Report, Eastern Europe, 18 Jan. 1978, D1. Also see PAP, 29 Dec. 1977, as reported in *FBIS,* Daily Report, Eastern Europe, 30 Dec. 1977, G3.

3. *Ideologiya i Polityka,* Feb. 1978, as reported in *FBIS,* Daily Report, Eastern Europe, 1 Mar. 1978, G5.

4. See Chap. 1, pp. 12, 13.

5. For criticism of what Carter said in Poland see *Rude Pravo,* 16 Jan. 1978, as reported in *FBIS,* Daily Report, Eastern Europe, 18 Jan. 1978, D1. TASS of 29 Dec. 1977, merely reported that Carter had arrived. See *FBIS,* Daily Report, Soviet Union, 30 Dec. 1977, B1; on Carter's State of the Union

see Prague Radio, 20 Jan. 1978 (and Warsaw Radio), as reported in *FBIS,* Daily Report, Eastern Europe, 23 Jan. 1978, D1 and G1; on Camp David see Warsaw Radio transcription, 2 Feb. 1978, as reported in *FBIS,* Daily Report, Eastern Europe, 3 Feb. 1978, G6.

6. Prague Television, 4 Jan. 1978, as reported in *FBIS,* Daily Report, Eastern Europe, 5 Jan. 1978, D3.

7. On this Eurocommunist "seminar" see *RFER,* RAD Background Report/12, 25 Jan. 1978.

8. See Adam Bromke, "Opposition in Poland," *Problems of Communism* 27(Sept.–Oct. 1978):49.

9. *La Vanguardia* (Spain), 3 Mar. 1978, as reported in *FBIS,* Daily Report, Eastern Europe, 10 Mar. 1978, G2–G3.

10. See *RFER,* RAD Background Report/51, 16 Mar. 1978, for this citation and an interesting discussion of nations and minorities in East Europe.

11. See *RFER,* Polish Situation Report/9, 21 Apr. 1978.

12. *Die Presse* (Vienna), 3–4 June 1978, as reported in *FBIS,* Daily Report, Eastern Europe, 6 June 1978, G5, and 17 May 1978, D1.

13. See *Pravda,* 19 Apr. 1978, 1; for further analysis of this meeting, see *RFER,* Polish Situation Report/10, 2 May 1978.

14. See PAP, 18 Apr. 1978, as reported in *FBIS,* Daily Report, Eastern Europe, 19 Apr. 1978, G1–G2. Also see *Trybuna Ludu,* 20 Apr. 1978, 1–2.

15. See *RFER,* RAD Background Report/80, 25 Apr. 1978.

16. Speculation on reasons for the change of ambassadors is in *RFER,* Polish Situation Report/11, 18 May 1978. It is interesting to note, in retrospect, Stanislaw Pilotowicz's fate. After this Soviet ambassador of Polish extraction was recalled from Warsaw, he was later reassigned as Deputy Chairman of the Council of Ministers of the *Belorussian* Soviet Socialist Republic. More significantly, still later at the Twenty-Sixth CPSU Congress, he was dropped from full membership in the CPSU Central Committee. He had been a full member of the Central Committee (CC) since the Twenty-Fourth CPSU Congress in 1971. These facts would indicate the strong possibility that the Kremlin was indeed displeased over the effect their "voice" in Warsaw was having during this time.

17. On the export-import problem see PAP, 4 May 1978, as reported in *FBIS,* Daily Report, Eastern Europe, 5 May 1978, G1, and also *RFER* RAD Background Report/111, 5 June 1978; see PAP, 27 Feb. 1978, as reported in *FBIS,* Daily Report, Eastern Europe, 1 Mar. 1978, G6 for admission of organizational problems existing.

18. Tanjug, 31 May 1978, as reported in *FBIS,* Daily Report, Eastern Europe, 2 June 1978, G1–G3.

19. See M. T. Iovchuk and M. I. Basmanov, eds., *Proletarskii, sotsialisticheskii internatsionalizm* (Moscow: Mysl', 1978), especially 155–58, 268–70, and 306–7; also see *RFER,* RAD Background Report/103, 31 May 1978, for the reaction of a Yugoslav writer to the appearance of such a book at this time. According to him, polemics had been revived "precisely at a time when ideological intensification on the international level issues has become so heightened."

20. See *Pravda,* 18 Oct. 1978, 4, and *Kazakhstanskaya Pravda,* 10 Oct. 1978, as reported in *FBIS,* Daily Report, Soviet Union, 25 Oct. 1978, CC1.

21. The French also announced another f75 million in credits to Poland to

purchase semifinished products. For the Gierek-Giscard meeting and its results, see *RFER,* Polish Situation Report/23, 6 Oct. 1978.

22. Vatican Radio, 17 Sept. 1978, as reported in *FBIS,* Daily Report, Eastern Europe, 18 Sept. 1978, G2; *RFER,* Polish Situation Report/22, 25 Sept. 1978.

23. See *L'Unita,* 22 Aug. 1978, as reported in *FBIS,* Daily Report, Eastern Europe, 25 Aug. 1978, D8. Also see *RFER,* RAD Background Report/210, 26 Sept. 1978 on this meeting.

24. Some referred to the "restraint" in PUWP's repression of the opposition during this time. See *RFER,* RAD Background Report/210, 26 Sept. 1978.

25. See various press commentaries on the Moscow declaration from this conference in *FBIS,* Daily Report, Eastern Europe, 7 Dec. 1978, G1. For speculation on Ceausescu's new posture, see *RFER,* RAD Background Report/271, 14 Dec. 1978; also see *RFER,* Romanian Situation Report/19, 1 Aug. 1978.

26. For the "new type of unity" comment see Bucharest Radio, 3 Aug. 1978, as reported in *FBIS,* Daily Report, Eastern Europe, 4 Aug. 1978, H12–15; on the Hua visit see *RFER,* Background Report/187, 24 Aug. 1978; "unity in diversity" was proclaimed in Agerpres (Bucharest), 12 Dec. 1978, as reported in *FBIS,* Daily Report, Eastern Europe, 13 Dec. 1978, H1.

27. This conference was presented in glowing terms by the CPCz. See *Bratislava Pravda,* 20 Dec. 1978, as reported in *FBIS,* Daily Report, Eastern Europe, 29 Dec. 1978, D8–9.

28. Ibid.

29. CTK (Prague), 28 Dec. 1978, in *FBIS,* Daily Report, Eastern Europe, 29 Dec. 1978, D8.

30. *Pravda,* 31 Jan. 1979, 5; also see *RFER,* RAD Background Report/31, 6 Feb. 1979.

31. For these polemics see *Rude Pravo,* 16 Feb. 1979, as reported in *FBIS,* Daily Report, Eastern Europe, 7 Mar. 1979, D3, and *Tribuna,* 28 Feb. 1979, as reported in *FBIS,* Daily Report, Eastern Europe, 8 Mar. 1979, D4. The subject of attack was PCE theorist M. Azcarate; for the Comintern reference see *Rude Pravo,* 5 Mar. 1979, as reported in *FBIS,* Daily Report, Eastern Europe, 8 Mar. 1979, D9–11.

32. PAP, 12 Mar. 1979, as reported in *FBIS,* Daily Report, Eastern Europe, 13 Mar. 1979, G1, and Tanjug, 13 Mar. 1979, as reported in *FBIS,* Daily Report, Eastern Europe, 14 Mar. 1979, I3.

33. PAP, 15 Mar. 1979, as reported in *FBIS,* Daily Report, Eastern Europe, 15 Mar. 1979, G3. Also see *Trybuna Ludu,* 15 Mar. 1979, 2.

34. Warsaw Television, 16 Mar. 1979, as reported in *FBIS,* Daily Report, Eastern Europe, 19 Mar. 1979, G1.

35. On the Camp David process compare *Rude Pravo*'s commentary of 15 Mar. 1979, and PAP's somewhat more objective (and brief) remarks on 17 Mar. 1979, as reported in *FBIS,* Daily Report, Eastern Europe, 19 Mar. 1979, G1, D1, and G4.

36. For Kania's speech see *Trybuna Ludu,* 2 Apr. 1979, as reported in *FBIS,* Daily Report, Eastern Europe, 5 Apr. 1979, G4–G8; for the Czech reaction see *Rude Pravo,* 5 Apr. 1979, as reported in *FBIS,* Daily Report, Eastern Europe, 6 Apr. 1979, D3.

37. See *Bratislava Pravda*'s coverage of 2 Apr. 1979, as reported in *FBIS,*

Daily Report, Eastern Europe, 4 Apr. 1979, D3; compare PAP, 11 Apr. 1979, as reported in *FBIS,* Daily Report, Eastern Europe, 12 Apr. 1979, G3.

38. Few references in the Soviet press, but see for example *Zarya Vostoka,* 19 Oct. 1978, as reported in *FBIS,* Daily Report, Soviet Union, 27 Oct. 1978, E4; see a multitude of Polish sources' appraisal of the election, all translated in *FBIS,* Daily Report, Eastern Europe, 17 Oct. 1978, G1, and 23 Oct. 1978, G1.

39. *Polityka,* 10 Mar. 1979, 1.

40. *Tribuna,* 30 May 1979, as reported in *FBIS,* Daily Report, Eastern Europe, 8 June 1979, D1.

41. Vatican Radio (in Polish), 3 June 1979, in *FBIS,* Daily Report, Eastern Europe, 5 June 1979, G2.

42. See PAP commentary in *FBIS,* Daily Report, Eastern Europe, 20 June 1979, G4. Also, for positive Polish coverage of the papal visit to the United States later in September, see *RFER,* Polish Situation Report/22, 12 Oct. 1979.

43. *Pravda,* 14 June 1979, 5. Although this article is citing *Trybuna Ludu,* it does put religion in the light of increased strength of Marxism-Leninism in Poland. The bizarre account of Catholicism and Khomeini is from a Moscow television broadcast on 4 June 1979, as reported in *FBIS,* Daily Report, Soviet Union, 18 June 1979, F2.

44. *Rude Pravo,* 6 July 1979, as reported in *FBIS,* Daily Report, Eastern Europe, 16 July 1979, D4.

45. *Polityka,* 20 Jan. 1979. See Jan B. de Weydenthal's excellent analysis of this article and the implications for Polish communism in *RFER,* RAD Background Report/22, 26 Jan. 1979.

46. See Chap. 2, 33–35.

47. See Jack Bielasiak, ed., *Poland Today: The State of the Republic* (Armonk, N.Y.: M. E. Sharpe, 1981), especially Chap. 5, 102–14. This volume comprises the work of Experience and Future (DiP). Also see *RFER,* RAD Background Report/22, 26 Jan. 1979, and *RFER,* Polish Situation Report/15, 9 Mar. 1979, for more on DiP.

48. For analysis of the CMEA session see *Le Figaro,* 25 July 1979, 7; for Polish criticism of Romanian gas rationing policy affecting East bloc tourists, see PAP commentary in *FBIS,* Daily Report, Eastern Europe, 2 Aug. 1979, G2; several different reports on the power ministry shake-up can be found in *FBIS,* Daily Report, Eastern Europe, 10 Aug. 1979, G1. Also see *RFER,* Polish Situation Report/18, 14 Aug. 1979.

49. See *New York Times,* 29 Sept. 1979, 26, and *RFER,* Polish Situation Report/22, 12 Oct. 1979.

50. *Rolnicke Noviny,* 24 July 1979, as reported in *FBIS,* Daily Report, Eastern Europe, 1 Aug. 1979, AA1.

51. See Reuters, 1 Aug. 1979, as reported in *FBIS,* Daily Report, Eastern Europe, 2 Aug. 1979, G2, and *Le Monde,* 19 Sept. 1979, 5. For the texts of both the nonaggression pact and the Soviet note of 17 Sept. 1939 to Poland, among other selected interwar documents on Soviet foreign policy and Poland, see George Kennan, *Soviet Foreign Policy 1917–1941* (New York: Van Nostrand, 1960), 176–80.

52. *Le Monde,* 19 Sept. 1979, 5.

53. For discussion of the KOR charter see *Daily Telegraph,* 7 Sept. 1979,

as reported in *FBIS,* Daily Report, Eastern Europe, 10 Sept. 1979, G6; on Polish protesters' unity with Czech dissidents, see *NRC Handelsblad* (Rotterdam), 4–5 Oct. 1979, as reported in *FBIS,* Daily Report, Eastern Europe, 10 Oct. 1979, G8–G9.

54. *Pravda,* 14 Oct. 1979, 4.

55. *Le Figaro,* 9 Oct. 1979, 1.

56. Ibid.; also see *RFER,* RAD Background Report/239, 2 Nov. 1979.

57. See *RFER,* RAD Background Report/221, 11 Oct. 1979.

58. See *RFER,* RAD Background Report/232, 23 Oct. 1979.

59. *Polityka,* 10 Nov. 1979, 3. For the English translation, see *FBIS,* Daily Report, Eastern Europe, 30 Nov. 1979, G3.

60. *Le Monde,* 19 Dec. 1979, 11.

61. *Polityka,* 17 Nov. 1979, 1–3; also see *RFER,* RAD Background Report/254, 21 Nov. 1979.

62. *Le Figaro,* 15 Jan. 1980, 5.

63. *Le Monde,* 19 Dec. 1979, 11.

64. See the extensive discussion in *L'Unita* of the PUWP Congress, as reported in *FBIS,* Daily Report, Eastern Europe, 27 Feb. 1980, G4, and *L'Unita,* 15 Feb. 1980, as reported in *FBIS,* Daily Report, Eastern Europe, 25 Feb. 1980, G3; TASS, 15 Feb. 1980, just announces the leadership changes with no explanations. See *FBIS,* Daily Report, Soviet Union, 19 Feb. 1980, F1.

65. *L'Unita,* 15 Feb. 1980, as reported in *FBIS,* Daily Report, Eastern Europe, 25 Feb. 1980, G3.

66. See Jiri Valenta, "Eurocommunism and the USSR," in *Eurocommunism between East and West,"* ed. Vernon Aspaturian (Bloomington: Indiana Univ. Press, 1980), 105.

67. *NRC Handlesblad* (Rotterdam), 14 Feb. 1980, as reported in *FBIS,* Daily Report, Eastern Europe, 25 Feb. 1980, G7; the pamphlet distribution occurred on 28 Apr. See *Le Figaro,* 28 Apr. 1980, 3.

68. The French press asked the question "Why?" to Gierek's sudden turn about in assisting the Soviets in this "suicidal propaganda attempt." It did appear out of character with Gierek's previous moderate position. Apparently he was now trying to identify himself more with Moscow in the face of domestic collapse, counting on the Kremlin's support as quid pro quo. See *Le Figaro,* 5–6 Apr. 1980, 2; Agerpres reported the Romanian position on this conference in *FBIS,* Daily Report, Eastern Europe, 23 Apr. 1980, H1.

69. *Pravda,* 30 Jan. 1980, 4.

70. Even the official Catholic daily blamed the weather. See *Slowo Powszechne,* 2 June 1980, as reported in *FBIS,* Daily Report, Eastern Europe, 5 June, 1980, G1; for continuing debt problems see *Trybuna Ludu,* 11 June 1980, as reported in *FBIS,* Daily Report, Eastern Europe, 13 June 1980, G5; on the massive dismissals see *Trybuna Ludu,* 7–8 June, 1980, as reported in *FBIS,* Daily Report, Eastern Europe, 12 June 1980, G6, and *Trybuna Ludu,* 25 June 1980, as reported in *FBIS,* Daily Report, Eastern Europe, 30 June 1980, G2. Also see *Trybuna Ludu,* 20 May 1980, when the high-level dismissals began; on discussion of meat prices see *Trybuna Ludu,* 28 May 1980, as reported in *FBIS,* Daily Report, Eastern Europe, 30 May, 1980, G6. Also see *FBIS,* Daily Report, Eastern Europe, 23 May 1980, G5.

71. *Le Figaro,* 10 June 1980, 4.

72. A. Brabets, "Vernye ideiam internatsionalizma," *Kommunist*

vooruzhenikh sil 10(May 1980):78–79; see article "Printsipial'nost' Partii," *Kommunist vooruzhenikh sil* 10(May 1968):4–5.

73. This observation was made by Professor Herbert Dinerstein of The Johns Hopkins University (SAIS), during a panel discussion of Eurocommunism and its impact on East Europe, at the AAASS Convention in Washington, D.C., 14 Oct. 1982.

74. See Adam Bromke, "The Opposition in Poland," *Problems of Communism* 27(Sept.–Oct. 1978):38, 46, for a similar view. Also implied by Andrezej Korbonski in "Eastern Europe as an Internal Determinant of Soviet Foreign Policy," in *The Domestic Context of Soviet Foreign Policy*, ed. S. Bialer (Boulder: Westview, 1981), 317.

75. Bromke, "Opposition," 38, 46.

76. See Agerpres, 4 Jan. 1980, as reported in *FBIS*, Daily Report, Eastern Europe, 8 Jan. 1980, H1.

77. See Tanjug for Yugoslav perspectives in *FBIS*, Daily Report, Eastern Europe, 31 Dec. 1979, I1, and 8 Jan. 1980, I1.

Chapter 6

1. See *Zycie Warszawy* and *Trybuna Ludu*, 3 July 1980, on the rationale for the need to raise prices, as reported in *FBIS*, Daily Report, Eastern Europe, 8 July 1980, G1–G2.

2. On the work stoppages see Reuters, 3 July 1980, as reported in *FBIS*, Daily Report, Eastern Europe, 3 July 1980, G1; on the necessity of price hikes see *Zycie Warszawy* and *Trybuna Ludu*, 3 July 1980, in *FBIS*, Daily Report, Eastern Europe, 8 July 1980, G1–G2; *Dziennik Polski* (Reuters copy), 7 July 1980, as reported in *FBIS*, Daily Report, Eastern Europe, 15 July 1980, G1; compare *Dziennik Polski* (Reuters copy), 7 July 1980, G2, with Rakowski's assessment in *Polityka*, 5 July 1980, as reported in *FBIS*, Daily Report, Eastern Europe, 17 July 1980, G1.

3. Reuters, 3 July 1980, as reported in *FBIS*, Daily Report, Eastern Europe, 15 July 1980, G1; Reuters, 17 July 1980, as reported in *FBIS*, Daily Report, Eastern Europe, 18 July 1980, G1. The strikes were initiated on 11 July.

4. *Tribuna*, 16 July 1980, as reported in *FBIS*, Daily Report, Eastern Europe, 24 July 1980, D3; see TASS, 18 July 1980, as reported in *FBIS*, Daily Report, Soviet Union, 22 July 1980, F1.

5. See *Trybuna Ludu*, 19–20 July 1980, as reported in *FBIS*, Daily Report, Eastern Europe, 22 July 1980, G3–G8.

6. Bucharest Domestic Service, 19 July 1980, as reported in *FBIS*, Daily Report, Eastern Europe, 21 July 1980, H1; *Bratislava Pravda*, 21 July 1980, as reported in *FBIS*, Daily Report, Eastern Europe, 22 July 1980, D1.

7. See *L'Humanité*'s (the PCF organ) analysis of 14 July 1980, as reported in *FBIS*, Daily Report, Eastern Europe, 22 July 1980, G8; Tanjug, 23 July 1980, as reported in *FBIS*, Daily Report, Eastern Europe, 24 July 1980, G2; the figures are according to *L'Humanité*, 14 July 1980.

8. For claims of return to "normalcy" see Warsaw Domestic Service, 23 and 31 July 1980 as reported in *FBIS* Daily Report, Eastern Europe, 23 and 31 July 1980, G1 and G6; railway connections were affected according to *Dziennik*

Polski of 19 July 1980, as reported in *FBIS*, Daily Report, Eastern Europe, 25 July 1980, G2, and *Borba* (Yugoslavia), 23 July 1980, in I1 of the same *FBIS* report.

9. For the economic side of this meeting see PAP, 31 July 1980, as reported in *FBIS*, Daily Report, Eastern Europe, 4 Aug. 1980, G1.

10. Ibid.

11. *NRC Handelsblad*, 23 July 1980, as reported in *FBIS*, Daily Report, Eastern Europe, 24 July 1980, G2.

12. *Pravda*, 2 Aug. 1980, 4.

13. See TASS, 31 July 1980, as reported in *FBIS*, Daily Report, Eastern Europe, 1 Aug. 1980, BB1.

14. Surprisingly, *L'Humanité*, 3-4 Aug. 1980, 4, reported this in an objective fashion. See *FBIS*, Daily Report, Eastern Europe, 5 Aug. 1980, G1-G3.

15. *Dziennik Polski*, 1 Aug. 1980, as reported by *FBIS*, Daily Report, Eastern Europe, 11 Aug. 1980, G1.

16. *Zycie Warszawy*, 6 Aug. 1980, as reported in *FBIS*, Daily Report, Eastern Europe, 6 Aug. 1980, G7.

17. Interview in *Der Spiegel*, 4 Aug. 1980, as reported in *FBIS*, Daily Report, Eastern Europe, 6 Aug. 1980, G3-G5.

18. AFP, 16 Aug. 1980, as reported in *FBIS*, Daily Report, Eastern Europe, 18 Aug. 1980, H1.

19. *Rude Pravo*, 23 and 25 Aug. 1980, 1, as reported in *FBIS*, Daily Report, Eastern Europe, 27 Aug. 1980, D2-D4.

20. See *Pravda*, 15 Aug. 1980, 3-4, in an article by E. Bagramov, "Proletarian Internationalism and the Struggle of Ideas"; TASS, 19 Aug. 1980, as reported in *FBIS*, Daily Report, Soviet Union, 20 Aug. 1980, F1. Also see *Pravda*, 20 Aug. 1980, 4.

21. *Pravda*, 15 Aug. 1980, 4; for a comprehensive survey of East bloc and Soviet coverage of the strikes and their immediate aftermath, see W. F. Robinson, ed., *August 1980: The Strikes in Poland* (Munich: Radio Free Europe Research, 1980).

22. TASS, 25 Aug. 1980, as reported in *FBIS*, Daily Report, Soviet Union, 25 Aug. 1980; speculation on no plans for use of force is by DPA, 19 Aug. 1980, as reported in *FBIS*, Daily Report, Eastern Europe, 20 Aug. 1980, G1. This is citing Polish officials.

23. DPA, 18 Aug. 1980, as reported in *FBIS*, Daily Report, Eastern Europe, 18 Aug. 1980, G1. Gierek's visit to the FRG was cancelled on 18 Aug. according to the German source.

24. The extensive citations are from *Rude Pravo*, 22 Aug. 1980, as reported in *FBIS*, Daily Report, Eastern Europe, 26 Aug. 1980, D5-D6 (emphasis in the original).

25. See Lawrence Sherwin's survey of this campaign in Robinson, *August 1980*, 239-43.

26. Ibid. This was the first in a series of similar innuendoes and accusations that appeared in the next few days. Also see TASS, 25 Aug. 1980, as reported in *FBIS*, Daily Report, Soviet Union, 26 Aug. 1980, F6.

27. TASS, 27 Aug. 1980, as reported in *FBIS*, Daily Report, Soviet Union, 28 Aug. 1980, F1.

28. Ibid.

29. See *Washington Post*, 13 Feb. 1981, A33.

30. BBC interview, 26 Aug. 1980, as reported in *FBIS*, Daily Report, Eastern Europe, 27 Aug. 1980, G5.

31. *L'Unita*, 23 Aug. 1980, as reported in *FBIS*, Daily Report, Eastern Europe, 28 Aug. 1980, G41 (emphasis added).

32. *Trybuna Ludu*, 29 Aug. 1980, as reported in *FBIS*, Daily Report, Eastern Europe, 4 Sept. 1980, G13.

33. Stefan Kisiliewski, retired *sejm* member in *Der Spiegel*, 25 Aug. 1980, as reported in *FBIS*, Daily Report, Eastern Europe, 27 Aug. 1980, G39.

34. This was reported by Prague Domestic Service, 31 Aug. 1980, as reported in *FBIS*, Daily Report, Eastern Europe, 2 Sept. 1980, D1. See the Gdansk Agreement in full in *Zycie Warszawy*, 2 Sept. 1980, and in Robinson, *August 1980*, 423–34. Also see Abraham Brumberg, ed., *Poland: Genesis of a Revolution* (New York: Random House, 1983), 285–95.

35. See "The Intrigues of the Enemies of Socialist Poland," *Pravda*, 1 Sept. 1980, 5. Also see *Trybuna Ludu*, 27, 28, 30, 31 Aug. 1980. The stepped-up attack in the bloc can be seen in a number of sources, as reported in *FBIS*, Daily Report, Eastern Europe, 2 Sept. 1980, D1–D2, G1, I3–I4.

36. *Pravda*, 1 Sept. 1980, 5.

37. Prague Television, 3 Sept. 1980, as reported in *FBIS*, Daily Report, Eastern Europe, 4 Sept. 1980, D1.

38. East Berlin Radio, as reported in *FBIS*, Daily Report, Eastern Europe, 3 Sept. 1980, E1.

39. See Tanjug's 31 Aug. 1980 appraisal of the situation as reported in *FBIS*, Daily Report, Eastern Europe, 2 Sept. 1980, I1–I2.

40. *Politika* (Belgrade), 28 Aug. 1980, as reported in *FBIS*, Daily Report, Eastern Europe, 3 Sept. 1980, I1.

41. Ibid.

42. *Zagreb Vestnik*, as reported in *FBIS*, Daily Report, Eastern Europe, 5 Sept. 1980, 14.

43. Along with *Pravda*, 1 Sept. 1980, 5, see also *Pravda*, 31 Aug. 1980, 4, for Gus Hall's criticism of Polish events.

44. *Izvestiia*, 2 Sept. 1980, 4.

45. Ibid.

46. *Rude Pravo*, 4 Sept. 1980, as reported in *FBIS*, Daily Report, Eastern Europe, 9 Sept. 1980, D1.

47. TASS, 5 Sept. 1980, as reported in *FBIS*, Daily Report, Soviet Union, 5 Sept. 1980, F1.

48. Prague Radio reported Gierek's "illness" rather bluntly on 6 Sept. 1980, as reported in *FBIS*, Daily Report, Eastern Europe, 8 Sept. 1980, D1. Bucharest Radio reported this on the same day, in H1; Kania's implicit criticism of Gierek is transmitted by Moscow Domestic Service, 9 Sept. 1980, as reported in *FBIS*, Daily Report, Soviet Union, 10 Sept. 1980, F1.

49. *Izvestiia*, 6 Sept. 1980, 4. This article made reference to a guarantee for the continued socialist development of Poland.

50. *Krasnaya Zvezda*, 9 Sept. 1980, as reported in *FBIS*, Daily Report, Soviet Union, 15 Sept. 1980, BB1.

51. See *New Times*, 12 Sept. 1980. Also see *Trud*, 27 Sept. 1980, as reported in *FBIS*, Daily Report, Soviet Union, 30 Sept. 1980, F6.

52. Moscow Radio (in Serbo-Croatian to Yugoslavia), as reported in

FBIS, Daily Report, Soviet Union, 11 Sept. 1980, F2. Also TASS, 12, 13 Sept. 1980.

53. Ibid., TASS, 12 Sept. 1980.

54. See PAP, 13 Sept. 1980, as reported in *FBIS,* Daily Report, Eastern Europe, 15 Sept. 1980, G1.

55. *Bratislava Pravda,* 27 Sept. 1980, as reported in *FBIS,* Daily Report, Eastern Europe, 1 Oct. 1980, D1; *Bratislava Pravda,* 30 Sept. 1980, as reported in *FBIS,* Daily Report, Eastern Europe, 2 Oct. 1980, D1.

56. *Tribuna,* 17 Sept. 1980, as reported in *FBIS,* Daily Report, Eastern Europe, 18 Sept. 1980, D1, and 30 Sept. 1980, D1–D6.

57. *Bratislava Pravda,* 10 Sept. 1980, as reported in *FBIS,* Daily Report, Eastern Europe, 17 Sept. 1980, D5. *Trybuna Ludu,* is cited by a Soviet commentator on the need for party reorganization, as reported in *FBIS,* Daily Report, Soviet Union, 16 Sept. 1980, F1.

58. See *RFER,* RAD Background Report/241, 10 Oct. 1980.

59. This is Jan B. de Weydenthal's perspective in ibid.

60. Ibid.

61. Ibid.

62. Ibid.

63. *RFER,* Polish Situation Report/18, 3 Oct. 1980.

64. Cited in *RFER,* RAD Background Report/241, 10 Oct. 1980.

65. *Bratislava Pravda,* 17 Oct. 1980, as reported in *FBIS,* Daily Report, Eastern Europe, 21 Oct. 1980, D1.

66. AFP, 21 Oct. 1980, as reported in *FBIS,* Daily Report, Eastern Europe, 21 Oct. 1980, G1.

67. See *Le Monde,* 22 Oct. 1980, 1.

68. AFP, 28 Oct. 1980, as reported in *FBIS,* Daily Report, Eastern Europe, 28 Oct. 1980, G1. Also *Trybuna Ludu* of 28 Oct. claimed that KOR was now trying to "penetrate Solidarity," as reported in *FBIS,* Daily Report, Eastern Europe, 31 Oct. 1980, G5.

69. *Zolnierz Wolnosci,* 27 Oct. 1980, as reported in *FBIS,* Daily Report, Eastern Europe, 13 Nov. 1980, G2 (boldface type in the original).

Chapter 7

1. For various reports on this visit, see *FBIS,* Daily Report, Eastern Europe, 30 Oct. 1980, D1, G1, G5. Also see *FBIS,* Daily Report, Soviet Union, 30 Oct. 1980, F1, and 3 Nov. 1980, F1; for the Brezhnev-Kania communiqué see Moscow Domestic Service, 1 Nov. 1980, as reported in *FBIS,* Daily Report, Soviet Union, 3 Nov. 1980, F1; Prague Radio, 31 Oct. 1980, as reported in *FBIS,* Daily Report, Eastern Europe, 3 Nov. 1980, D1.

2. See *Krasnaya Zvezda,* 1 Nov. 1980, as reported in *FBIS,* Daily Report, Soviet Union, 5 Nov. 1980, BB1.

3. Warsaw Domestic Service, 9 Nov. 1980, as reported in *FBIS,* Daily Report, Eastern Europe, 10 Nov. 1980, G2.

4. Ibid.

5. *Bratislava Pravda,* 1 Nov. 1980, as reported in *FBIS,* Daily Report, Eastern Europe, 4 Nov. 1980, D1.

6. Ibid.

7. Ibid.

8. *Ljublana Delo,* 25 Oct. 1980, as reported in *FBIS,* Daily Report, Eastern Europe, 31 Oct. 1980, D2.

9. See *Rude Pravo,* 6 Nov. 1980, as reported in *FBIS,* Daily Report, Eastern Europe, 10 Nov. 1980, F2.

10. Cited by *Le Monde,* 4 Nov. 1980, 10.

11. Ibid.

12. DPA (Hamburg), 10 Nov. 1980, as reported in *FBIS,* Daily Report, Eastern Europe, 10 Nov. 1980, E2.

13. See *Krasnaya Zvezda,* 11 Nov. 1980, as reported in *FBIS,* Daily Report, Soviet Union, 14 Nov. 1980, F4. Similar accusations preceded the incursions into both Hungary and Czechoslovakia.

14. See *Pravda,* 17 Nov. 1980, 4, for the strong Soviet assertion of this point.

15. *Daily Telegraph,* 14 Nov. 1980, as reported in *FBIS,* Daily Report, Eastern Europe, 14 Nov. 1980, G2.

16. See *Borba's* (Belgrade) optimism on this new development, as reported in *FBIS,* Daily Report, Eastern Europe, 17 Nov. 1980, I1, 20 Nov. 1980, I1–I2.

17. See the citation of *Trybuna Ludu,* 26 Nov. 1980, in *Pravda,* 27 Nov. 1980, 4.

18. TASS, 24 Nov. 1980, as reported in *FBIS,* Daily Report, Soviet Union, 25 Nov. 1980, F1, and Warsaw Domestic Service, 24 Nov. 1980, as reported in *FBIS,* Daily Report, Eastern Europe, 25 Nov. 1980, G1; Polish Radio, 25 Nov. 1980, as reported in *FBIS,* Daily Report, Eastern Europe, 26 Nov. 1980, G1.

19. See note 17.

20. *Rude Pravo,* 27 Nov. 1980, as reported in *FBIS,* Daily Report, Eastern Europe, 3 Dec. 1980, D1. It is interesting to note that in this article, Hungarian nationalism during the Soviet intervention in 1956 is referred to directly by the Czechs.

21. Ibid.

22. Polish Radio, 2 and 3 Dec. 1980, as reported in *FBIS,* Daily Report, Eastern Europe, 3 Dec. 1980, G1, 4 Dec. 1980, G1.

23. See various reports on the CC Plenum of 1–2 Dec. 1980, as reported in *FBIS,* Daily Report, Eastern Europe, 4 Dec. 1980, D7–G11; also see CTK, 2 Dec. 1980, in *FBIS,* Daily Report, Eastern Europe, 4 Dec. 1980, D8.

24. Warsaw Radio, 3 Dec. 1980, as reported in *FBIS,* Daily Report, Eastern Europe, 3 Dec. 1980, G10; Polish Radio, 3 Dec. 1980, as reported in *FBIS,* Daily Report, Eastern Europe, 4 Dec. 1980, G8.

25. Rakowski was now "eschewing radicalism." See *Trybuna Ludu,* 3 Dec. 1980, 5.

26. *Svenska Dagbladet* (Stockholm), as reported in *FBIS,* Daily Report, Eastern Europe, 2 Dec. 1980, G25–26, for the text of this interview.

27. *Trybuna Ludu,* 1 Dec. 1980, 1.

28. See PAP, 10 Dec. 1980, in *FBIS,* 11 Dec. 1980, G1.

29. See *Washington Post,* 5 Dec. 1980, AA17, where it is claimed that the Soviets decided on 27 Nov. 1980 "in principle" to intervene. See Yugoslav

159

commentary on these warnings, as reported in *FBIS,* Daily Report, Eastern Europe, 5 Dec. 1980, I2.

A comment on an interesting development should be added here. Despite the noticeable retrenchment in the Polish press because of increased Soviet pressure, PAP broadcast *in Russian* on 2 Dec. 1980, that in some *voivodships,* 70–90 percent of party members had become members of Solidarity. The report was extremely positive in its depiction of need for renewal "ever in the party" as well as cooperation with Solidarity! This could hardly have been a bold attempt on the part of Solidarity to further intimidate the Russians. One could speculate that the Russians were *planting* such reports to further justify possible military action against Poland. See *FBIS,* Daily Report, Eastern Europe, 3 Dec. 1980, G2.

30. For example, see Belgrade Domestic Service, 4 Dec. 1980, as reported in *FBIS,* Daily Report, Eastern Europe, 5 Dec. 1980, I2.

31. Polish Domestic Service, 3 Dec. 1980, as reported in *FBIS,* Daily Report, Eastern Europe, 4 Dec. 1980, G11.

32. See the communiqué from this meeting in *Pravda,* 6 Dec. 1980, 1; *Le Monde,* 5 Dec. 1980, 3, also reported that by 3 Dec. Poland's armed forces were on 36-hour alert.

33. *Le Monde,* 9 Dec. 1980, 3.

34. *L'Unita,* 6 Dec. 1980, as reported in *FBIS,* Daily Report, Western Europe, 10 Dec. 1980, L1. In this regard, a stringent letter was sent by the PCI to the CPSU and other bloc parties in early December. See *RFER,* RAD Background Report/49, 20 Feb. 1981.

35. *L'Humanité,* 6 Dec. 1980, as reported in *FBIS,* Daily Report, Western Europe, 12 Dec. 1980.

36. TASS, 8 Dec. 1980, as reported in *FBIS,* Daily Report, Soviet Union, 8 Dec. 1980, F3; *Rude Pravo,* 9 Dec. 1980, as reported in *FBIS,* Daily Report, Eastern Europe, 11 Dec. 1980, D1; Paris Radio, as reported in *FBIS,* Daily Report, Eastern Europe, 10 Dec. 1980, G1.

37. Tanjug, 25 Nov. 1980, as reported in *FBIS,* Daily Report, Eastern Europe, 28 Nov. 1980, I2.

38. *Le Figaro,* 11 Dec. 1980, 1, 3.

39. Ibid.

40. See the Zagladin interview in *La Republica,* 11 Dec. 1980, as reported in *FBIS,* Daily Report, Eastern Europe, 15 Dec. 1980, G1–G3. Also see Joan Urban, "The West European Communist Challenge to Soviet Foreign Policy," in Roger Kanet, *Soviet Foreign Policy in the 1980s* (New York: Praeger, 1982), 179–80.

41. *Der Spiegel,* 15 Dec. 1980, as reported in *FBIS,* Daily Report, Soviet Union, 16 Dec. 1980, F2–F13.

42. *Pravda,* 15 Dec. 1980, 4; TASS, 22 and 25 Dec. 1980, as reported in *FBIS,* Daily Report, Soviet Union, 23 and 29 Dec. 1980, F1, F5.

43. See Warsaw Radio transcript, 26 Dec. 1980, as reported in *FBIS,* Daily Report, Eastern Europe, 29 Dec. 1980, G1 and *Pravda,* 27 Dec. 1980, 4.

44. *Pravda,* 26 Dec. 1980, 2–3. (Translated version reported in *FBIS,* Daily Report, Soviet Union, 30 Dec. 1980, CC8–12.)

45. Moscow Radio, 30 Dec. 1980, as reported in *FBIS,* Daily Report, Soviet Union, 31 Dec. 1980. F1.

46. Reported by Tanjug, 14 Jan. 1981, as reported by *FBIS*, Daily Report, Eastern Europe, 15 Jan. 1981, I1.

47. Polish Radio (in Russian to the Soviet Union), 19 Jan. 1981, as reported in *FBIS*, Daily Report, Eastern Europe, 19 Jan. 1981, G1.

48. *Rude Pravo*, 16 Jan. 1981, as reported in *FBIS*, Daily Report, Eastern Europe, 21 Jan. 1981, D7.

49. See the exploration of these new problems in *RFER*, RAD Background Report/16, 22 Jan. 1981; Warsaw Radio, on both 24 and 26 Jan. repeated this TASS evaluation, as reported in *FBIS*, Daily Report, Eastern Europe, 26 Jan. 1981, G1.

50. *Rude Pravo*, 27 and 26 Jan. 1981, as reported in *FBIS*, Daily Report, Eastern Europe, 29 and 28 Jan. 1981, D2, D1.

51. See *RFER*, RAD Background Report/16, 22 Jan. 1981.

52. Ibid.

53. See *RFER*, RAD Background Report/53, 25 Feb. 1981.

54. See note 15, this chapter.

55. See *RFER*, RAD Background Report/53, 25 Feb. 1981. Rural Solidarity was accepted only as an "association"; see *RFER*, RAD Background Report/59, 2 Mar. 1981.

56. See *RFER*, RAD Background Report/53, 25 Feb. 1981; also see *Washington Post*, 13 Feb. 1981, A33. According to the *Post* apparently a discipline problem faced the Soviets with their reservists in the Trans-Carpathian region. Desertions were noted while some who were called up failed to appear.

57. *Avanti*, 11 Feb. 1981, as reported in *FBIS*, Daily Report, Eastern Europe, 19 Feb. 1981, D5.

58. My discussion on CPSU-PCI tensions during this time is based on the analysis in *RFER*, RAD Background Report/49, 20 Feb. 1981.

59. *Pravda*, 24 Feb. 1981, 2–9. For translation, see *Current Digest of the Soviet Press* 33, no. 8(1981):6–7, for Brezhnev's address.

60. See *RFER*, Polish Situation Report/6, 7 Apr. 1981 and *Pravda*, 8 Apr. 1981, 4. Also see the reprint of Husak's speech on "any aid necessary" to Poland in *Pravda*, 7 Apr. 1981, 3–4.

61. See *RFER*, Polish Situation Report/7, 24 Apr. 1981; Suslov visited Warsaw 23 Apr. after the announcement that Rural Solidarity was to be registered.

62. See Warsaw Radio, 19 May 1981, as reported in *RFER*, RAD Background Report/155, 26 May 1981; Stefan Olszowski and Tadeusz Grabski, hard-liners, reportedly offered to resign from the Politburo after the 29 Mar. CC Plenum, which came on the heels of the Bydgoszcz incident, but they did not. See *RFER*, RAD Background Report/109, 23 Apr. 1981 for this analysis.

63. *Pravda*, 12 June 1981, 2. Also see App.

64. Ibid.

65. See *RFER*, RAD Background Report/176, 19 June 1981.

66. *RFER*, RAD Background Report/196, 10 July 1981.

67. For analysis of the congress, see *RFER*, RAD Background Report/219, 3 Aug. 1981.

68. *RFER*, RAD Background Report/221, 3 Aug. 1981.

69. See *RFER*, Polish Situation Report/17, 5 Oct. 1981, for in-depth view of the congress; on the military maneuvers see *RFER*, RAD Background Report/285, 9 Oct. 1981.

70. Radio Warsaw, 9 Sept. 1981, as reported in *RFER*, RAD Background Report/270, 21 Sept. 1981.

71. *Pravda*, 13 Sept. 1981, 4. Also, Soviet ambassador to Poland Boris Aristov communicated a message to Kania from the Soviet leadership on 10 Sept. warning against "further leniency" toward the opposition. See *RFER*, RAD Background Report/285, 9 Oct. 1981.

72. For Rakowski's change of heart, see *RFER*, RAD Background Report/298, 28 Oct. 1981, and *RFER*, RAD Background Report/291, 19 Oct. 1981.

73. *RFER*, RAD Background Report/291, 19 Oct. 1981; *Trybuna Ludu*, 20 Oct. 1981, as reported in *RFER*, RAD Background Report/298, 28 Oct. 1981.

74. This summit is described in *RFER*, RAD Background Report/314, 13 Nov. 1981.

75. Richard Spielman, "Crisis in Poland," *Foreign Policy* 49(Winter 1982–1983):30.

76. Ibid., 31.

77. Cited in Ibid. The Poles were not the only ones "scared." Soviet Marshal Viktor Kulikov was "conspicuously present" in Warsaw a few days before the Jaruzelski takeover. See Dimtri K. Simes, "Clash over Poland," *Foreign Policy* 46(Spring 1982):50.

78. Spielman, "Crisis," 30–31.

Chapter 8

1. See Alexander Smolar, "The Rich and the Powerful," in *Poland: Genesis of a Revolution,* ed. Abraham Brumberg (New York: Random House, 1983), 42–43.

2. Eric Willenz of the U.S. Department of State characterized as "cross-fertilization" the interplay of East and West European communist ideas during a roundtable discussion of "The Impact of Eurocommunism on Poland and East Europe," at the AAASS, 14 Oct. 1982, Washington, D.C.

3. Richard Spielman, "Crisis in Poland," *Foreign Policy* 49(Winter 1982–1983):30–31.

4. I am indebted to Paul Shoup for the suggestion that this might indeed have been the case.

5. Ibid.

6. Apparently pressure is coming from the Soviet Union, according to recent accounts, requiring some $10 billion from Poland during the remainder of the century for various energy projects. See the remarks of Zdislaw Rurarz, former Polish ambassador to Japan, in the *Wall Street Journal,* 19 June 1985, 31. Also see Deputy Prime Minister Rakowski's more oblique but relevant comments on the postmartial law economic situation in the *Wall Street Journal,* 14 June 1985, 20.

More evidence of this stress can be found in Poland's continued requests for Western governments to reschedule Polish debt payments of $1.3 billion (due in 1985). Such a deferment was granted by Western creditor governments. See the *Wall Street Journal,* 21 Nov. 1985, 34.

7. J. F. Brown, *Relations between the Soviet Union and Its East European*

162

Allies: A Survey, R-1742-PR (Santa Monica: Rand Corporation, 1975), vi.

8. *Pravda,* 21 June 1985, 3–4.

9. Ibid. Also see the *Christian Science Monitor,* 10 July 1985, 11.

10. *Christian Science Monitor,* 10 July 1985, 11. The CMEA Summit took place 25–27 June. See the Soviet presummit stress on "unity and cohesiveness" in *Pravda,* 24 June 1985, 4. The communiqué from this meeting is in *Pravda,* 29 June 1985, 1, 4.

11. The three generals added were Czeslaw Kiszczak, Jozef Baryla, and Florian Siwicki. Also Mieczyslaw Rakowski was retained in the Central Committee, while offers of partial amnesty were made to 300 political prisoners. See *Trybuna Ludu,* 3 and 4 July, 1986, 1. For Gorbachev's speech see *Trybuna Ludu,* 1 July 1986, 3. See also *New York Times,* 2 July 1986, A2.

Selected Bibliography

Books and Articles

Anderson, Richard D., Jr. "Soviet Decision-Making and Poland." *Problems of Communism* 31(Mar.–Apr. 1982):22–36.

Angelov, S., ed. *Sotsialisticheskii internatsionalizm.* Moscow: Politizdat, 1979.

Ash, Timothy Garton. *The Polish Revolution: Solidarity.* New York: Scribner's, 1983.

Aspaturian, Vernon, Jiri Valenta, and David P. Burke. *Eurocommunism between East and West.* Bloomington: Indiana Univ. Press, 1980.

Basmanov, M. I., and M. T. Iovchuk, eds. *Proletarskii, sotsialisticheskii internatsionalizm.* Moscow: Mysl', 1978.

Beck, Jozef. *Final Report.* New York: Speller, 1957.

Bethell, Nicholas. *Gomulka: His Poland, His Communism.* New York: Holt-Rhinehart, 1969.

Bialer, Seweryn. "Poland and the Soviet Imperium." *Foreign Affairs* 59(1981):522–39.

_____, ed. *The Domestic Context of Soviet Foreign Policy.* Boulder: Westview, 1981.

Bielasiak, Jack. *Poland Today: The State of the Republic.* Armonk, N.Y.: Sharpe, 1981.

Borkenau, Franz. *World Communism.* Ann Arbor: Univ. of Michigan Press, 1962.

Bromke, Adam. *Poland's Politics: Idealism vs. Realism.* Cambridge: Harvard Univ. Press, 1967.

_____. "A New Juncture in Poland." *Problems in Communism* 25(Sept.–Oct. 1976):1–17.

_____. "The Opposition in Poland." *Problems of Communism* 27(Sept.–Oct. 1978):37–51.

Bromke, Adam, and John W. Strong, eds. *Gierek's Poland.* New York: Praeger, 1973.

Brown, J. F. *Relations between the Soviet Union and Its East European Allies: A Survey.* R-1742-PR. Santa Monica: Rand Corporation, 1975.

Brumberg, Abraham, ed. *Poland: Genesis of a Revolution.* New York: Random House, 1983.

Brun-Zejmis, Julia. "The Russian Idea and the Polish Question: Some Russian

Views on the Polish Insurrection of 1830." *East European Quarterly* 14(Fall 1980):315–26.

Brzezinski, Zbigniew. *The Soviet Bloc: Unity and Conflict.* New York: Praeger, 1961.

Butenko, A., et al. *The World Socialist System and Anticommunism.* Moscow: Progress, 1972.

Caldwell, Lawrence T. "The Warsaw Pact: Directions of Change." *Problems of Communism* 24(Sept.–Oct. 1975):1–19.

Carr, Edward H. *The Bolshevik Revolution: 1917–1923.* 3 vols. New York: Penguin, 1953.

Carrillo, Santiago. *Eurocommunism and the State.* Westport, Conn.: Lawrence Hill, 1978.

Connor, Walter D. "Social Change and Stability in East Europe." *Problems of Communism* 26(Nov.–Dec. 1977):16–32.

_____. "Dissent in East Europe: A New Coalition?" *Problems of Communism* 29(Jan.–Feb. 1980):1–17.

Davies, Norman. *White Eagle, Red Star: The Polish-Soviet War, 1919–20.* New York: St. Martin's, 1972.

_____. *Heart of Europe: A Short History of Poland.* Oxford: Oxford Univ. Press, 1984.

Dawisha, Karen. *The Kremlin and the Prague Spring.* Berkeley: Univ. of California Press, 1984.

Degras, Jane. *The Communist International, 1919–1943: Documents.* 3 vols. London: Oxford Univ. Press, 1960.

Devlin, Kevin. "The New Crisis in European Communism." *Problems of Communism* 17(Nov.–Dec. 1968):57–68.

_____. "The Inter-Party Drama." *Problems of Communism* 24(July–Aug. 1975):18–34.

Dziewanowski, M. K. "Jozef Pilsudski, 1867–1967." *East European Quarterly* 2(Jan. 1969):359–83.

_____. *The Communist Party of Poland.* 2d ed. Cambridge: Harvard Univ. Press, 1976.

_____. *Poland in the Twentieth Century.* New York: Columbia Univ. Press, 1977.

Fallenbuchl, Zbigniew. "The Polish Economy in the 1970s." In Joint Economic Committee U.S. Congress, *East European Economies Post-Helsinki.* Washington, D.C.: U.S. Government Printing Office, 1977:816–64.

Fejto, Francois. *A History of the People's Democracies.* New York: Praeger, 1971.

Fountain, Alvin. *Roman Dmowski: Party, Tactics, Ideology, 1895–1907.* Boulder: East European Monographs, Columbia Univ. Press, 1980.

Gati, Charles, ed. *The International Politics of East Europe.* New York: Praeger, 1976.

Gieysztor, A., et al. *History of Poland.* Warsaw: Polish Scientific, 1969.

Golan, Galia. *Reform Rule in Czechoslovakia: The Dubcek Era, 1968–1969.* Cambridge: Cambridge Univ. Press, 1973.

Hammond, Thomas T., ed. *The Anatomy of Communist Takeovers.* New Haven: Yale Univ. Press, 1975.

Herspring, Dale R. "The Warsaw Pact at 25." *Problems of Communism* 29(Sept.–Oct. 1980):1–15.

Herspring, Dale R., and Ivan Volgyes, eds. *Civil-Military Relations in Communist Systems.* Boulder: Westview, 1978.

Hutchings, Robert L. *Soviet-East European Relations: Consolidation and Conflict, 1968-1980.* Madison: Univ. of Wisconsin Press, 1983.

Inozemtsev, N. "O Leninskom metodologii analiza mirovogo obshchestvennogo razvitiia." *Kommunist* (Moscow) 12(Aug. 1976):66-77.

Ionescu, Ghita. *The Break-up of the Soviet Empire in East Europe.* New York: Penguin, 1965.

Jamgotch, Nish, Jr. *Soviet-East European Dialogue: International Relations of a New Type?* Palo Alto: Stanford, Hoover Institution, 1968.

Johnson, A. Ross. "Polish Perspectives, Past and Present." *Problems of Communism* 20(July-Aug. 1971):59-72.

Jones, Christopher D. *Soviet Influence in East Europe: Political Autonomy and the Warsaw Pact.* New York: Praeger, 1981.

Kanet, Roger E. *Soviet and East European Foreign Policy: A Bibliography of English and Russian Language Publications.* Santa Barbara: ABC-Clio, 1974.

————. *Soviet Foreign Policy in the 1980s.* New York: Praeger, 1981.

Kanet, Roger E., and M. D. Simon. *Background to Crisis: Policy and Politics in Gierek's Poland.* Boulder: Westview, 1981.

Kennan, George. *Soviet Foreign Policy, 1917-1941.* New York: Van Nostrand, 1960.

Khrushchev, Nikita. *The Soviet Stand on Germany.* New York: Crosscurrents, 1961.

————. *Khrushchev Remembers.* Trans. and ed. Strobe Talbott. Boston: Little-Brown, 1974.

Korbel, Josef. *Poland between East and West: Soviet and German Diplomacy towards Poland, 1919-1933.* Princeton: Princeton Univ. Press, 1963.

Kovrig, Bennett. *The Myth of Liberation: East Central Europe in U.S. Diplomacy and Politics since 1941.* Baltimore: Johns Hopkins Univ. Press, 1973.

Kuhlman, James A. *The Foreign Policy of East Europe: Domestic and International Determinants.* Leyden: Sijthoff, 1978.

Kulski, W. W. *Germany and Poland: From War to Peaceful Relations.* Syracuse: Syracuse Univ. Press, 1976.

Kux, Ernst. "Growing Tensions in East Europe." *Problems of Communism* 29(Mar.-Apr. 1980):21-37.

Lane, Arthur Bliss. *I Saw Poland Betrayed.* Indianapolis: Bobbs-Merrill, 1948.

Leitsch, Walter. "Russians and Poles in the Nineteenth Century." *East European Quarterly* 8(Fall 1974):288-94.

Legvold, Robert. "The Problem of European Security." *Problems of Communism* 23(Jan.-Feb. 1974):13-33.

Leslie, R. F. *Reform and Insurrection in Russian Poland, 1856-1865.* Westport, Conn.: Greenwood, 1969.

Leslie, R. F., et al. *History of Poland since 1863.* New York: Cambridge Univ. Press, 1983.

Linden, Carl. *Khrushchev and the Soviet Leadership, 1957-1964.* Baltimore: Johns Hopkins Univ. Press, 1966.

London, Kurt. *The Soviet Union in World Politics.* Boulder: Westview, 1980.

————, ed. *East Europe in Transition.* Baltimore: Johns Hopkins Univ. Press, 1966.

Lukasiewicz, Juliusz. *Diplomat in Paris, 1936–39.* New York: Columbia Univ. Press, 1970.

Machiavelli, Niccolo. *The Prince.* Ed. T. G. Bergin. New York: Appleton-Century Crofts, 1947.

Mastny, Vojtech. *Russia's Road to the Cold War: Diplomacy, Warfare, and the Politics of Communism, 1941–1945.* New York: Columbia Univ. Press, 1979.

Meyer, Alfred G. *Marxism: The Unity of Theory and Practice.* Ann Arbor: Univ. of Michigan Press, 1966.

Naimark, N. "Problems in the Historiography of the 'Proletariat': Poland's First Marxist Party." *East European Quarterly* 12(Summer 1978):234–51.

Orlik, I. I. *Imperialisticheskie derzhavy i Vostochnaia Evropa.* Moscow: Izdatel'stvo Nauka, 1968.

———. *Politika zapadnykh derzhav v otnoshenii Vostochnoevropeiskykh sotsialisticheskykh gosudarstv (1965–75).* Moscow: Izdatel'stvo Nauka, 1979.

Ortmayer, Louis. *Conflict, Compromise and Conciliation: West German-Polish Normalization, 1966–1976.* Denver: Univ. of Denver Press, 1975.

Osnos, Peter. "The Polish Road to Communism." *Foreign Affairs* 56(1977):209–20.

Parsadanova, V. S. *Sovetsko-Pol'skie otnosheniia v gody Velikoi Otechestvenoi Voiny, 1941–45.* Moscow: "Nauka," 1982.

Pastusiak, Longin. "A Marxist Approach to the Study of International Relations." *East European Quarterly* 3(Sept. 1969):285–93.

———. "East-West Relations and Arms Control: Achievements and Prospects." *East European Quarterly* 9(Spring 1975):1–13.

Potichnyj, Peter. *The Ukraine and the Czechoslovak Crisis.* Australia: Canberra National Univ. Press, 1970.

———, Peter, ed. *Poland and the Ukraine: Past and Present.* Toronto: Canadian Institute of Ukrainian Studies, 1980.

Rachwald, Arthur R. *Poland between the Superpowers: Security vs. Economic Recovery.* Boulder: Westview, 1983.

Rakowska-Harmstone, Teresa. "Socialist Internationalism and East Europe: A New Stage." *Survey* 22(Winter 1976):38–54.

Rakowski, Mieczyslaw F. *Polityka Zagraniczna PRL.* Warsaw: Interpress, 1974.

———. "The Image of Democracy." *Contemporary Poland* 9(Apr. 1977):1–3.

Reddaway, W. F., ed. *The Cambridge History of Poland.* 2 vols. Cambridge: Cambridge Univ. Press, 1951.

Remington, Robin. "Czechoslovakia and the Warsaw Pact." *East European Quarterly* 3(Sept. 1969):315–36.

———. *The Warsaw Pact.* Cambridge: MIT Press, 1971.

Riasanovsky, Nicholas. *A History of Russia.* New York: Oxford Univ. Press, 1969.

Robinson, William F., ed. *August 1980: The Strikes in Poland.* Munich: Radio Free Europe Research, 1980.

Roos, Hans. *A History of Modern Poland.* London: Eyre and Spottiswoode, 1966.

Rubinstein, Alvin Z. *The Foreign Policy of the Soviet Union.* New York: Random House, 1972.

Sanford, George. *Polish Communism in Crisis.* New York: St. Martin's, 1983.

Schwartz, Morton. *The Foreign Policy of the USSR: Domestic Factors.* Encino, Calif.: Dickenson, 1975.

Seabury, Paul. "On Detente." *Survey* 19(Spring 1973):62–76.

Seton-Watson, Hugh. *East Europe between the Wars, 1918–1941.* Cambridge: Cambridge Univ. Press, 1945.

_____. *The East European Revolution.* New York: Praeger, 1956.

Simes, Dmitri K. *Detente and Conflict: Soviet Foreign Policy 1972–77.* London: Sage, 1977.

_____. "Clash over Poland." *Foreign Policy* 46(Spring 1982):46–66.

Simmonds, George W. *Nationalism in the USSR and East Europe.* Detroit: Univ. of Detroit Press, 1977.

Skilling, H. Gordon. *Czechoslovakia: The Interrupted Revolution.* Princeton: Princeton Univ. Press, 1976.

Skilling, H. Gordon, and Franklyn Griffiths. *Interest Groups in Soviet Politics.* Princeton: Princeton Univ. Press, 1971.

Sokolewicz, Wojciech. *Konstytucja PRL po zmianach z 1976 r.* Warsaw: Panstwowe Wydawnictwo Naukowe, 1978.

Sonnenfeldt, Helmut, and William Hyland. "Soviet Perspectives on Security." *Adelphi Papers 150.* London: International Institute for Strategic Studies, Spring 1979.

Spielman, Richard. "Crisis in Poland." *Foreign Policy* 49(Winter 1982–1983):20–36.

Stone, Daniel. "The Cultural Life of Conservative Polish Nobles in the Late Eighteenth Century." *East European Quarterly* 9(Fall 1975):271–77.

Szporluk, Roman, ed. *The Influence of East Europe and the Soviet West on the USSR.* New York: Praeger, 1975.

Taras, Ray. *Ideology in a Socialist State: Poland, 1956–1983.* Cambridge: Cambridge Univ. Press, 1984.

Terry, Sarah M. *Poland's Place in Europe.* Princeton: Princeton Univ. Press, 1983.

_____, ed. *Soviet Policy in East Europe.* New Haven: Yale Univ. Press, 1984.

Tökes, Rudolph, ed. *Opposition in East Europe.* Baltimore: Johns Hopkins Univ. Press, 1979.

Trapeznikov, S. "Obshchestvenaia nauka, ideinoie bogatstvo partii i naroda." *Kommunist* (Moscow) 12(Aug. 1976):19–31.

Triska, Jan. "Messages from Czechoslovakia." *Problems of Communism* 24(Nov.–Dec. 1975):26–42.

Ulam, Adam. *Expansion and Coexistence: The History of Soviet Foreign Policy, 1917–73.* New York: Praeger, 1974.

_____. "The Destiny of East Europe." *Problems of Communism* 23(Jan.–Feb. 1974):1–12.

Ulč, Otto. "Czechoslovakia and the Polish Virus." *Current History* 80(Apr. 1981):154–58.

Valenta, Jiri. "Eurocommunism and Eastern Europe." *Problems of Communism* 27(Mar.–Apr. 1978):41–54.

_____. *Soviet Intervention in Czechoslovakia: Anatomy of a Decision.* Baltimore: Johns Hopkins Univ. Press, 1979.

_____. "Eurocommunism and the USSR." *Political Quarterly* 51(Apr.–June 1980):127–40.

_____. "Soviet Options in Poland." *Survival* 23(Mar.–Apr. 1981):50–59.

Volgyes, Ivan. *The Reliability of the Warsaw Pact Armies: The Southern Tier.* Durham: Duke Univ. Press, 1982.

Wandycz, Piotr. "Polish Federalism 1919–20 and Its Historical Antecedents." *East European Quarterly* 4(Mar. 1970):25–39.

_____. *Soviet-Polish Relations: 1919–1921.* Cambridge: Harvard Univ. Press, 1970.

_____. *The United States and Poland.* Cambridge: Harvard Univ. Press, 1980.

Wesson, Robert, ed. *The Soviet Union: Looking to the 1980s.* Palo Alto: Hoover Institution Press, 1980.

Weydenthal, Jan B. de. *The Communists of Poland: An Historical Outline.* Stanford: Hoover Institution Press, 1978.

_____. *Poland 1980–1982: The Making of the Revolution.* Lexington, Mass.: Lexington Books, 1982.

_____. "Workers and Party in Poland." *Problems of Communism* 29(Nov.–Dec. 1980):1–15.

Wojtaszek, Emil. "Poland's Foreign Policy and European Security Problems." *International Affairs* (Moscow) 8(Aug. 1978):19–30.

Woodall, Jean, ed. *Policy and Politics in Contemporary Poland: Reform, Failure, and Crisis.* New York: Pinter, 1983.

Zarodov, Konstantin. *Leninism and Contemporary Problems of Transition from Capitalism to Socialism.* Moscow: Progress, 1972.

_____. *Tri revoliutsii v Rossii i nashe vremya.* Moscow: Mysl', 1977.

Zauberman, Alfred. "The East European Economies." *Problems of Communism* 27(Mar.–Apr. 1978):55–69.

Zawodny, J. K. *Death in the Forest: The Story of the Katyn Forest Massacre.* South Bend: Univ. of Notre Dame Press, 1962.

_____. *Nothing but Honour: The Story of the Warsaw Uprising.* Stanford: Hoover Institution Press, 1978.

Zimmerman, William. *Soviet Perspectives on International Relations, 1956–1967.* Princeton: Princeton Univ. Press, 1969.

_____. "Soviet Foreign Policy in the 1970s." *Survey* 19(Spring 1973):188–98.

Zimmerman, William, and Zvi Gitelman, eds. *East-West Relations and the Future of Eastern Europe.* London: George Allen, 1981.

Newspapers and Other Sources

Current Digest of the Soviet Press. New York: Joint Committee on Slavic Studies.

Foreign Broadcast Information Service. Washington, D.C.: Joint Publications Research Service.

International Affairs (Moscow).

Izvestiia (Moscow).

Journal of the Institute of World Economics and International Relations. Moscow: IMEMO.

Kommunist (Moscow).

Kommunist vooruzhenikh sil [Communist of the armed forces (Moscow)].

Le Figaro (Paris).

Le Monde (Paris).

New Times (Moscow).
The New York Times.
Polityka (Warsaw).
Pravda (Moscow).
Problems of Peace and Socialism [World Marxist Review in the English version (Prague)].
Radio Liberty Reports. Munich: RFE/RL Inc.
Radio Free Europe Research. Munich: RFE/RL Inc.
Review of International Affairs (Belgrade).
Trybuna Ludu (Warsaw).
Voprosy istorii KPSS (Problems in the history of the CPSU). [Moscow].
Wall Street Journal.
Washington Post.
Zycie Warszawy (Warsaw).

Index

Acts of Lublin, 11
Adenauer, Konrad, and Hallstein Doctrine, 28
Afghanistan, 85, 89, 91, 126, 131
Anti-Zionism, in Poland, 29
Aristov, Boris I., as Soviet Ambassador, 74; warns Kania, 161 n. 71

Babiuch, Edward, and constitutional debate, 45-56; and PUWP CC, 106; visits Moscow, 64
Baybakov, Nikolai K., 117
Beck, Jozef, 18-19
Belorussia, parts to Poland, 17; Poland absorbed into, 19; and Russian imperialism, 73
Berlin Conference of Communist Parties. See East Berlin Conference of Communist Parties
Berlinguer, Enrico, 134; and Kania, 78; and Polish dissent, 50-51; and 26th CPSU Congress, 119
Bierut, Boleslaw, 20-21, 26
Bilak, Vasil, and Carrillo, 60, 63, 76; on CSR renegades, 59; on reforms, 110
Brandt, Willy, 29
Brezhnev, Leonid I., 29, 90; congratulates Jaruzelski, 123; and detente, 48; receives Kania and Pinkowski, 109; and 26th CPSU Congress, 120
Brezhnev Doctrine, 5, 6, 26, 31, 91, 93; and Poland, 103, 126, 131-32
Bromke, Adam, 27
Bydgoszcz incident, 121

Camp David, 72
Carrillo, Santiago, 65-66; and 26th CPSU Congress, 119

Carter, President Jimmy, 59; and Polish press, 72; visit to Poland, 72. *See also* Human rights in Eastern Europe
Catherine the Great, 12
Ceausescu, Nicolae, and East Berlin Conference of Communist Parties, 50; and Gierek, 58; and mediating between Poland and WTO, 115; and Polish crisis, 111
Charter '77, 59-60; and KOR, 76; and members, treatment of, 83
China, People's Republic of (PRC), Chairman Hua visits Romania, 76-77; and relations with USSR, 32; and Soviet polemics, 28; splitting tactics of, 41
Cold War, 4, 82
COMECON. *See* Council for Mutual Economic Assistance
Cominform (Communist Information Bureau), 21
Comintern (Communist International), 5; CPCz on legacy of, 78; Second Congress and membership, 17; and Soviet-Polish war, 20
Committee for the Defense of the Workers (KOR), establishment of, 57; political aims of, 98; and right to strike charter, 83
Communist Party of Czechoslovakia (CPCz), 9, 29-30, 32, 59; and criticism of Poland, 72-73; and Pope John Paul II, 80
Communist Party of the Soviet Union (CPSU), 4; Congresses of: Twentieth, 5; Twenty-fourth, 41, Twenty-fifth, 47-48, Twenty-sixth, 119; and *kto-kogo* in East Europe, 3, 6, 31; and "June letter," 121-22, App.; and Polish economy, 64; and Polish party affairs, 58-59, 64, 128-29; and "secret letter" to PCI, 119
Communist Workers' Party of Poland, 17-18

171

Yugoslavia (*continued*)
ian revolution, 27; and Prague Spring,
31; and self-management, 5

Zagladin, Vadim V., and PCI, 115–16
Zarodov, Konstantin, 56
Zhivkov, Todor, at East Berlin Con-
ference of Communist Parties, 49; as
host of conference, 76
Zimyanin, Mikhail V., and delegation to
Warsaw, 59
Zinoviev, Grigory E., 17

900014

900 14